Liberals: America's Termites

or

It's a Shame that Liberals,
Unlike Hamsters,
Never Eat Their Young

Burt Prelutsky

Scorched Earth Press
Published by Scorched Earth Press
North Hills, CA
Copyright (c) 2009 by Burt Prelutsky

ISBN# 978-0-9746732-1-9

Scorched Earth Press are distributed by:
Scorched Earth Press
16604 Dearborn Street
North Hills, CA 91343-3604

Printed in the United States of America

This book, like my life,
is dedicated to my wife, Yvonne,
who proves that the
third time really is the charm.

FOREWORD

I've never spent much time thinking about reincarnation. Don't get me wrong; if you want to believe that you're coming back as a chicken or a turtle or Barbra Streisand after you die, be my guest. Live and let live is my motto. Even when you're dead.

But now I'm having second thoughts. Now, I think I'm turning into a believer.

Because now I have reason to suspect that Mark Twain may have come back. Not as one of his leaping frogs of Calaveras County or anything like that, but that he somehow pulled a few strings with whomever's in charge of such things and managed to return as an updated version of his old self, as a witty and perceptive chronicler of the great American scene.

But for show business reasons he changed his name. Now he goes by Burt Prelutsky. I got to know Burt slowly, over many years, one witty and perceptive essay at a time. His writing made so much sense. And like a great center fielder, he made it all look easy. That, probably more than anything else, is why I detest him. It's why I loathe him to this day. No one should be this good, this often, and make it look like he isn't even breaking a sweat.

Nevertheless, despite my contempt for the author (which only looks like envy), this book is a triumph of common sense over the foolishness we see all around us in America these days. Burt sticks pins in all the right bubbles.

Referring to left-of-center cultural elitists, Tom Wolfe, the great author and journalist, spoke for many of us when he said, "There is something in me that particularly wants it registered that I am not one of them."

Rest assured, Burt Prelutsky is not one of them either. As he puts it, "Most of the conservatives I know, including myself, started out somewhere else on the political spectrum, and evolved through time and knowledge and experience. I personally do not know of a single case of an individual evolving in the other direction. I will leave it to the Darwinists to make of that what they will."

The other Mark Twain couldn't have said it better.

Bernard Goldberg
Miami, Florida

TABLE OF CONTENTS

INTRODUCTION

Frankly, I think the title of this book is self-explanatory, but on the chance that some people might disagree, I will take this opportunity to explain.

Unlike hurricanes, cyclones, earthquakes and other such phenomena, which are defined as Acts of God in your homeowners insurance policy, termites can wreak equal amounts of structural damage without making a lot of noise as they go about their nefarious business. So it is with liberals - whether they're calling themselves Socialists, progressives, radicals or just plain Democrats, this particular week.

I can see where Barack Hussein Obama and his cronies in the White House and on Capitol Hill might disagree with my assessment. In their own minds, I'm sure they regard themselves as being on the side of the angels. Whether this obvious disconnect from reality is the result of a mental disorder, I'll leave to the pathologists. What should be apparent, though, is that George Soros and those who dance to his well-financed tune are doing their best to undermine America's historical values and traditions, and turn our nation into a latter day version of the late, generally unlamented Soviet Union.

Behaving exactly like termites, those on the Left are nibbling away at the foundation of a nation that was created by such remarkable architects as Washington, Jefferson, Madison, Monroe, Franklin and Adams. What compels the likes of Barack Obama, Nancy Pelosi, Harry Reid, Charles Schumer, Henry Waxman, Barbara Boxer, John Murtha, Charles Rangel, Olympia Snowe, Barbara Lee, John Conyers, Patrick Leahy, Barney Frank, Dick Durbin, and the rest of that tawdry crowd to destroy the single greatest nation ever conceived is beyond me. Frankly, I wish we could simply call up a professional exterminator and have him remove the ugly, crawly creatures from our nation's capitol, but, alas, that's not possible.

However, the truth is we are all exterminators if we choose to be. Unfortunately, while we can't spray these two-legged termites out of existence, we can surely vote them out. Do I hear an amen?

Regards,
Burt Prelutsky
North Hills, California

1

CHAPTER ONE

How I Learned Left from Right,
and Right from Wrong

People often ask me just exactly when I stopped being a liberal and, depending on their own political persuasion, saw the light or sold my soul to the Devil. My fellow conservatives assume I had something akin to an epiphany. Liberals simply wonder if I tripped and fell on my head.

When I fail to come up with anything specific, I can invariably read disappointment in their eyes. The truth is that it was a fairly gradual process. I grew up in a typical middle-class Jewish home, the third son of Russian immigrant parents. In other words, Franklin Roosevelt was our patron saint. In our house, the feeling was that he could walk - or at least roll - on water. Then, after FDR's death, when Harry Truman recognized the state of Israel in 1948, that clinched it. After that, if the Republicans had run God for president, my parents wouldn't have voted for Him.

I suspect that every family has its share of skeletons in the closet, black sheep that are only mentioned in passing, in whispers, at, say, Thanksgiving gatherings. In the old days, they might have been horse thieves, rustlers and card sharks. These days, they're more likely to be defense attorneys, journalists or judges.

In my own case, most of the black sheep were red. That is to say, they were Communists. Most, if not all, were from my mother's side of the family. Between my uncles, and first and second cousins, you could have put together a fairly good-sized cell.

The poorer relatives, many of whom worked in the garment business, cut and sewed for very low wages. Even as a kid, I was able to understand the appeal that Communism held for them. My relatives were Jewish and had been born in Czarist Russia, a pigsty of a country notable for its Cossacks and its pogroms. So far as my relatives were concerned, the Russian Reds rid the land of the much-despised Nicholas II. For them, the enemy of their enemies was considered a friend.

After coming to America, they found that it was the Communists who not only talked about the dignity of the working man, but who often got their heads busted by hired goons when they attempted to unionize the sweatshops. I, on the other hand, was born in the U.S. and was aware that Stalin was every bit as evil as Hitler and every bit as anti-Semitic as Nicholas and the rest of the Romanovs. Still, under the circumstances, I could understand why these folks might not see things my way.

But I had these other relatives, uncles who had made a killing on Chicago's thriving black market during WW II. Once the war ended, they decided that, between Russia and the Windy City, they'd had enough lousy weather to last a lifetime. So, in 1946, they moved their families and their ill-gotten gains to Los Angeles, where they proceeded to buy up parking lots, bowling alleys and apartment houses.

That was bad enough. But having to hear them rhapsodize about Joseph Stalin - Uncle Joe to his stooges - and the wonders he had wrought in the Soviet Union used to drive me crazy. Whenever I'd suggest they should consider moving back to the worker's paradise they kept yakking about, they'd just nod sagely and say, "Comes the revolution, America will be another Soviet Union."

Once, when I'd finally had my fill, I said to one of them, "Uncle Meyer, you're not only a wealthy capitalist, but you made your money as a war profiteer, and now you're making even more as an absentee landlord. For good measure, you're a Jew. Don't you realize that, comes the revolution, the comrades will line you up against the wall and shoot you even before they get around to the Rockefellers?"

If I live to be a hundred, I'll never forget the expression on his face. He gave new meaning to apoplexy as his face turned as beet red as his politics, and he managed to stammer, "That's how you talk to an uncle?"

I have no way of knowing if he was shocked more by my statement or by the fact that his young nephew could not only envision his facing a firing squad, but actually chuckle at the thought.

Obviously I don't know how my rich Commie relatives carried on when I wasn't around, but at least I never again had to listen to any of my uncles sing the praises of their favorite uncle.

In any case, by the time I got to cast a vote in my first presidential election in 1964, naturally I cast it for Lyndon Johnson. Then, in '68, I voted for Hubert Humphrey. After that, things only got worse. Over the course of the following years, I actually voted for McGovern, Carter and Mondale. I would say that sounds like the name of a sleazy law firm, but that would be unfair to sleazy law firms. The thing is, even back then, I'd wake up the day after voting for one of these clowns and I'd hate myself.

Back in the early '80's, I was still one of those shmoes who laughed at jokes about Ronald Reagan nodding off during cabinet meetings. Somewhere along the line, though, it began to sink in that the sleepyhead had managed to turn around an economy that had a 21% rate of inflation and

11% unemployment under his predecessor, and, for an encore, managed to help bring down the Soviet Union. Even a dope like me who had voted for a sanctimonious phony like Jimmy Carter had to admit that was a pretty sensational performance. It turned out that the actor had finally found his perfect role.

Then, in the early 1990's, two things happened that convinced me that I could no longer vote Democratic or identify myself as a liberal, even if it meant that my parents were going to start spinning in their graves. I could only hope that, were they still alive, they would have felt that being a liberal no longer meant that you opposed the poll tax and segregated lunch counters, but, rather, that you were blindly beholden to well-heeled defense attorneys; the morally bankrupt ACLU; and the self-serving likes of Jesse Jackson, Al Sharpton, Al Gore and Ted Kennedy.

From 1987-1991, I served on the Board of Directors of the Writers Guild of America. It was my first hands-on experience in the political arena. I think it's safe to say that the three officers and sixteen board members were all registered Democrats. A handful of the older members had been blacklisted forty years earlier because they'd been card-carrying Communists. Nearly everyone in the boardroom, I should hasten to say, was a polite and at least moderately intelligent human being. There were certainly no more than two or three whom I would have gladly fed to the sharks.

Because the agonizing six-month strike of 1988 took place during my first term in office, I had seen my colleagues at their best and at their worst. But it wasn't until one of my last days in office that I realized how far apart I was from the others. The way the by-laws of the WGA were written, the Board could, without putting it to a vote of the general membership, elect to bestow sums up to $5,000 to any cause we felt deserving of our largesse.

On this occasion, the defense attorneys for photograper Robert Mapplethorpe had contacted us, requesting that the Guild sign on as amicus curiae in the pornography case that had recently been filed against a gallery owner who had exhibited his photos.

Mapplethorpe, in case his name has slipped your mind, had received a grant from the National Endowment of the Arts over the strong objections of North Carolina's Senator Jesse Helms. The senator felt that the U.S. government had no business subsidizing a man who devoted his career to photographing naked children. Naturally, in elite circles, that made Sen. Helms a buffoon, a lunkhead, a southern rube who couldn't tell the difference between a pedophile and an artiste. So far as I was concerned, if an artist couldn't earn a living in a wealthy country with 300 million people in it, he didn't need a federal subsidy, he needed vocational guidance.

When it came time to take a vote that night at the Guild, I was the only person who spoke out against supporting the gallery owner legally or financially.

Furthermore, I didn't think the WGA should be wasting the hard-earned money of its members supporting the artistic freedom of some creep who could only have his creative vision satisfied by having an eight or nine year old child stripped down and posed for his camera.

That night, when I was outvoted 18-1, I clearly saw the enormous gulf that separated me from the liberals in the room. It wasn't simply that we disagreed about whether or not to support this guy, either. It was the fact that they didn't even need to consider what I was saying. It was enough that the ACLU was on Mapplethorpe's side and a southern Conservative was opposed. That was really all they needed to know.

The second thing that turned me into a raging Republican? That's easy. After naturally assuming that the Democrats couldn't possibly do any worse after selecting Michael S. Dukakis to be their standard-bearer in 1988, they accomplished that seemingly impossible feat in 1992 by nominating Hillary Rodham Clinton's husband.

CHAPTER TWO

The Little Red School House

Down through the years, there have been a great many movies in which school teachers have been portrayed as decent and hard-working, even heroic. Just a handful that come to mind are "Goodbye, Mr. Chips," "Holland's Opus," "This Land is Mine," "Up the Down Staircase," "Good Morning, Miss Dove," "Cheers for Miss Bishop," "Dangerous Minds," "Blackboard Jungle," "To Sir, With Love," "Stand and Deliver" and "Dead Poet's Society."

But when it comes to college and university professors, they tend to be portrayed either as comical buffoons ("The Nutty Professor," "Monkey Business," "Son of Flubber," "The Absent Minded Professor," "It Happens Every Spring," "Horse Feathers") or as petty, demented and, often as not, alcoholics ("Who's Afraid of Virginia Woolf," "People Will Talk," "Proof," "The Squid and the Whale"). In fact, the last time I recall a movie about a professor that any normal person would wish to spend time with was the 1948 release, "Apartment for Peggy," and even in that one, Edmund Gwenn spent most of his time planning to commit suicide.

Feeling, as I do, that most professors, aside from those teaching science or math, are over-paid, under-worked, left-wing narcissists infatuated with the sound of their own voices, it makes perfect sense that it would be nearly impossible to make a movie about them that wasn't a slapstick comedy.

Some of the issues that we on the right usually agree about involve affirmative action, taxes, capital punishment, bilingual education, welfare, illegal aliens, the military, the Constitution, and the belief that logic and common sense should always trump emotion when it comes to making national policy.

Like all my conservative colleagues, I have often taken up a cudgel or even an axe in the ongoing battle with liberals, leftists, Socialists, progressives, Maoists, Castroites, Communists, and all the other whack-jobs on the wrong side of history.

There is one issue, however, of some importance about which nobody else seems even the slightest bit concerned. And, no, I am not referring to my book sales, but, rather, to the cost of what is amusingly referred

7

to as higher education. Higher than what, you well might ask, considering that a good number of college graduates cannot do simple math or write a coherent sentence, and would be better served if they repeated the eighth grade. Still, countless American families are mortgaging their homes and future solvency so that their kids can attend college. Unlike waterboarding, which served a higher purpose, there is simply no excuse for mortarboarding.

Frankly, I'm not certain just when it became so darn imperative for every 18-year-old to traipse off to some ivy-walled ivory tower. I understand colleges and universities serving as trade schools for such occupations as engineering, physics, architecture and medicine. But why are all those other people hanging around, wasting their parents' hard-earned cash? It can't merely be to fill the stands at football and basketball games, but perhaps the answer really is as simple as that.

It seems obvious to me that our education system, which costs us billions and billions of dollars, is a wreck. While not all of it is the fault of the teachers' unions, affirmative action, bi-lingual education and the emphasis on promoting self-esteem in youngsters, a lot of it is. But if there was any one thing I could change tomorrow, it's the loony notion that everyone should get a college degree.

Now, please understand, I have nothing against education. My only objection is the way the system is set up. Why, for instance, do you think students are required to devote four years to undergraduate studies? It's simply because that's how the colleges make their money. It's just like the movies. They don't make their profit selling you a ticket, they clean up at the concession stand selling you stale popcorn, over-priced candy and watery sodas.

When it comes to the price of things like oil and health care, Americans are very vocal in their resentment. But the truth is that it costs a lot of money to explore for oil, to drill for it, transport it and refine it. Likewise, health care, which runs the gamut from orphan drugs and heart monitors to MRI's and specialized surgical procedures, is understandably costly. I bet that half the people over 75 would have been dead 10 or 20 years ago, were it not for all the amazing medical advances.

I have long-wondered why it costs so much dough to be a student in the humanities. After all, it's not as if novels and books of poetry are terribly pricey items. It's not as if cyclotrons or chemistry labs were required. Paper is paper, and it doesn't cost all that much. However, thanks to Michael Medved, I just recently learned that the average salary for American professors is more than $90,000-a-year, and that doesn't factor in what they might earn as researchers, consultants and writers. Even that nutjob,

Ward Churchill, I've read, was pulling down well over the national average, and that was just base salary, and didn't include personal appearance fees.

The second reason the colleges and universities charge so darn much is simply because, again like movie theaters that charge three or four dollars for 10 cents worth of popcorn or a nickel's worth of soda pop, they can.

P.T. Barnum, in his famous reference to suckers, remarked that there was one born every minute. He was wrong, of course. As the world of academia proves conclusively, it's far more frequently than that.

As a result, the biggest con game, the slickest racket, in America is the so-called college education.

I feel silly even referring to it as an education.

For some time now, I've heard age-conscious people claim that 70 is the new 60, and 60 is the new 50, and 50 is the new 40, and so on and so forth. The point is that because of diet and exercise, not to mention cosmetic surgery, today's 60-year-old could pass for yesterday's 50-year-old. But lately I've heard it being said that today's college is yesterday's high school, meaning that the level of education a 20-year-old is receiving is equal to what a 15-year-old used to receive. I happen to disagree with that assessment. I think it's comparable to junior high.

I honestly feel sorry for all those dutiful and loving parents who feel they must hock the silverware in order to finance junior's liberal arts education. Guilt, being as ingrained in some people as it is, I know that even if I started screaming from a rooftop that they'd all be better off if they gave the kids $10,000 and a library card my words would fall on deaf ears.

What the heck is the matter with you people? More and more, I feel like Howard Beale in "Network," urging his apathetic TV viewers to get up, go to the window, open it, stick their heads out, and yell: "I'm as mad as hell, and I'm not going to take this anymore!"

It's as if the nation's water supply had been tampered with by one of those fairytale witches who was always up to no good, poisoning apples, putting people into comas, locking them up in towers and placing curses on newborn babies. One day, it seems, everybody in America woke up convinced that he or she was the parent of a young scholar. No matter what sacrifice they had to make for their budding Albert Einstein or Marie Curie, they would see to it that their young sprouts made it safely through the groves of academe.

When I think about how little time professors actually spend in the classroom and how much of the really tedious, time-consuming work is handled by their assistants, their hourly wage is downright scandalous.

The waste of money is bad enough, but the waste of time should not be overlooked. Frankly, I don't care if my doctor has ever read Baudelaire or my accountant can tell a Manet from a Monet, not that they could even if they'd spent four years on a college campus. Thanks to computers and the local library, anybody can bone up on just about anything he's interested in, and it doesn't cost upwards of $100,000 to do it.

What college administrators claim is that they want to turn out well-rounded individuals, but that is such an obvious lie, it's a wonder they can say it with a straight face. Hardly anyone in America has been all that well-rounded since Thomas Jefferson passed away. Aside from learning how to drink themselves into a stupor and smooth-talk members of the opposite sex, those first four years have no other purpose than to drain off thousands of dollars from mom and dad in order to pay exorbitant salaries to deans, professors and a gaggle of athletic coaches. Speaking of athletics, I used to complain that subsidized athletes had no place on a college campus. I have now come to see the error of my ways. The truth is, they are just about the only under-grads who do belong there. At least they're preparing for their future careers, assuming they make it into the pro ranks.

These days, a liberal arts education is essentially no education at all. It's a catch-all that can include such feel-good curriculums as Black Studies, Chicano Studies, and even Lesbian Studies. There are even classes devoted to comic books, science fiction, burlesque and TV shows of the 50's. After four years of goofing around with this stuff, the young grads are prepared to do nothing except become professors themselves and regurgitate this drivel to the next herd of sheep.

I mean, how is it that Americans who lived hard scrabble lives 150 years ago could read, write, do math problems and quote at length from Shakespeare and the Bible, while today, in spite of "Sesame Street," preschool, Operation Head Start, computers and mind-numbing hours of homework, millions of youngsters entering college can do none of those things? And four years later, many of them still can't!

Really, what is there about being a grade school teacher, a social worker or a professor of English Literature, for that matter, that requires a major expenditure of time or money?

Millions and millions of 18-year-olds are being herded like cattle to the ivy-covered pens. These are people who have no intention of becoming scientists, engineers, mathematicians, architects, physicians or lawyers. So, assuming they can't dribble a basketball or pass a football, what the heck are they doing at what we might call trade schools for the elite?

There is a solution to this madness, but it would require that we quit pretending that anyone should be devoting four years to listening to lazy left-wing professors nattering on about 20th Century comic books, 19th Century French poetry, the movies of Sam Fuller, the scribbling of Noam Chomsky or the sex life of Henry Miller.

I once confessed that if any child of mine ever said he planed to get a liberal arts degree, I'd give him a library card and wish him all the best.

What I propose is that they turn colleges and universities into libraries, zoos, hospitals or, for all I care, parking lots or low income housing. And in place of these ivory towers, I would institute an assortment of trade schools. But not just those traditional trade schools where high school graduates learn to be mechanics, plumbers and carpenters, but trade schools for lawyers, doctors, dentists, accountants and architects.

Or if you don't think that's a swell idea, why not give diplomas to anybody who wants one and says "Please"? At least that way, with all the goobers off campus, there would be additional parking spaces for the youngsters studying the hard stuff.

My proposal, which owes a lot to the Wizard of Oz, who turned the Scarecrow into a virtual William F. Buckley, Jr., simply by handing him a sheepskin, would be far more honest and efficient than what we have today, plus parents wouldn't have to mortgage their homes just so Johnny and Susie can attend a school that has ivy on its walls or a nationally ranked team on its football field.

For the time being, though, I must accept the sad fact that on this issue at least, I remain the lone haranguer.

Even if we overlook the expense of a college education, we shouldn't ignore the damage done by left-wing professors.

For instance, 80-90% of those so-called educators in the humanities will devote 90-100% of class time propagandizing for the left, and trying to convince the kids that their parents are political troglodytes if they don't happen to agree that Che Guevara was a saint; that the members of al-Qaida and Hezbollah are freedom fighters; and that any war, otherwise known as a quagmire, in which America engages is motivated by oil, empire building and/or racism; unless, of course, the war is begun or at least waged during a Democrat's administration.

In addition, millions of young people who won't be able to write a cogent sentence or do long division without using a calculator will end up absolutely convinced that they're intellectually, not to mention morally, superior to their parents and their grandparents.

To paraphrase George Bernard Shaw: those who can, teach; those who can't, indoctrinate.

Another aspect of college that bears looking into is Affirmative Action and the notion that, for the sake of racial diversity, a quota system that rewards Black and Hispanic students at the expense of Asian students is a good thing.

Diversity in the student body is, according to those on the left, the ideal. But, as you may have noticed, there is no diversity among the faculties. In the humanities departments of most major colleges, professors run the gamut from liberal to radical. Given a choice between Ahmadinejad and a Republican, a large majority would vote for the little schmuck in the windbreaker.

It has always seemed to me that actual diversity is to be found among people who have different points of view, not different pigmentation. I, for instance, have far more in common with the likes of Thomas Sowell, Clarence Thomas and Walter Williams than I do with Keith Olbermann, Chris Matthews and Rachel Maddow.

Even though left wing professors profess that the college experience is enhanced by making certain that members of certain minority groups are allowed to leap-frog over other more deserving students, I have yet to hear of a single white professor who resigned so that a Black or Hispanic person could have his job.

If diversity is so wonderful, why limit it to people of color, and why give scholarships to students just because they're smart? If a mix of humanity is what they're really seeking, I say they should throw open the doors to idiots. And, no, I'm not referring to those aforementioned professors in the humanities who get paid a lot of money for doing nothing more than foisting their asinine politics on a bunch of highly impressionable 18-year-olds. No, I'm talking about the genuine article - people with subterranean I.Q.s.

In case you haven't gotten the word, the religious left, as I like to think of them, inasmuch as they live their lives according to a specific dogma, have now determined that poor people are terribly under-represented on America's college campuses. It was, I suppose, only a matter of time. After all, if no institute of higher education can justify its existence unless its student population is composed of X-percent of women, Hispanics, Blacks, gays and Islamic terrorists, some Democrat was bound to notice that there still remained an untapped source of future votes; namely, poor, young whites.

But we know that smart white kids already get scholarships, so it can only be the really dumb bunnies they have in mind.

Honestly, I haven't a clue why college would be a more exalting experience just because the student in the next seat has different pigmentation or hails from a country where indoor plumbing is optional.

Admittedly, it's been many years since I was a collegian. Still, as I recall, the real value of the four years, aside from learning how to drink and how to talk to women without stuttering, was the enforced proximity to the minds and works of Socrates, Newton, Freud, Shakespeare, Plato, Milton, Michelangelo, Einstein, Da Vinci and Jefferson, and was neither enhanced nor diminished by the color or creed of the other students.

The truth of the matter was that my interest in my fellow scholars, and I don't think my attitude was at all atypical, was limited to wanting to date the more attractive coeds and wanting to eviscerate those troublemakers most likely to raise the class curve.

Academics pride themselves on their accumulated knowledge, even though their focus is extremely narrow and their life experiences have rarely taken them very far from a school building from the time they were four or five years old.

In spite of their paying lip service to integrity and high principles, many academics see no need to be honest, tolerant or even logical. My friend, Larry Purdy, a Minnesota-based lawyer who worked on the University of Michigan cases regarding racial preferences, has written a book, "Getting Under the Skin of 'Diversity': Searching for the Color-Blind Ideal," that makes mincemeat of the Supreme Court's fatuous decisions, while reminding many of us why we celebrated Sandra Day O'Connor's departure from the bench. It was back in 1998, that Derek Book, former president of Harvard, and William Bowen, former president of Princeton, collaborated on a book, "The Shape of the River," which greatly influenced O'Connor and a majority of her associates.

The entire purpose of the book was to prove that racial preferences (aka Affirmative Action) were beneficial for the elite schools and for society at large. For openers, Purdy proves that Book and Bowen were deceptive, to say the least, because they never released the data that allegedly made their case. Instead, we're all simply expected to take their word for it even though, as clearly spelled out in Brown vs. Board of Education, the government is prohibited from treating citizens differently because of their race. According to Book and Bowen, the benefits of racial diversity on elite college campuses, no matter how it's achieved, simply outweighs all other considerations.

However, they admit that they don't have any idea how many of the minority students they claim to have studied made it to the university on their own merits and not simply because a bunch of elitist pinheads decided that leapfrogging them over more deserving white and Asian students was the American way.

Something else that Book and Bowen neglected to mention was the large number of minority students who graduated from historically Black colleges and universities and went on to achieve a reasonable amount of fame and fortune in spite of not attending Ivy League schools.

As much as I'd like to, I can't deny that Ivy League graduates tend to go on to greater success than most people. But that has far less to do with the quality of education than with the fact that the students so often come from families that are already wealthy and powerful because their ancestors owned railroads, banks and oil companies, and they therefore have dibs on Senate seats and the Oval Office.

This brings us to one of my major gripes with the Groves of Academe or, as I prefer to think of it, Hackademe.

First, I should confess that I am, at heart, a crusader, but, by temperament, a couch potato. To be really good at altering the status quo, you have to be ready to join with others in a mission, and I don't happen to like group activities. Even when a group consists of people I like as individuals, as soon as they organize, some bossy person is handing out marching orders, and somebody else is putting me to sleep reading the minutes of the last meeting.

Ideally, the way it should work is that I come up with great ideas and then get to lie down on the sofa and take a nap while other people run off and do the heavy lifting.

My latest campaign is to do away with tenure. If there's a dumber idea floating around than the guarantee of lifetime employment I'm not sure I want to hear about it. A person can take only so much stupidity in a single lifetime and I believe I've just about reached my quota.

So far as I'm aware, the only two groups that receive tenure in our society are federal judges and college professors. The theory is that these people need to be protected from undue political pressure. Well, these days, as we're all very much aware, there is as much or more blatant politicking involved in a Supreme Court appointment than in a presidential election. For the life of me, I don't see why a duly-elected president can only serve eight years, but a justice can serve forty or fifty.

It makes even less sense that professors are guaranteed a job for life. Guys on the assembly line don't have tenure. Gardeners and waitresses don't get tenure. Why should professors who already work short hours for good money be treated like English royalty?

One of the things that makes them particularly offensive is their hypocrisy. They all pretend that tenure is essential - not because it guarantees them a generous livelihood just so long as they don't burn down a dormitory or give a star athlete a failing grade - but because it ensures them the right to voice unpopular, even unpatriotic, opinions. The truth, however, is that, more often than not, they're the bullies censoring free speech and punishing with low marks those students with the gumption to speak their own minds.

I keep hearing the argument that, without such protection, they might be fired for political reasons. The fact of the matter is that, as more and more colleges and universities are infested with left-wing radicals, professors are far more likely to be hired because of their juvenile politics.

As for the risk that a professor of any political stripe might be shown the exit because the administration disapproves of his leanings, the question should be moot. Even if his field of study happens to be history, philosophy or even the Republican party in the 21st Century, no professor worth his salt has any business dragging his own partisan politics into the classroom. But suggest that to a left-wing academic, and he starts yelling about censorship, as if the job description includes proselytizing. In the Socratic method, to which academics are always paying lip service, the function of the professor isn't telling young people what to think, but, rather, helping pave the way so that they can think for themselves; to encourage them to ask hard questions, even to question their own beliefs, not to provide them with easy, half-baked answers.

Frankly, I think most parents would do better if they forgot about spending all that money at the tail end of their children's education. Instead, they should spend it earlier on. Those parents who, for one reason or another, are unable to home-school their offspring, should give serious consideration to taking them out of the public school system and placing them in private or parochial schools. By the time, the typical student has gone from kindergarten through high school, the teacher's union has had over a dozen years in which to indoctrinate him or her and turn your kid's head into a pile of mush.

Recently, I read of yet another fine example of why liberals should not ever be in charge of anything – not Congress, not the White House, not the military and certainly not education. In fact, I think that parents who don't do everything in their power to keep their kids out of the public school system should be charged with child abuse. In case you missed the story, Zachary Christie, age 6, was so proud of joining the Cub Scouts that he brought his new camping utensil, a combination fork, knife and spoon, to school, intending to use it at lunchtime. But he hadn't taken into account the knuckleheaded administrators running the Christina School District of Newark, Delaware.

For violating the zero-tolerance policy regarding "weapons," young Dillinger was not only kicked out of his grammar school, but faced 45 days of detention in reform school.

In a related matter, a year earlier, a third grader in Delaware was booted out of school because her grandmother sent her to class with a birthday cake, along with a knife for cutting it. One can only hope that Granny then baked her a second cake with a file in it so she could manage to bust her way out of jail.

Some of us have long puzzled over how a dunce like Delaware's Joe Biden could keep getting re-elected to the U.S. Senate. Well, we can stop wondering. That mystery has now been solved.

According to young Zachary's parents, the boy takes school so seriously that he sometimes insists on wearing a suit and tie to class. Now, however, it seems he's afraid he'll be teased because he's gotten into so much trouble. I just hope somebody assures this six-year-old that if he hasn't been ribbed over the suit and tie, he has very broad-minded schoolmates and probably has nothing to worry about.

But, what, I ask you, is the world coming to when a nice little boy gets into hot water for taking a Cub Scout tool to class so he can be the cool kid eating soup with his own personal spoon, but nobody thinks a thing about it when Henry Waxman or Barney Frank gets anywhere near a microphone or Barack Obama gets within 50 feet of a teleprompter?

A while back, in response to a piece I had written ridiculing the state of allegedly higher education, a reader wrote: "I remember when 'Lesbian, Gay, Bisexual and Transgender Studies' meant trying to figure out what's wrong with these people. In fact, if your child is majoring in something that ends in 'Studies,' you better not turn their bedroom into a den, because that one is coming home after college."

To which, I replied, "That's assuming you still own your home after taking out a second mortgage so your kid can waste four years studying how to be Black, Hispanic, bisexual or a lesbian."

Not too long ago, I read about a student in a debate class here in L.A. whose professor called him a "fascist bastard" and refused to allow him to conclude his remarks in opposition to same-sex marriages. Although I am aware that this betrayal of the First Amendment occurs regularly in classrooms and lecture halls all across America, the reason I heard about this particular case is because the student, Jonathan Lopez, decided to sue. For good measure, when Lopez, a devout Christian, asked his professor what grade he was getting for his speech, he was told to go ask God!

So, on some college campuses, it's okay to ridicule a student's religious convictions, but not to voice an objection to homosexual marriages.

Instead of tenure, I'd give these academics the gate.

Finally, when all is said and done, most college graduates aren't really smarter than other people. They just think they are.

CHAPTER THREE

Justice is Blind, Also Deaf & Dumb

There are so many things wrong with our legal system it's hard to know where to begin. There are the laws, the lawyers, the judges, the juries and the criminals.

Let us begin by considering judges, those God-like characters who get to wear their bathrobes to work and lord it over us mere mortals.

Anytime I hear my fellow conservatives talk about sitting out presidential elections, I want to grab them and shake them until their teeth rattle. Anything that puts Democrats even an inch closer to appointing federal judges should be more than enough reason to get every right-winger off the couch and down to his or her polling place.

In case you think I'm engaging in hyperbole, consider Judge Stephen Roy Reinhardt. He has been the mainstay of the U.S. Court of Appeals for the 9th Circuit for over a quarter of a century, ever since Jimmy Carter foisted him off on us.

What sort of disaster has Judge Reinhardt been? For openers, it was his court that first got our attention when it decided that "under God" had no place in the Pledge of Allegiance.

Not a court to rest on its laurels, the 9th Circuit garnered media attention with its rulings in a couple of high-profile murder cases. In the first, Reinhardt and his colleagues decided that a convicted killer was entitled to a new trial because the relatives of his victim had worn small buttons with their loved one's picture to court. The 9th Circuit decided this had undue influence on the jurors, although the trial judge had ruled otherwise, and the relatives, in any case, had only worn the buttons for the first two days of the lengthy trial.

In the other case, the defendant had murdered a young woman by bashing in her head with a dumbbell. No, an actual dumbbell, not Judge Reinhardt. In this instance, a three judge panel decided 2-1, Reinhardt providing the swing vote, that when the jurors back in 1982 sentenced the killer to die, they might not have taken into account "the defendant's potential for a positive adjustment to life in prison"!

Scary, isn't it?

But I'm only getting started. Judge Reinhardt is also the fellow who said, "I don't believe the Constitution says that individuals have a right to bear arms." Judge Reinhardt, let me introduce you to the Second Amendment.

There's more. When someone suggested that the 9th Circuit was the most liberal court in the country, he replied with a straight face: "When people say that, what they mean is that this court, unlike most of the circuit courts, isn't totally dominated by a group of conservative judges who have a view of the Constitution that is, to put it mildly, rather narrow and tends to resemble the view of the federal courts before the age of enlightenment." I guess he means way back in the old days when the Second Amendment was still part of the Constitution.

Not knowing the judge personally, I don't know if he drinks or is simply a visitor from a very strange planet, but in what was even for him a particularly loony moment, he actually said, "When President Clinton was appointing judges, he did not appoint liberals to the Supreme Court. He appointed people that would be acceptable to the Republicans in the Senate, and that's why he got some of his appointees nominated. But anyone who seemed to be slightly liberal would not even get a hearing." Judge Reinhardt, let me introduce you to Ruth Bader Ginsburg.

Sometimes those on the Left accuse those of us on the Right of putting words in their mouth. But the truth is, we don't need to. Besides, even if we tried, we wouldn't succeed because they usually have one or more of their feet jammed in there, and there's simply not enough room to get a stupid word in edgewise!

Lately, every time some scofflaw is convicted of a crime, the presiding judge and the media seem to place an enormous amount of weight on whether or not the creep was properly contrite. Am I the only person who doesn't care? If anything, I am more sympathetic towards the felon who doesn't add hypocrisy to his sins. The obvious fact is that, like a six-year-old who's caught with his hand in the cookie jar, criminals are only sorry that they've been caught.

Even worse than those who claim in court that they've seen the error of their ways are those sanctimonious phonies who suddenly make a big show of having found God in prison, hoping they'll be able to use this sudden epiphany to get time lopped off their sentences. If it were up to me, I'd throw the book at them. The Good Book. Let's face it, if you can't find God before you're behind bars, you really haven't been looking. After all, it's not like He's been hiding.

If I were serving on a parole board and some chucklehead tried to convince me I should grant him early release because he'd discovered religion, I'd tack on extra time for attempting to perpetrate a con game. So far as I'm concerned, if he'd truly seen the light, he'd understand better than most people why he should be punished to the full extent of the law.

I think I first developed this attitude during the aftermath of Watergate. Back in those days, I was a Democrat and, like most of my friends, I was delighted to see Nixon leave the White House under a cloud of his own making. We were equally delighted to see his crew-cut cronies, Halderman and Ehrlichman, crash and burn. But only I seemed to resent the fact that White House insider John Dean got so many Brownie points for essentially ratting out his chums and colleagues.

I begrudgingly accept that plea bargaining is a part of modern life, but it seemed terribly inappropriate that people were bestowing heroic stature on somebody whose claim to glory was nothing more than his managing to be the first rodent off the sinking ship. I felt that if his self-serving testimony meant lawyer Dean wasn't going to go to jail, he should at least have been shunned by society. Instead, Hollywood, well-known for its own highly flexible code of morality, rolled out the red carpet for Dean and the missus. The way John and Mo were feted, you'd have thought he'd done something brave and wonderful, instead of having merely cut himself a deal with the prosecution, just like any other petty hood.

The only one of the lot who came out of Watergate with his dignity intact was weird G. Gordon Liddy. He didn't whine, he didn't apologize and he served his time without trying to convince anybody that he had found Jesus in the next cell.

I would suggest that it's only remorse if it takes place before you're arrested. After that, it's merely defense strategy.

For a long time, I've realized that the only people who place more emphasis on blood than certain aboriginal tribes, Islamic fundamentalists and Dracula, are American judges.

Some years ago, in a highly-publicized case, the Illinois Supreme Court removed a young child from his adopted family, and handed him over, as if he were a used car or a stick of furniture, to some foreign jerk-off who hadn't even been married to the boy's biological mother. But blood, these black-robed idiots decided, counted for more than love and sacrifice, and for far more than what the child wanted or needed.

There have been countless cases in which the children of women who used crack cocaine even during their pregnancies were taken away from the only home and only parents the children had ever known because, at some point and for however long, the woman managed to get off drugs. These women endangered the child even before it was born, they're unwed, and usually have no parenting skills or any other skills beyond hooking for a living. But none of that matters, not so long as they're connected by blood. So far as these mutton-headed jurists are concerned, blood trumps everything, including common sense and common decency. So far as these judges are concerned, blood is indeed thicker than water. But nothing is quite so thick as their own heads.

Another such outrage took place in Memphis, Tennessee. In 1999, little Anna Mae's biological parents, Shaoqiang and Quin Luo He, gave up their infant daughter, and Jerry and Louse Baker became her foster parents. You still remember 1999, don't you? Bill Clinton was occupying the White House, the Twin Towers were still standing, and nobody but her parents had even heard of Paris Hilton. If you think that was a long time ago, imagine how long it would seem if it were your entire life.

Suddenly, in 2007, the He's decided that they wanted Anna Mae snatched away from everything and everyone she had ever known. And, naturally, the members of the Tennessee Supreme Court agreed. If I were running things, it would take me all of five minutes to determine that these judicial guttersnipes were aiding and abetting in what is clearly nothing more than a court-sanctioned kidnapping. Then I'd send the bunch of them off to the salt mines, there to reflect on the error of their ways.

Oh, did I forget to mention that, on top of everything else, Shaoqiang and Quin Luo He were illegal aliens?

Mrs. Baker said at the time, "Our sweet, loving little girl is full of anger, and she's yelling that nobody understands her."

On the other hand, David Siegel, the attorney for the He's, accused the Bakers of attempting to stir up public sentiment, ruining what "has otherwise been a very peaceful transition."

First, I'd ask, which of these two people do you actually believe? Next, I'd like to know how it is that some lawyers aren't compelled, like lepers in the old days, to ring little bells and say, "Unclean...unclean" whenever they appear in public. I'd also like to know who marries these creatures, and why.

In conclusion, let me merely say that the blindfold on Justice is intended to be taken symbolically, not literally. Justice, after all, is supposed to be blind, not stupid.

Moving on, I think I understand the reason why so many politicians are reluctant to take a tough stand against the illegal aliens pouring across our southern border. It's partly pandering for votes, partly providing corporate America with cheap labor, and partly a natural reluctance to be branded as racists by the liberal media, Latino leaders on the make, and the moral cretins in the ACLU.

I don't like it, but at least I can understand their tawdry motives. However, when it comes to our legal system, I am totally at a loss. More often than not, I feel as if I've fallen down the same rabbit hole as Alice, and found myself lost in Lewis Carroll's Wonderland.

Perhaps it's because I was summoned for jury duty a few weeks ago that I have been hyper-aware of criminal matters. My attention was particularly grabbed by a couple of news items. The setting for the first was the small Colorado city of Fort Lupton. It's there that Municipal Judge Paul Sacco has been making a name for himself by employing a Solomon-like sense of justice in dealing with young scofflaws.

Previously, when teenagers stood accused of blasting their car stereos or otherwise disturbing the peace and assaulting the ears of those residents whose taxes pay his salary, Judge Sacco was in the habit of levying fines. But then one day, it occurred to him that the tickets weren't changing anything. The parents would pay the $95, and the kids would continue their noisy ways. It was then that he came up with the brilliant idea of giving the offenders a dose of their own medicine. Ever since then, he has sentenced them to spend an entire hour on a Friday evening in the courtroom listening to everything from Barry Manilow to Boy George, from Beethoven's Ninth to Barney's theme song.

As a result, noise offenses in Fort Lupton dropped from 56 in 2007 to 20 in 2008. Even more telling, the recidivism rate is now less than 5%.

I realize it's probably too much to ask, but the next time there's an opening on the Supreme Court, I hope that Judge Sacco makes the short list.

The other matter concerns the LAPD's announcement the other day that they had finally arrested the mastermind behind the gang that had been dubbed the "Hillside Burglars." Over the last few years, this guy and his crew had apparently committed more than 150 break-ins, absconding with over $10 million in cash and loot from the homes of Hollywood executives, celebrities and sports stars.

As I read the news, I couldn't help thinking that if I were a lawyer hired to defend this guy in the current political climate, I'd try to convince the jury that he wasn't really a thief, but that he was merely doing his part to help the government redistribute wealth.

Why, for instance, do we go so far out of our way to protect criminals? It's as if we're playing a game and all the rules are in their favor. For instance, why should a cop making an arrest have to pause to read the perp his rights and run the risk that the case will be blown if he happens to forget? Why shouldn't jurors be made aware of the defendant's criminal history? Why should a cop's honest mistake work to the felon's advantage? The liberals would have us believe that all of these so-called safeguards serve to protect us from police malfeasance, but most of us, I dare say, would prefer to take our chances with the cops and be protected from madmen, thugs and their defense attorneys.

Before you rush forward to defend this cockeyed legal system, allow me to conclude with yet another example of this lunacy. I recall reading about a man who was found guilty of killing his young bride. The judge gave him six years-to-life. I ask you, what kind of sentence is that? What is the message? The killer gets a mere six years for cold-blooded murder, perhaps with time off for good behavior, but if he doesn't make his bed or eat all his vegetables, he could rot in jail for the next sixty years?

A question that bears looking into is, whether a career in politics inevitably turns people into four-flushers or whether four-flushers are born, not made, and are simply drawn to the field the way that metal shavings are drawn to a magnet.

Being a conservative, naturally I hold Democrats in far lower regard than I do Republicans. But, overall, I don't think that politicians of any stripe should be trusted anywhere near a live microphone or anybody's wallet. In fact, I find most people's infatuation with office holders completely infantile and unseemly, and on a par with an adolescent girl's crush on some slack-jawed rock star.

After all, what does a politician do that is so admirable? He spends most of his waking hours shaking down friends and strangers for campaign funds so that he can remain in office...and, thus, continue shaking down friends and strangers for campaign funds.

In those odd moments when he takes a break from lining his own coffers, his work consists in coming up with novel and foolish ways to spend our tax dollars. And, ninnies that we are, we applaud him as if he'd just written a personal check!

Up to now, I've merely been generalizing about politicians as a group. But, for sheer unadulterated duplicity, you can't beat the left-wing members of the U.S. Senate, and don't even think about trying. You'd only hurt yourself.

As loathsome as they are on any given day, they rise to truly unimaginable heights on those occasions when they're sitting in judgment of a prospective jurist. Consider, for instance, the back alley mugging they administered to Judge Charles Pickering, a man who had faced down the Ku Klux Klan, condemning him as a racist, of all things, thus ensuring that this gallant gentleman would never be allowed to sit on the bench beside Ruth Bader Ginsburg. Well, perhaps there was an upside, after all, for Judge Pickering.

One only has to look at the way they attacked Sam Alito, by all accounts a decent man in both his public and private life, to realize the depths to which these moral pygmies will stoop in order to promote their leftist agenda. I find myself wondering how such fellows as Robert Byrd and the late Ted Kennedy would have dealt with judicial nominees who'd been carting around their own respective baggage.

Can't you imagine the blood-letting that would occur if a Republican president dared nominate a judge who, like Senator Byrd, had been a member of the Ku Klux Klan?

Better yet, can't you picture the grilling that Kennedy, the swizzle stick kid himself, would give a candidate who had earned a well-deserved reputation as a college cheat, a life-long sot, an unrepentant womanizer and, for good measure, had committed manslaughter?

Finally, can't you envision the late senator from Massachusetts leaning forward in his chair, peering down at the judicial wannabe over those glasses he always wore on such occasions, and saying in that overbearing voice that could curdle milk: "How dare you even think about sitting on the highest court in the land! Who are you to sit in judgment of any man? Does the name Mary Jo Kopechne not ring any bells for you? It surely does for me, sir. It surely does for me."

Even in this so-called enlightened age, I have no problem admitting I am in favor of capital punishment. I don't view it as a deterrent, understand, I consider it the only appropriate punishment for cold-blooded murder. Actually, I have only two objections to it. The first is that the killer with more than a single murder to his credit can only be executed the one time. Next, I resent the fact that no matter how much he may have tortured his victims, society has seen fit to send him off as painlessly as possible. I find it bizarre that in a country where mercy killings are illegal even for the terminally ill, only our beloved pets and vicious psychopaths are guaranteed a merciful death.

That brings me to Stanley Williams, better known as Tookie. Speaking of which, I, for one, resent that the media - as if beholden to his defense team - kept calling this stone-cold killer "Tookie," as if he were some child's teddy bear.

Stanley Williams used a shotgun to blow the heads off four people. That's some teddy bear.

I knew that Williams was being held up as a reformed character because he supposedly used his influence to steer young people away from gangs. Considering the escalating number of gang-related murders, it seems that Mr. Williams, who was the founding father of the Crips, was much better at getting kids into gangs than out of them.

Although, intellectually, I can grasp the point of view of those morally opposed to capital punishment, emotionally I am unable to fathom how they can congregate outside prisons and hold candlelight vigils for mass murderers. Wouldn't their time be better spent visiting the burial sites of the victims, and leaving flowers instead of candle wax behind?

There are those who claim that Williams, who never even voiced remorse for his crimes, had found redemption behind bars. They point out that he had even written a children's book. Never having had occasion to read it, it took Michael Medved to point out that Williams had dedicated it to Nelson Mandela. To Nelson Mandela, that is, along with a slew of cop killers!

Some of his fans argue that Williams, having spent over a quarter of a century in prison, was a totally different person than the guy who'd been convicted. Well, it's true that he hadn't shot-gunned anybody to death in all that time. But I happen to believe it's far more relevant that his victims had been deprived of a cumulative hundred years of life by this brute, and that doesn't even include what their friends and families lost.

Claiming that it was immoral, after all those years of incarceration, to execute Williams makes as much sense as appearing as amicus curiae on behalf of the man who murders his parents and then pleads for mercy as an orphan. If Williams and his mouthpieces hadn't filed appeal after appeal, he would have been executed in a far more timely fashion.

To me, the only amusing aspect of this entire matter is that the man was constantly being identified as a Nobel Prize nominee. Sometimes, he was a nominee for literature, other times for peace. For all I know, he may have been nominated for both. He may even have been nominated for medicine, physics and economics. The truth of the matter is that anybody can nominate anyone for a Nobel Prize. In fact, considering that the likes of Le Duc Tho, Kofi Annan, Al Gore, Barack Obama, Jimmy Carter and his friend Yasser Arafat, have actually been honorees, you can see that not only can any ne'er-do-well get nominated, he can even win. Quite frankly, I was surprised that Gov. Schwarzenegger allowed the execution to take place. With all the campaigning on behalf of Williams by the Hollywood elite, I fully expected him to capitulate.

I'm glad my instincts were wrong. It took gumption for Schwarzenegger to do the right thing. The Terminator may be long gone, but the Exterminator showed up just in time.

Hasta la vista, Tookie.

Still, I can nearly, but not quite, comprehend why some people object to capital punishment. After all, if they're unaware that Thou Shall Not Kill is a bad translation of Thou Shall Not Murder, you can see where they might wind up believing that the execution of a serial killer is as sinful as the original crime. On the other hand, I happen to think that, at this late date, there's no excuse for a grown-up not having bothered to find out what the Sixth Commandment actually says. That's especially the case if he's going to carry on as if he has dibs on the moral high ground, and accuse those who disagree with him of being bloodthirsty savages.

That said, what I can't begin to fathom are the people who seem to have the same tender feelings for sexual predators that the rest of us have for our dogs and cats. Unfortunately, these aren't the same mushy-headed simpletons holding candlelight vigils outside San Quentin. Instead, they're judges and legislators.

Each time I hear any of these people discuss how many feet away from a school playground or a park some pedophile should be allowed to live, I'm reminded of those nuts in the middle ages who whiled away their days arguing over how many angels could dance on the head of a pin. It's as if I had just awakened in Oz to discover that my farmhouse had landed smack dab on top of a witch named Common Sense.

For what reason would any sane society ever release such a person from jail? The notion that kids are safe if the creep lives 2,000 feet away from where they play is perfectly idiotic. What about the kids walking to and from those parks and playgrounds? Are we supposed to take the freak's word that he'll behave himself? If so, why not release all the bank robbers, making certain that none of them lives closer than two blocks away from the nearest branch of First National? I believe it's safe to assume that robbers can far more easily control their desire to knock over a bank than perverts can be counted on to control their urge to rape a child.

Only judges and lawmakers seem happy to ignore the rates of recidivism among rapists and pedophiles. Is there anyone else, aside from defense attorneys, who would argue that a man who's raped a child deserves a second chance?

Whenever I read about the problems of resettling these creeps once they're out of jail and then trying to keep track of them until the day they die, I can only shake my head. Why should anyone be able to destroy the life of a little child and the child's family and ever be allowed to see the light of day again?

So far as I'm concerned, the only place they belong isn't 700 yards from the nearest see-saw, but in a dungeon or in Hell. Next best would be having them move in with a politician or a judge.

As a general rule, I try to make allowance for human failings. That's because, more often than not, they do no lasting harm. On top of which, they're usually pretty darn funny.

But there's one subject which simply has no amusing aspects. If you thought I was going to say child molesters, you're only partly right. For as vile these bottom-feeding scum-suckers are, there are others who are even worse, if only because they are far more numerous.

For openers, there are the lawyers who use all their guile to con juries into letting these freaks run loose. I have no idea how these shysters sleep at night, knowing full well that their own children and grandchildren could be the creep's next prey.

Next we have the judges, the parole boards, the ACLU and the legislatures, who are all in cahoots to pretend that these degenerates are just like other criminals. It's just not so. Sentence a burglar or a thief to a few years in jail, and there's always a chance he'll come out a changed man. He may not be a saint, but it's just possible he'll decide it's not worth knocking over a 7-11 for a few hundred bucks if it's going to land his sorry butt back in the clink.

But there is no group of evildoers with a higher rate of recidivism than those who brutalize children. In order to live out their sick fantasies, they would risk being drawn-and-quartered. There is a very good reason that parents don't want them moving into the neighborhood once they're out of prison. Parents instinctively know the truth about them, but unfortunately parents do not make the laws or determine the sentences.

The question with these devils isn't whether they'll strike again, but only when. I hear some of you demurring. What about those, you ask, who somehow see the light? Is it fair that they don't get to prove they've had an epiphany? Is it fair that they don't get to prove they're rehabilitated? Yes, it is fair and just and moral. For one thing, if they fool us, the price of their freedom is far too high. Far better for them to rot in jail than for one more child to be at risk. Besides, how many chances should anyone have to brutalize a three-year-old?

Some years ago, a man in California abducted a young girl, raped her, and then, just for the hell of it, chopped off both her arms. I wonder how many other people, like me, were amazed when a few years later we read that he had served his sentence, moved to Florida, and been arrested for murdering a woman. For God's sake, what the hell does a guy have to do in order to spend the rest of his miserable life behind bars?

A short time later, we all heard about the monster who snatched a little 11-year-old at a carwash, murdered her and left her body in a church parking lot. He had already been imprisoned for molesting a child and then, upon being released, in spite of violating his parole, the judge in the case refused to send him back to jail. But if the D.A. had had his way, the man would have been serving an additional 15 years in the pen, and the child would have arrived home safely.

Finally, we have Kenneth Parnell, who first achieved fame as the ogre who kidnapped little Steven Stayner, molesting and torturing him for seven long years, and then abducted a five-year-old before being captured. After all that, he served a five-year term in Soledad. Five years! In other words, his sentence was shorter than Steven's!

At the age of 72, lest you think the freaks out-grow their dementia, Parnell was arrested for attempting to buy a four-year-old boy for $500.

What does it say about a society when it takes such a casual attitude towards crimes against children? I believe that sexual perverts really can't control their obscene behavior. That's why I think they should be locked up once and for all in asylums for the criminally insane.

By now, some of you, realizing that I am a big proponent of capital punishment, are probably thinking I've turned into a big softy, shocked that I'm willing to let these abominations go on living.

But, then, you haven't asked me what I'd do to their lawyers.

We pretend that registering these perverts is a deterrent and that our kids are safe if we order the monsters to stay a certain distance away from parks and playgrounds when any sane person knows that an adult who can't be trusted within a thousand yards of a four-year-old should be locked away in a dungeon and gnawed on by rats. Or at least be forced to watch "The View" or re-runs of "Hardball With Chris Matthews" for the next fifty or sixty years.

The only message we send when we allow those without souls to walk free is that we care more about them than we do about their innocent and inevitable victims. What is especially disgusting is that for each one of them, there are scores of lawyers eager to defend their right to live amongst us. Why is it we don't register these members of the bar as sex offenders? After all, they aid and abet criminals just as much as the guy driving the getaway car for bank robbers. One day, my hometown newspaper, the L.A. Times, carried the headline "Fixes in Jessica's Law Are Urged." The sub-head read: "Tight residency curbs on sex offenders can leave them homeless and propel them to re-offend, a panel says."

For those of you fortunate enough to live someplace where the Times isn't your local daily, let me assure you that a similar news story runs nearly as regularly as Doonesbury and Dennis the Menace.

It dismayed me the first time I came across a story bemoaning the difficulty of finding homes for these perverts. By this late date, it leaves me seething with rage.

The state's Sex Offender Management Board is urging Gov. Schwarzenegger and the state legislators to change Jessica's Law, insisting that its restrictions on where sex offenders can live are counter-productive and calling the $25 million-a-year spent to house them, mainly in motels and halfway houses, a poor use of tax dollars.

The law, which was passed in 2006 with the approval of 70% of California's voters, bars sex offenders from living within 2,000 feet of schools, parks and other areas where children gather. The Board is concerned that it drives the offenders "into homelessness, an unstable situation that can propel them back to crime."

Scott Kernan, undersecretary for adult operations at the California Department of Corrections and Rehabilitation, announced that his agency is discussing plans to scale back its housing of sex offenders, some of whom have their rent paid for several years while they're on parole.

Okay, first off let me say that some "sex offenders" shouldn't be branded as such. If a 15-year-old girl decides to have sex with her 18-year-old boyfriend, I'd have to be even sillier than I am to suggest the guy should go to jail or have to spend the rest of his life under a black cloud. Heck, if anyone's going to jail, it should probably be the young Jezebel. Everyone knows that 15-year-old girls are smarter and wilier than 18-year-old boys. In fact, as a rule, males don't even begin to narrow the gap until they're well into their 40's and 50's, and often not even then.

When I think of a sex offender, I have rapists and pedophiles in mind, as I suspect most people do. What's more, I'm willing to wager that the reason that 70% of us voted for Jessica's Law was out of frustration because the state doles out such light sentences to these monsters. The very idea of a pedophile being paroled is totally absurd. What's he being rewarded for? Not raping any five-year-olds while he was behind bars?

What could be any more ridiculous, or demented, than declaring that a child molester can live 2,001 feet from a neighborhood playground, but not 1,999 feet? What's to prevent him from going out his front door and taking a walk? What about the kid who doesn't go to the playground, but, tragically, lives next door or around the corner? For such potential victims, the bogeyman isn't a figment of his or her imagination, it's that freak up the block.

As for the contention that being homeless or restricted as to where he can live would propel a man to molest a child, one can only shake one's head and hope the double-strength Excedrin kicks in. A normal human being might feel driven by homelessness to rob a bank or knock over a McDonald's, but molest a child? Who, aside from a bottom-feeding defense attorney, would even suggest such a rationale?

The Sex Offender Management Board has 17 members whose salaries are paid by the taxpayers. Frankly, I could do the job by myself and I wouldn't even ask for a paycheck. I would simply go before the state legislature and tell them I had the perfect solution to the problem of housing rapists and pedophiles. You either execute them, I'd say, or keep them locked up in dungeons until they die, at which point housing them becomes Satan's responsibility.

Then, my mission completed, I would next pull off an honest-to-goodness miracle. I would resign, thus making the Sex Offender Management Board the first government bureaucracy in human history to actually disappear.

There are very few things you can confess to these days that will garner you a raised eyebrow, let alone public censure. After all, a day doesn't go by that people don't go on TV and admit to all sorts of crimes and misdemeanors that may elicit an ovation from Oprah's audience, but rate no more than a shrug and a stifled yawn from the rest of us, sated, as we are, with such disclosures. Use drugs? Commit serial adultery? Beat your kids? Kick your dog? Date sheep? Ho hum.

I, on the other hand, am about to admit something that will rub a lot of people the way that steel wool rubs pewter. I hereby confess that I never presume that anybody who's been arrested and indicted is innocent. While I realize that some of them are, that the eye-witness made a mistake or the cops nabbed the wrong guy or the D.A. was overzealous, my assumption is that the mug on trial is as guilty as sin.

Although I understand that our legal system is based on the presumption of innocence and the notion that every person, however vile his history, is entitled to the best defense his money can buy, I can't help believing that he wouldn't be in hot water if he hadn't committed the crime.

What's more, I don't stop thinking he's guilty just because one goofball on the jury got flimflammed by some fast-talking shyster, and wound up handing him a Get Out of Jail Free card. Furthermore, I'll go so far as to state that, whatever folks may say to the contrary, most of you feel the same way.

As we all saw in the O.J. Simpson case, even the term "a jury of his peers" has been turned on its head. Whatever it may have meant in the past, in our silly age it has come to mean that Blacks have to be well-represented on a jury trying a Black defendant, even if he happens to be a wealthy ex-jock who has spent most of his adult life chasing blondes, and has nothing in common, aside from pigmentation, with those fans sitting in the jury box.

Those who insist that we mustn't ever presume guilt inevitably commandeer the moral high ground. It just sounds so nice, this presumption of innocence, so highly principled, so doggone American. The problem is that once you cut through the malarkey, what it really is, is laughable.

Do we presume Hitler was innocent? Or Idi Amin? How about Stalin? Pol Pot? Saddam Hussein? Why not? Not one of those bastards was ever been found guilty of mass murder by a jury of his peers.

To believe that we must presume these butchers were therefore innocent makes you a fool. Wishing you'd had the opportunity to plead their case makes you something even worse. It makes you an ACLU lawyer!

Up until now, I have been dealing with the theoretical. That's because, aside from having been the plaintiff in a few small claims cases, I had been able to avoid courtrooms for most of my life. In fact, until about a dozen years ago, I hadn't even been called in to do jury duty.

But once I got on the list, not a year has gone by that I don't get called to fulfill my civic responsibility. And being who I am, I resent the rigmarole. I mean, why on earth can't they just erase my name and pretend I don't exist?

Why do I have to keep calling the court's hotline every night for a week to find out if I have to show up the next morning when any sane person would realize that even if I got down on my knees and begged, no defense attorney in his right mind would ever let me slip by. For one thing, I wrote for several TV crime shows, ranging from Dragnet and McMillan and Wife to Diagnosis Murder, and I never had any qualms about doling out justice to the bad guys. In fact, on one memorable occasion, I found myself at loggerheads with Dragnet's producer-director, Jack Webb. In an episode I wrote involving a young woman who had abandoned her newborn baby, Webb argued for an ending in which the infant would be placed in her arms and the woman would undergo a transformation from monster to Madonna in five tear-jerky seconds. "Jack," I still recall saying, "she dumped her baby in a dumpster. I'm not letting her walk. She's going to do time!" You'd have thought I was talking about an actual person. In any case, Webb backed down, and we ended up giving her two-to-five.

Even now, when my own TV writing career is over, the only things I ever watch on the tube, aside from baseball games and old movies, are "Monk" and re-runs of "Columbo." As you may have noticed, these are shows in which nogootniks, no matter how rich and clever they are or how wily and underhanded their defense attorneys, get their just deserts right before the final commercial.

As if that weren't bad enough, I once wrote an article in which I confessed that one of the few things, aside from his spirited defense of Israel, ever written by Alan Dershowitz that I accepted as gospel was his contention that over 90% of all criminal defendants are guilty as charged.

And, finally, at the point during voir dire when I'd be asked if I would vote for acquittal if, in spite of a preponderance of evidence, the defense could show that the police had committed a technical error in making the arrest, I'd have to admit that I couldn't imagine myself ever doing anything quite that ridiculous.

So far as I'm concerned, if the cops make a simple human error, that in no way entitles the criminal to walk free. If, on the other hand, the cops make an intentional error, I would put the cops on trial, but I'd still be unable to grasp the logic of letting the felon scoot. I mean, short of planting evidence, employing the third degree in order to obtain a confession or committing perjury, I fail to see how the behavior of the cops should ever affect the outcome of a criminal trial.

As you can plainly see, I simply am not cut out to be a juror. On the other hand, I think I'd make a hell of a judge.

Recently, though, I thought that just possibly a miracle had occurred, something along the lines of the earth not spinning or hell freezing over. For the first time ever, I was going to undergo questioning during an honest to goodness voir dire. In the past, I had sat by while other potential jurors went through the process, but the jury box was always filled before they got around to me.

I had arrived at the Burbank courthouse, identified as Juror 3343, at 8 a.m. It was now seven hours later, during which time we potential jurors had been handed a sheet of paper with 15 questions to ponder. A few of the initial group of 40 or so had already been questioned and admitted they were related to police officers or lawyers, and, so far as I could tell, they had been excused with thanks.

By the time it was my turn to be questioned, I was feeling self-conscious because, as I stated in open court, I had a problem with three of the questions that nobody else had even mentioned. The judge cast what I regarded as a jaundiced eye in my direction, and asked me to explain myself.

The first of the three questions had to do with the presumption of innocence. I told Judge Lubell that, try as I might, I couldn't quite accept the idea that it was just an accident that 40 of us in the room were potential jurors and one of us was the defendant. So while I was prepared to assume that the rest of us were innocent, I would have a much harder time believing it about the fellow sitting at the table next to a defense attorney. I did promise, though, to make a sincere effort if I wound up on the jury.

Next, I was asked if I was prepared to give equal weight to any witness giving testimony in the witness box. I confessed that I couldn't in good faith make such a promise. "What if one of the witnesses is a priest," I asked, "and another is a convicted drug dealer? Who in his right mind would give their sworn testimony equal weight?"

There was a third question, which slips my mind, but it was along similar lines, and like the other two, required that I leave my logic and commonsense sitting outside on the courtroom steps.

Finally, the defense attorney decided he'd take his turn at trying to crack this nut: "Well," he said, "what if the prosecutor states in his opening remarks that he's going to prove four points, but by the end of the trial he had, to your mind, only proven three of them? Would you then be able to vote for acquittal?"

"It's impossible for me to play that theoretical game with you because I don't know what those four points are or if they'd be of equal importance. Right now, the best I can do is suggest we wait for the end of the trial and see how it all plays out." Five seconds later, I was excused. I didn't hear the judge say, "Thanks."

Some of you probably think I gave those answers because I was trying to get out of doing my civic duty. Not so. I answered as I did because I was telling the truth, the whole truth, and nothing but the truth, so help me God. Which, I'm willing to wager, is more than the 12 people who wound up sitting in that jury box can say with a straight face.

CHAPTER FOUR

Islam is a Peaceful Religion,
And if You Don't Believe It,
They'll Cut Off Your Head

I, for one, am sick and tired of hearing how wonderful the followers of Islam are. First it was George Bush and Condoleezza Rice singing their praises, insisting in the wake of the Ayatollah Khomeni taking hostages; the destruction of two U.S. embassies; the first attack on the Twin Towers; the attack on the USS Cole and the Marine barracks; and, finally, 9/11; that Islam was a religion of peace.

The big lie continued after the Republican cheerleaders left office and Barack Obama moved into the White House. He went to Turkey and boasted about the contributions Muslims have made to America down through the years. He wasn't specific, so I tried to figure out what he was referring to, but the only thing that came to mind was the way they had dramatically changed the look of lower Manhattan.

Some people might assume that my antipathy to the people and nations of the Middle East, aside from the Jews in Israel, is explained by the fact I'm Jewish. Some people could win gold medals if jumping to conclusions was an Olympic event.

Just for the record, I am a non-observant Jew. That means that my mother's father, Max Lashevsky, who kept kosher and attended an orthodox synagogue twice-a-day every day of his life, would probably have considered me a heathen, while Adolf Hitler would have had me exterminated.

I want to be perfectly clear so that when I declare my concern for Israel, nobody will simply assume it's because I'm Jewish. I am on the side of Israel because it's a Western democracy, an ally of America, and because I regard her enemies to be our enemies, people dedicated to our mutual annihilation.

Israel's foes believe in targeting women and children just so long as they're Jewish or Christian. They are not only intolerant of the freedoms we take for granted - speech and religion - but they are adverse to liberty, they treat their women as chattel and encourage their children to achieve martyrdom as suicide bombers. Moreover, the abomination known as honor killings are part of what passes for their culture.

In order to realize what a paternalistic society they have, you need only look at a photo of an Islamic mob carting a corpse through the streets of Gaza; even when it's the corpse of a child, I challenge you to find a woman anywhere in sight. So far as they're concerned, the mother, grandmother, aunts and sisters, are of absolutely no consequence, unless, of course, they can be persuaded to strap several sticks of dynamite to themselves and pay a visit to an Israeli pizza parlor.

Yet here in America and even more so in Europe, you will find millions of presumably civilized people, particularly in Hollywood and on our left-wing college campuses, who theoretically find a moral equivalence between Israel and her sworn enemies - while invariably siding with the Islamics.

In a recent Rasmussen Poll, 62% of Republicans in America were aligned with Israel, while a mere 31% of Democrats favored the Israelis in their life-and-death conflict.

As you may have noticed, the world's media rarely if ever remarked on the thousands of missiles Hamas fired into Israel over the past few years. However, once Israel finally got around to announcing that enough was enough, and went on the offensive, Condoleezza Rice and the European Union didn't waste a second before crying "Foul!" and throwing a penalty flag. Going them one better, the present administration has earmarked nearly a billion dollars for Hamas, while they distracted us over the $165 million in AIG bonuses.

This same pattern is followed each and every time that Israel responds to unprovoked attacks. You can inevitably count on the nations of the world agreeing that Israel is out of line. While it's nice they can agree on something, it's a shame that "something" never seems to be Islamic terrorism, Arab barbarism, or slavery and black genocide in modern-day Africa. As someone once observed, "If Israel's enemies laid down their arms, there would be peace tomorrow in the Middle East; if Israel laid down its arms, there would be genocide."

Can you imagine anyone in his right mind in 1941 claiming that America was over-reacting to Pearl Harbor? Would anybody but an idiot have suggested that once America had sunk an equal number of Japanese battleships or killed an equal number of Japanese soldiers and sailors that we should have ceased hostilities and turned things over to European diplomats, especially after seeing how well those fellows in striped pants had kept Hitler and Mussolini in check?

The fact is, it's a con game to continue referring to the folks in Gaza as refugees. The only reason that there were any Arab refugees back in 1948 was because Egypt, Jordan and Syria, promised to exterminate the Jews and divide the spoils, not because Israel had exiled its Arab population. Once Israel fought off the invaders, no Arab nation would open its doors to the refugees, and to this day no Arab nation ever has.

But that was over 60 years ago! Who ever heard of people being refugees for six decades? How can people who have never lived in Israel, whose fathers and mothers never lived in Israel, continue to lay claim to a place where they've never set foot - and which, according to Arab textbooks, doesn't even exist? They might as well insist they have a claim to Oz, Atlantis or Brigadoon.

For those who would claim that the Jews weren't entitled to their own state, the truth is that most of the land that is now Israel was purchased from Arabs, at exorbitant prices, over the course of several decades by Zionists who began settling there in the 19th Century.

Finally, I marvel at Israel's spiritual fortitude and her reluctance to seek Biblical retribution. Even one missile would be enough to get me riled up. To absorb 10,000 missile attacks strikes me as verging on the masochistic. I honestly think Israel continues to be far too concerned with world opinion. After decades of hearing one's enemies parroting Hitler's plans for the final solution, collateral damage would be the least of my concerns.

I understand that civilized societies are expected to worry about the deaths of women and children. But in civilized societies, parents don't raise their youngsters to be suicide bombers, they don't elect their leaders from the ranks of a terrorist group and they certainly wouldn't dance in the street when 3,000 innocent Americans were incinerated on 9/11.

Some people used to refer to Ronald Reagan as the Teflon president because no matter how much mud his political foes threw at him, nothing stuck. That was because he was so much wiser, more principled, charming and charismatic, than his left-wing detractors.

These days, those who seem to come equipped with Teflon are the world's Islamics. What's so mystifying about this is that they share none of Reagan's finer qualities. Theirs is a religion which calls for the domination of all others, and yet the majority of Christians, Jews, atheists and agnostics, continue treating them with the utmost respect and sensitivity. Frankly, I don't think it's even appreciated. Instead, I believe it's perceived quite rightly as fear and cowardice.

Although Muslims are committing acts of barbarism all over the globe, our leaders continue paying lip service to the followers of Allah. These people blow up trains, planes and school buses, and the British prime minister orders his cabinet members never to use the term "Islamic terrorists," while our own president and secretary of state feel compelled to keep reminding us that Islam is a religion of peace. Funny how often they need to keep reminding us. When is the last time that anybody needed to be told that Buddhism, for instance, or Shintoism, is a religion of peace? Do we require constant reassurance that the Amish mean to do us no harm? But, then, when's the last time that a Quaker blew up a pizza parlor?

In America, there appear to be far more chowderheads who fear the followers of Christ than of Muhammad. It gives me a headache trying to psychoanalyze the liberals who side with the so-called Palestinians against the Israelis, when Israel is an ally of ours, is a nation of laws and is, unlike all the Islamic tyrannies, an honest-to-goodness democracy.

I fear that millions of our fellow citizens are as gullible as little kids. But instead of believing in the Easter Bunny, Santa Claus and the Tooth Fairy, these lunkheads choose to believe that what the members of Fatah and Hamas desire is to simply live in freedom in their own homeland. When Yasser Arafat was offered that very thing, he left Camp David in a huff. What the Muslims want is to destroy Israel for no other reason than that it's inhabited by Jews. Once they finish the job begun by Hitler, the different factions can then get back to doing what Islamists do best - namely, killing off one another.

Some Americans, the truly befuddled, actually believe that what the rest of us recognize as Islam's intolerance of all non-Muslims is actually a matter of economics. But, then, that's what Communists, Socialists and other assorted left-wing loonies, always think. Because they have no morals themselves, they like to think that economic deprivation is the basis of all violence. They believe it's poverty that leads Muslims to be suicide-bombers, but fail to explain how killing innocent civilians cures that particular problem. They don't seem to find it peculiar that Osama bin Laden and Yasser Arafat were multi-millionaires, and that those behind the plot to set off explosions in London and Glasgow were all a bunch of doctors.

Apologists for Islam will go to any length, no matter how absurd, to spin the truth. They contend, for example, that the initial attack on the Twin Towers and the attack on 9/11 took place because we had waged war against Saddam Hussein, while ignoring the fact that in 1991, we were coming to the defense of Kuwait, a Muslim country under siege by Iraq. Furthermore, when you ask these crazies to explain all the prior Islamic attacks on the U.S., dating back to the Ayatollah Khomeni's taking hostages in 1979, they suddenly remember they were supposed to be somewhere else half an hour ago.

The fact remains that Muslims hate not only the West, but the five billion non-Muslims on the face of the earth. As for their liberal defenders in this country, the sad truth is that they aren't really pro-Islam as much as they're anti-America. Like Muslims, they regard us as the Great Satan. It explains why the same people who openly despise all the symbols of Judaism and Christianity went ballistic over the Korans allegedly being trashed in Guantanamo; and why the ACLU, always so quick to oppose religious displays at Christmas and Chanukah, went to the mat on behalf of the Islamic woman who insisted that her face be veiled on her Florida driver's license.

Two news items caught my attention in the recent past, and although they occurred 3,000 miles apart, they are definitely connected.

In New York, Muzzammil Hassan, who started a cable TV network after 9/11 to prove to America that American Muslims are moderate, peace-loving people, beheaded his wife, Aasiya, because she was planning to divorce him. In moderate Muslim circles, that happens to be grounds for a so-called honor killing. I believe other grounds include daring to touch the TV remote and over-seasoning the humus.

At nearly the same time, a Dutch politician, Geert Wilders, was invited by a member of the House of Lords to come to England and screen his 17-minute film. The documentary, "Fitna," links text from the Koran with footage of Islamic terrorism around the world.

Well, a funny thing happened on his way to Parliament. It seems that England's Home Secretary, Jacqui Smith, uninvited Mr. Wilders. On the grounds that the Dutchman would incite civil unrest if allowed entry to the country, Wilders was met at Heathrow and sent packing back to the Netherlands.

Although his own government has raised an official objection, England hasn't budged. They feel that Wilders and his little movie would be the equivalent of someone yelling "Fire!" in a crowded theater. The question that's always plagued me is what a decent person is supposed to do if he smells smoke and sees flames in a theater? Quietly grab his coat and popcorn and sneak out?

The English politicians are defending their craven act on the grounds of cultural sensitivity. Which is of course a highfalutin' euphemism for censorship. But, then, you can always count on bureaucrats to pass off cowardice as principle.

When I see the way Muslims have bullied one country after another into kowtowing to their demands, one can't help thinking that Hitler's biggest mistake was being born 70 years too soon.

That whirring sound you hear is Winston Churchill spinning in his grave.

In the matter of Mr. Hassan, some people have wondered why he was only charged with second degree murder, while others are naturally puzzled by the fact his grisly crime didn't capture more media attention. While I can't claim to know the answers, I am, as usual, willing to hazard a guess. Even though nobody, aside from a defense attorney, would dare suggest that it wasn't a clear-cut case of premeditated murder, I suspect Hassan has been charged with the lesser crime because, as is often the case, a double standard is in play. It's as if, in spite of all our lip service to the contrary, we all know that people given to treating women like trash, suicide bombings and honor killings, are not really civilized - and therefore cannot be judged by civilized standards. As for the fact that the media hasn't given this story the gruesome attention one would normally expect, the most obvious answer is that the MSM is as lily-livered as the English government when it comes to offending Islamics.

Believe me, if Mr. Hassan had been a Christian or a Jew, he'd have gotten more coverage than Paula Abdul's departure from "American Idol," and long before now we'd all know how to spell Muzzammil.

Although I have never claimed to be as politically correct as, say, the N.Y. Times, I like to think of myself as a reasonably open-minded fellow where people who are different from me are concerned. And, inasmuch as most people are very different from me - and glad of it - I get a lot of practice. Furthermore, I have always contended that bigots are just plain lazy, and that if you just take the trouble to know people as individuals, almost invariably you will discover more and better reasons to despise them other than their race, religion or sexual orientation.

So it is that when American Muslims insist that they're loyal to the United States, I'd like to believe them. The trouble is, in the wake of 9/11, I heard them complaining about being racially profiled; what I didn't hear was their damning the monsters who hijacked the planes and flew them into the Twin Towers, a Pennsylvania field and the Pentagon. I was also aware that, until the F.B.I. put a stop to it, a great many of them were funneling money to Hamas and Hezbollah. What they weren't doing with their money was passing the hat in their mosques and offering a reward for Osama bin Laden, dead or alive.

So you'll have to excuse my lack of decorum when I refuse to accept their contention that bin Laden, Mohammed Alta and Sheik Omar Abdul-Rahman, are aberrations, unholy defilers of their peace-loving religion. As people used to say, tell it to the Marines.

No, I have not read the Koran. And while I have heard highly inflammatory excerpts from those who had read the book, I'm aware that Satan can quote or even misquote scripture to his own purpose. Another ancient adage, however, states that the proof is in the pudding. In the case of Islam, I would suggest that the pudding is to be found in every nation where Muslims hold the reins. Or, perhaps, one should say, the whip.

Can it be mere coincidence that, although democracy has long flourished in nations that are predominantly Protestant, Catholic, Hindu, Jewish, Shinto, Buddhist, Lutheran and Anglican, it's never taken root where Muhammad's word is law? Can it be mere happenstance that wherever you look in the Muslim world, from Sudan to Syria, from Iran to Yemen, from Libya to Saudi Arabia, wherever Islam holds sway, you will find one totalitarian state after another? Only time will tell if Iraq will be the exception, but, frankly, I'm not willing to bet on it.

True, you will find a variety of national leaders, including oil-rich sheiks, fanatical ayatollahs and run-of-the-mill tyrants like Qaddafi, Assad and Mahmoud Ahmadinejad, but one and all could dine comfortably with a Russian czar or a Chicago gangster.

For an allegedly peaceful religion, isn't it remarkable that wherever Islam gains a stranglehold, you will find a nightmare of slavery, genocide and female stoning and mutilation, the norm?

I have heard folks say that the historical reason for all this is that, of all the founders of the major religions, only Muhammad was a warrior. Although a merchant by trade, he led his followers in the bloody conquest of Mecca. So perhaps the die was cast thirteen centuries ago. Hell, for all I know, maybe it all goes back to climate. I know I'm a perfect grouch when the temperature goes through the roof and the air conditioning conks out.

Maybe it has something to do with too much sand in one's diet. Or perhaps sharing one's life with camels, a notoriously nasty beast, is the reason behind the cult of death that celebrates suicide bombings throughout the Arab world and makes a hero out of a lout who throws his shoes at an American president. And not just any president, mind you, but the one who got rid of the tyrant who would have killed the so-called journalist if he'd even dared look at him cross-eyed, let alone hurl a size-ten in his direction.

To tell you the truth, when I first heard tell of the awards that supposedly awaited Islamic martyrs, even I began to see the attraction. I mean, on the face of it, moving from Jenin, say, to Paradise sounds like an awfully good deal. Toss in 72 beautiful virgins, and what healthy, red-blooded Palestinian wouldn't gladly blow himself to Kingdom Come?

The problem, of course, is that, like most youngsters, they never bother thinking things through and looking at the big picture. For instance, in the natural course of events, what the impetuous young idiot will inevitably have on his hands are six dozen ex-virgins.

And if he thinks he has it bad now, just wait until he winds up spending eternity with 72 women who while away each and every day complaining that he's always leaving his burnoose on the floor, doesn't help out with the kids, and never takes them dancing.

Even though I may not look it, I am essentially a pretty happy guy. Like most people my age, I get out of sorts when I consider the steady decline of art, culture and baseball. But so long as nobody puts a gun to my head and makes me listen to Hip Hop and so long as I don't have to watch MTV or suffer through yet another Jim Carrey movie, I don't let myself get too perturbed by current trends. I don't even object to the mud-slinging one associates with presidential campaigns. I just remind myself that nobody ever got to sling mud at Joseph Stalin or Idi Amin.

One of the few things that I do find truly depressing, aside from Islamic fanatics, are those Americans on the radical left who defend their atrocities. I can't be the only person who finds it peculiar that the very same people who break out in a cold sweat over the slightest overlap of church and state in the U.S., who despise evangelical Christians and distrust Orthodox Jews, have no problem arguing on behalf of people who saw the heads off civilian hostages, who treat their camels better than their women, and who will happily conduct blood-baths over a few dumb cartoons.

What I find most disconcerting about these Muslims is that they almost manage to make the Nazis look normal by comparison. This is not to suggest that Hitler and his butchers weren't abominable. Hitler was an evil lunatic who waged war on mankind, and dreamed of turning "Deutschland uber alles" into more than a catchy slogan. But at least the world he set out to conquer was the world of the 20th Century. You have only to look at Berchtesgaden, his palace in the mountains, to understand that the man loved excess. He may have been a vegetarian, but the little bastard was a hedonist at heart.

Der fuhrer and his cohorts appreciated art and music, architecture and film, beautiful women, fine cigars and schnapps. Really, the only thing that made the Nazis worse than the barbaric Islamics is that, being technologically advanced, they were more efficient killers.

The world of the mullahs is the world of the Dark Ages. It is an ugly place and it smells like a sewer. It is as enlightened as a cesspool. It turns its back on life and it celebrates death. Its heroes are suicide bombers. Its motto is, better a dead martyr than a living child. Who would choose to live in such a world? Only the hopelessly insane.

I say, whatever it costs to defeat this plague is well worth the price, just as the costs were justified to rid the world of the Third Reich.

At times, I confess, I get downhearted because it seems such an impossible task. The Muslim terrorists, after all, seem to be everywhere in the world, blowing up buildings, blowing up people. We bring down Saddam Hussein as we brought down Hitler, but still the killing rages on in Iraq. How can we hope to defeat people who aren't merely fighting for a leader or a nation, but because of their religion, because Muhammad gave them their marching orders fourteen hundred years ago?

Well, in spite of all that, I find reasons to be hopeful. For instance, think about the French Revolution. One day, the French were ruled by a despotic king, the next day, "Voila!" they weren't.

One day, here in America, we had slavery, the next day, after two hundred years, we didn't.

One day, Italy was being bossed around by a two-bit thug named Mussolini; the next day, he was in the town square, hanging upside down like a side of beef.

One day, the Soviet Union had a few hundred million Eastern Europeans under its brutal thumb; the next day it barely had a thumb.

But even more to the point, consider Japan. The Japanese who invaded China, Korea, Shanghai and Manchuria, and bombed the hell out of the American fleet at Pearl Harbor, thought they were on a holy mission on behalf of their emperor. Think of it as a jihad with a sake chaser.

Emperor Hirohito was more than a national leader, he was a god. He was as distant and mysterious as the great and powerful Wizard of Oz. When he went on the radio in 1945, after Hiroshima and Nagasaki, to announce to the nation that the war was over and that Japan had lost, his countrymen didn't know what to make of it. They had never heard his voice. Gods, for god's sake, don't talk on the radio.

Because Hirohito was regarded as a deity, dying on his behalf had been regarded as a holy act. The Japanese, as you may recall, had their own version of suicide bombers; they were called Kamikazes. They were pilots whose sole mission was to fly their explosive-laden Zeros directly into allied battleships and destroyers. Next stop, they were told: Paradise. Sound vaguely familiar?

So ingrained in the Japanese was blind devotion to their emperor that, long after the war was over, isolated soldiers were found on South Pacific Islands still defending their turf. They simply hadn't heard God on the short-wave.

Who would have guessed that in no time at all, Japan would not only be a peace-loving democracy, but that its citizens would feel as free as the English to gossip about the royal family, and would revere baseball players above all other mortals?

In other words, what so often seems impossible to imagine only means that sufficient imagination is often lacking.

From all this, I find hope that the Islamic necrophiliacs will go the way of the Japanese kamikazes.

I believe that we will destroy them because, having vowed to destroy all of us, even those who speak on their behalf, they really leave us no choice in the matter.

I am curious about one thing, though. When Arab terrorists speak about martyring themselves so that they can go directly to Paradise, is their vision of the place as desolate and as gruesome as the world they're trying to foist off on the rest of us?

Does it at least have indoor plumbing?

Speaking of plumbing reminds me that I have grown weary of hearing left-wingers, who think they're being tortured if they have to fly coach, insisting that if we caused Islamic terrorists the slightest discomfort we're as bad as the Nazis.

Let weasels like Dick Durbin, John Kerry or John Murtha call our soldiers storm troopers and America's MSM hails these louts as true patriots. Sometimes, I get the idea that the media is nothing more than an off-shoot of Al Jazerra, a well-oiled propaganda machine for all things Islamic. The way they start jabbering about the Geneva Conventions, you might get the idea that they've actually read them.

The fact is, Islamic terrorists aren't covered. They don't wear uniforms, they don't fight under a flag, and they represent no nation. Even the argument that if we treat them badly, they'll do the same to us is absurd. In case liberals were busy demonstrating and missed the news, these people cut off the heads of their prisoners. Compared to that, depriving them of sleep and dunking them in water strikes normal people as being as torturous as a fraternity initiation.

Speaking of torture, we've been hearing for the longest time that torture is the worst possible way by which to extract information from the enemy. Who says so? When something that is so patently nonsensical is passed off as common knowledge, I, for one, get very suspicious.

I'm willing to believe that every so often there are those who are willing to absorb any amount of punishment and take their secrets to the grave with them. But, aside from those occasional saints and masochists, I'll wager that most people - and that definitely includes Osama bin Laden, if we were ever to get our hands on him - would cough up everything they knew.

I think a problem we have when discussing, say, water-boarding is one of semantics. The question isn't whether water-boarding constitutes torture to some degree. (If it doesn't, then it's just a big waste of time and a small waste of water). Rather, the question is: What purpose does it serve? When Muslims cut off the head of an American such as Daniel Pearl, they do it in order to prove how barbaric they are, and to put the fear of Allah in our hearts. However, when a terrorist is water-boarded so that we can avoid experiencing another 9/11 or prevent some American soldiers from being ambushed, I'm all for it. I do wonder, though, why we don't just cut to the chase and threaten to feed them pork intravenously or bury their miserable remains in pigskins.

When you get right down to it, torture takes many forms. For one man, it's being dunked repeatedly in water, while for another it's being forced to sit through a Sean Penn speech or a Dixie Chicks concert.

Lately, I've been wondering if the folks who spread the rumor about the failure of torture to garner results are the same ones now insisting that Iran is not trying to develop a nuclear weapon. My understanding is that our so-called intelligence community came to this absurd conclusion based on having overheard a single telephone call, probably one between Ahmadinejad and the guy who supplies his windbreakers. I suspect that at least a few of these clowns on the CIA payroll were members of the O.J. jury.

The logical question is: Why Iran, a nation under the thumb of fanatical ayatollahs, fronted by a dwarf who spends half his time denying the Nazi holocaust and the other half promising to initiate one of his own, wouldn't spend a sizable portion of its oil revenue in developing a nuclear bomb for the purpose of annihilating Israel?

That brings us to the final question of the day, class: Why are America's liberals so anxious to believe the best of Islamic fanatics but only the worst of Christian fundamentalists?

There are times when I feel as if I have tumbled down the same rabbit hole as Alice. One understands that if you live long enough, the world will change. Sometimes for the better, sometimes not. But, more and more often, I feel like Rip Van Winkle. How long was I asleep? Where did all these people who admire people like Hugo Chavez, Ahmadinejad and the Castro brothers, come from? Do these folks really find something admirable in the way these tyrants govern or is it simply enough that they hate America?

I think that enough time has now elapsed since Ahmadinejad addressed the old fools at the U.N. and the young fools at Columbia so that we can view those singular events with a clear and dispassionate eye.

So, first off, let me just suggest for about the ten thousandth time that we get out of the U.N. and then tell the U.N. to get out of the U.S. The organization serves no useful purpose, unless you count the number of New York bars, restaurants and bordellos, the various foreign diplomats keep afloat, thanks to their generous expense accounts.

The sad fact is that so long as we tolerate having the U.N. housed on our turf, we're going to see the likes of Ahmadinejad, Yasser Arafat, Fidel Castro and Hugo Chavez, taking advantage of our hospitality to wipe their dirty boots all over our welcome mat.

As you may recall, there was a great deal of controversy swirling around President Lee Bollinger's inviting Iran's president to address the student body at Columbia University. So, in order to show that he wasn't just a pushover for any sweet-talking despot, Bollinger proceeded to insult the guy in his introductory remarks. Among other things, as I recall, he called him a petty dictator. I believe Ahmadinejad took exception to being called petty. As to be expected, the students showed their displeasure - not with the fellow who's made a career of denying the Nazi Holocaust while simultaneously threatening Israel with a nuclear holocaust - but, instead, with Bollinger! They thought he was rude to their guest of honor. I guess they must all be boning up for their final in Moral Equivalency by watching Steven Spielberg's "Munich."

Actually, the event wasn't a total loss. For one thing, Bollinger showed himself to be a complete dunce. Like a rube who sits down to play poker with guys called Doc, Slick, Fingers and the Old Professor, he not only lost his shirt, but his shoes, socks and underpants.

In defense of extending the invitation to the Iranian gnome, Bollinger blathered on about Columbia's dedication to free speech. The fact that he passed off that drollery without giggling suggests he may have a career as a stand-up comic. Apparently, Columbia's approach to free speech is not unlike Iran's. It extends to Islamic tyrants, but not to American conservatives. This is, let us not forget, the same Bollinger who fought against the ROTC's being reinstated at his university, thus going on record as a proponent of free speech so long as the speaker is not affiliated with the U.S. military.

The students, liberals all, took advantage of the opportunity to show the entire world what absolute airheads they are. To them, making a few rude remarks to a tyrant was far worse than sponsoring Islamic terrorism. The fact that Ahmadinejad, on a regular basis, threatens to annihilate Israel, supplied arms to the rabble in Iraq who were killing American G.I.s, and is the front man for the vile mullahs, means nothing to them. Bollinger insults the dictator, and the students boo. Their pal Mohammed insults America, and they applaud. And for that, their dopey parents are mortgaging their homes?

The other benefit of Ahmadinejad's speech is that he took the opportunity to denigrate homosexuals. That will cost him the support of Hollywood's own mullahs should he ever decide that what he'd really like to do is direct.

I have heard that Ahmadinejad dined that night with NBC's Brian Williams and Christiane Amanpour, the pride of CNN. I expect that the three of them took turns telling jokes about George Bush and ridiculing conservatives.

What is it with these New York media types? Is it simply that normal, decent people will no longer eat with them? Perfectly understandable, if true.

Some left-wing lunkheads are convinced that, as Rev. Jeremiah Wright put it, 9/11 was simply a case of America's chickens coming home to roost. They believe that if only America would keep its nose out of the Middle East, the Islamics wouldn't hate us. What they fail to explain is why they massacre innocent people in the Philippines, Bali, Scandinavia, India, Russia, Spain and France. But, then, the media and those who believe the media never blame Muslims for anything.

When thousands of Islamics took to the streets of France, setting fires and attacking Jews, it wasn't their fault. The blame was laid on the French for failing to assimilate Muslims into their society. Far be it from me to defend France, something you may have noticed over the past century the French, themselves, are extremely reluctant to do. However, you might as well condemn Old MacDonald for not assimilating with his farm animals. It's not French snobbery that isolates the Muslims or creates their embarrassingly high rate of illiteracy and unemployment. The fact of the matter is that their young men are too spoiled and too lazy to do manual labor, and too ignorant to do anything else. Combine a welfare state that provides them with food and lodging with a vulgar religion that condemns all non-believers as infidels, and you have gasoline just waiting for a lighted match.

Most liberal pundits, I've found, justify riots, blaming society at large for its marauders. I, on the other hand, am not so easily hoodwinked. Check out the photos of every riot you've ever seen and you will discover that it's the very same riff-raff in every mob, no matter where the vandalism takes place. Remove the 16-25 year old male punks from the pictures, and you'd be left with a lot of lampposts and telephone poles minding their own business.

Whether it's the Rodney King mob burning down stores in L.A., the PLO bums throwing stones in Jenin, or the lay-a-bouts in Paris, they're exactly the same as those punks in America who run amok every time their home team either wins or loses a Super Bowl or an NBA title. There is a reason why you rarely see anybody over the age of 30 out in the streets. Could it be that only youngsters are ever oppressed or downtrodden? Hardly. It's because even their own parents know that the young hoodlums would be just as likely to stone them as to stone the cops; far likelier, in fact, because their folks are less likely to be armed and dangerous.

It's no secret that testosterone-driven young males enjoy busting windows, spray-painting graffiti and starting fires. Unfortunately, just as with certain parents who are in denial when it comes to the antics of their own bratty children, social workers, members of the liberal media and other assorted pacifists, habitually blame riots on capitalism, western imperialism and, for all I know, premature potty training.

Frankly, what I most fear is that in a world in which multi-culturalists feel obligated to bow and scrape to Muslims, in a world so overflowing with infantile feel-good rhetoric about the joys of Islam, that it will eventually and inevitably give rise to an opposing force rooted in fascism.

Each time I hear people defending Islam, pretending that it's merely another humanistic faith like Christianity, Judaism and Buddhism, I wonder if they would have insisted that National Socialism was just another political party, and that being a Nazi was no different from being a Republican or a Democrat.

I worry that in a world filled with folks lying about the emperor, it will finally take a monster like Hitler to point out he's as naked as a jaybird.

Frankly, I'm sick and tired of hearing people parroting the lie that Islam is a religion of peace. I suppose so long as you're willing to set aside your bible and pick up the Koran and start kneeling to Mecca, they'll let you live in peace; unless, of course, you belong to a different sect. In which case, in the name of the great and merciful Allah, they'd have no choice but to lop your head off.

As for the rest of us, it's high time we stopped trying to come up with pretentious, high-sounding excuses for murderous mobs.

The answer, nearly always, to why young people riot is simple. It's fun.

The best thing about the rioting in France is that it proved once and for all that pandering to Islamics is always a bad idea. Even when you provide them with all the perks available to sluggards in a socialist society, it's no guarantee they won't turn right around and bite the hand that feeds them. So, just in case anybody ever asks you to name the biggest difference between a French Muslim and a French poodle, you now know the answer.

France made the mistake of throwing open its doors 40 years ago to cheap Arab and African workers, and came to discover, to its dismay, that the children and grandchildren of those original immigrants, don't care for the French any more than the rest of us do.

A few years ago, I wrote a piece in which I took American Muslims to task for displaying greater loyalty to their murderous brethren than they did to the victims of 9/11. The piece was posted at several blogs and received a great deal of attention.

Frankly, I expected that a lot of people were going to take me to task for denouncing millions of our fellow Americans. That didn't happen. In fact, only one person, a Muslim living in England, took strong objection to the piece.

In the following exchanges, I believe he represents what we would regard as the moderate wing of his religion. As usual, I represent only myself. It's a dirty job, but someone has to do it.

Michael opened with the following: "Your article was extremely ignorant, incorrect and inflammatory. It is clear that you are pleased to use atrocities being committed today by some wayward individuals to attack Islam itself. It is a great pity that men such as yourself should be given such a platform to express their prejudice and spread misinformation. Muhammad never converted anyone to Islam by the sword. This is not my opinion, but is established fact. Islam being the newest and most influential of the great world religions, is also the most accurately documented in history, so there is simply no basis for what you are saying.

"People like you would fan the dangerous flames that are threatening to engulf the world at the moment, without regard for truth or the consequences of your lies.

"What a shame that you have such a platform. What a shame. One wonders how many more there are like you, seeking to engulf the world in your ignorance. No wonder the world is in such a perilous situation."

Burt: "Michael, please get a grip. The world is not in peril because of my words, whether or not you like them, but because of the disgusting misdeeds of your co-religionists. But you obviously prefer to direct your righteous indignation at me instead of at the people who are committing cold-blooded murder in the name of Allah."

Michael: "How do you know that I have not already directed my 'righteous indignation' at my erring co-religionists? I'll have you know that nine or ten years ago, before September 11th, I spoke directly to one of the leaders of Hamas during a live BBC radio phone-in. I told him that he and his group were committing grave crimes in the name of Islam. He said they had the right to defend themselves. I told him that Islam laid out clear rules of engagement which Hamas and other similar groups broke, and I listed those rules on the air. I told him that I sympathized with the suffering of his people, but I believed that what he was doing was wrong and, as a Muslim, he did not represent me. He had no answer to any of that."

Burt: "You sympathized with his suffering?! What suffering that hasn't been brought on by the leaders of the PLO and the other terrorist organizations? Were you perhaps sympathizing with his having to exist in a world contaminated by the existence of 5,000,000 Jews in Israel?"

Michael: "So why don't you get a grip? Instead of playing dangerous games with your lies and misinformation, why don't you try to work to address the real causes of these problems and I'm not talking about the Middle East."

Burt: "So far you haven't been talking about anything except what a bad man I am for writing what most Americans are merely thinking. If not the Middle East, what did you have in mind? Perhaps the Islamic killings that have taken place in Russia, Spain, the Philippines, Indonesia, Africa, France, Holland and New York City?"

Michael: "Whatever the cause, the inequalities that exist between those two peoples who inhabit the same land (Jews and Muslims) have led to suffering on all sides. Palestinians are living in (sometimes extreme) poverty and have to watch the luxurious living of the Jews. This leads to suicide attacks which means Israelis can't enjoy their high standard of living with peace of mind. I think this is acknowledged by people of all persuasions."

Burt: "So jealousy is your idea of a rational motive for mindless butchery? If poverty is the issue, why don't the oil-rich Arabs help their brethren? How is it that Arafat died a multi-millionaire and his widow lives like a queen in Paris? Why didn't the Arab nations welcome in the Palestinians instead of allowing them to rot in Gaza in "sometimes extreme" poverty for the past six decades? Why is it that when Israel gained statehood in 1948, the Arab nations immediately confiscated the land and property of its Jewish citizens and sent them packing?"

Michael: "But this is not the point. The point is that the episode I described to you, my exchange with the man on the radio, demonstrated that true Islam and the actions of people like Hamas, Al Qaeda, etc. are not related. Instead of acknowledging this, you keep trying to provoke me with your pathetic cock-eyed reasoning, which I don't even think you subscribe to yourself. You probably just want some inflammatory jihadist quotes from a 'real life' Muslim you talked to on line, for your unfortunate column."

Burt: "Au contraire. My point is that it is exactly people such as yourself who provide aid and comfort and excuses for the actions of the terrorists. You even excuse suicide bombers who target school buses and pizza parlors on the basis of poverty. Would you be so quick to use the same reason to excuse poor Baptists, Jews and Catholics, in England if they suddenly began blowing up civilians?"

Michael: "The real cause of the world's problems is that 25% of the world's population (Britain, the U.S., Europe, rich Arabs who are their puppets, etc.) are living on 85% of the world's resources. They would like it to stay that way, while the 75% of people living on 15% of the world's resources would like a better standard of living."

Burt: "Why so reluctant to mention jihad? Many people in the world are poorer than Arabs, but they don't use poverty as an excuse to sever the heads of their victims. How exactly does blowing up school children raise anybody's standard of living? Since most of the people that Muslims murder are other Muslims, your argument doesn't hold even a thimble's worth of water. And the fact is, America has gone to the assistance of Muslims more often than their fellow Muslims have ... in Serbia, Somalia, Kuwait and, yes, even in Iraq, by removing Saddam Hussein."

Michael: "That is the root cause in my opinion. If for example the West (for want of a better description) was seen as seriously addressing this by basically rejecting protectionism in all of its forms, including wars for oil, then the problem of Arab/Mid Eastern inspired terrorism (which is really only a problem for the West and those connected to it; the rest of the world has other more serious problems that perhaps Americans don't know about) would fade, I believe."

Burt: "You have no basis for thinking that. Islamic terrorism is a concern of people all over the world. And what makes you think we went to war over oil? You've been watching CNN way too much. Apparently you failed to notice that we didn't confiscate Kuwait's oil fields in 1991. And we could certainly have done business with Saddam Hussein; we might even have wrangled sweetheart deals the way France, Russia, Germany and China, did."

Michael: "Don't reply unless you are going to say something serious and sensible. Also, as a Muslim, I would like an apology for what you said about the prophet Muhammad. I don't expect one, but I think I should ask for one, and it would be sensible if you did so."

Burt: "Apologize for what? For pointing out that he created a religion whose holy book dismissed non-Muslims as infidels, and referred to Jews and Christians as monkeys and pigs? So far as I am concerned, our discussion is at an end. You have written nothing thoughtful or informative. You have merely excused the barbaric acts of your fellow Islamics; you have not indicated revulsion at their butchery. At the same time, I suspect that if I had written a piece attacking England, you wouldn't have been offended or defensive. Like most of your kind, you have no allegiance or loyalty to your homeland, only to Mecca, and then you wonder why your country-men distrust you. Farewell...and try not to blow up any trains today."

Muslims are people who believe that freedom is a naughty word, who believe that women are no better than cattle, and who refer to the ninth century as the good old days. As if it wasn't bad enough when they used a newspaper cartoon as an excuse to go berserk, these Neanderthals in the Sudan actually wanted to torture and execute English school teacher Gilliam Gibbons because, at the behest of a seven-year-old in her class, she had named a stuffed toy Muhammad.

These simpletons seem to spend half their lives on their knees pray-ing and the other half up in arms, looking to kill somebody for some utterly stupid reason. They are a blot on humanity, and humanity, I think we'd all agree, isn't all that great to begin with.

As bad as Bush and Rice were when it came to offering bouquets to the Muslims, they can't hold a candle to Obama. During one of his Damn America Tours, he not only insisted that the U.S. is one of the larg-est Muslim nations in the world, but that Muslims played a major role in the creation of our republic. That one really had me reeling, so I went back to my trusty old history book and looked it up and, sure enough, he was correct. Right there in black and white, I discovered that among the most influential of the Founding Fathers were Abdullah Washington, Mahmoud Adams and Osama Bin Jefferson.

Imagine if Catholics were as psychotic as Islamists. Just having a creche in a person's front yard or a picture of Jesus on a Christmas card would be like signing his own death warrant.

So, even though I haven't a religious bone in my body, I have every reason to be grateful I was born in a country in which it's Christ's birth-day, and not Muhammad's first slaying of an infidel, that's celebrated as a national holiday.

CHAPTER FIVE

Why Do 80% of Jews
Vote Like 90% of Blacks?

Over the years, I have found that if I write a piece arguing on behalf of Israel, I will hear from anti-Semites. They will accuse me of being on the payroll of the Jewish lobby - I only wish! - and will feel free to call me a kike.

If, on the other hand, I take my fellow Jews to task for always voting for the left-winger in every election, I know I will get word that I'm a self-hating Jew.

The truth is, I'm a Jew because my parents were Jewish, as were my grandparents. So, even though I am not in the least bit religiously observant, I call myself a Jew. Besides as the Albert Einstein-like character portrayed in "Gentlemen's Agreement" by Sam Jaffe said, "With this nose, if I denied it, who would believe me?"

Still, the fact remains I wasn't even bar mitzvahed, although my two older brothers were. By the time I was approaching my 13th birthday, my folks, who were not the least bit religious, allowed me to make the call. Although a lot of my friends opted for the ceremony, I told my folks that six hours of public school each day was punishment enough, without tacking on an hour or two of Hebrew school. I preferred spending my afternoons playing ball and getting my homework out of the way.

The way I look at it, my maternal grandfather, Max Lashevsky, would probably regard me - me with my love of shrimp and BLTs - as a heathen, but Hitler, who wasn't nearly as finicky about such things, would have pulled down my pants and sent me straight to Buchenwald.

Usually, when people say they're not religious, they're looking to pick a fight or at least start an argument. That's probably because people who identify themselves as atheists or agnostics are often as dogmatic as Cotton Mather and have merely made a religion of their own non-belief.

In my case, however, religion simply plays no role in my life. Or perhaps I should say institutionalized religion, seeing as how I very much subscribe to the Judeo-Christian value system. It's the reason that I'm so grateful that two sets of Russian Jewish grandparents had the guts to pack up their kids and caboodle, and come to America.

51

Unfortunately, they and many others like them included in their baggage several hundred years worth of religious antagonisms. In far too many cases, these fears and prejudices, although initially well-founded, have been passed along like precious heirlooms from one generation to the next.

Even among some of my friends and relatives, there are those who half-expect their Christian neighbors to start organizing pogroms any day now. They remain unconvinced that Hitler and the Nazis were pagans, and ignore me when I point out that their symbol was the swastika, not the cross . Unfortunately, even when I point out that it was American and British soldiers, mainly Christians, who brought down the Third Reich and liberated the concentration camps, it often falls on deaf ears.

So, although I do not accept that we are all fallen creatures or that Jesus Christ died for my sins, I am thankful that I live in a Christian nation. I realize that it's only my dumb luck to be an American. The fact of the matter is that when it comes to one's religion, it is usually determined by geography, not by choice. If you're born in Japan, you are likely to be Buddhist; if you're born in Italy, you're likely to be a Roman Catholic; in India, a Hindu; in England, an Anglican; in Utah, a Mormon; and in New York City, a knee-jerk liberal.

This is not to suggest that, even in my eyes, all religions are equally valid. You'd have to be one of those non-judgmental ninnies who sound the trumpets for cultural diversity, pretending to believe that all nations, all religions and all ideologies, are equally good. So long as Islam is around, only an idiot could seriously promote such nonsense.

If I am asked one question by my readers far more frequently than any other, it's why do so many American Jews insist on aligning themselves with the far left. Believe me, being Jewish myself, it's the question I most frequently ask myself. That is, when I'm not simply banging my head on the wall.

It's certainly not because Jews are stupid, evil, unpatriotic or dependent on government handouts for their survival, four reasons that certainly explain why millions of my fellow Americans will eagerly line up to vote for any political crackpot so long as he or she is running as a Democrat.

Having given it a great deal of thought, I believe the explanation is to be found in the way we tend to be raised. It's not so strange if you think about it. After all, most people are Catholics or Protestants, Mormons or Quakers, because that was the religion practiced in their homes. Well, for most Jews, liberal politics played an essential role in their upbringing. It's why a much higher percentage of us vote for Democrats than attend synagogue on a regular basis or keep kosher. In fact, I often think that in the way that conservatives often identify moderate Republicans as RINOs, Republicans In Name Only, secular Jews such as myself should be referred to as JINOs.

Another question that gets kicked around quite a lot is why Jews, unlike every other identifiable group in America, consistently votes against its own apparent self-interest. No matter what the issue - be it capital punishment, school vouchers, affirmative action, illegal immigration - Jews can nearly always be counted on to vote with those who wish them ill.

I believe there are two primary reasons for this. The first of these is that, thanks to Franklin D. Roosevelt, most first and second generation Jews in America came to identify themselves with the Democratic Party. It was the party, after all, that opposed Hitler, Jim Crow laws and the concept of separate-but-equal. So, even though the Democratic agenda has come to mean support of same-sex marriages, open borders, litmus tests for judicial appointments, the canonization of criminal defense attorneys, and entitlements-for-votes, Americans, by and large, are loath to change their political affiliation. In what is increasingly a secular society, most of us are far more willing to change our religion than our party.

The second reason, I believe, is that American Jews tend to be raised in matriarchal homes. Now, in some ways that can be a positive, and helps explain not only why so many Jews end up as doctors, but so often wind up in the arts and show business (not very high on the machismo scale). But, on the downside, such an upbringing, I would suggest, saps them of a certain virility of thought and will and action. It also helps to explain why Jews would love to have the Second Amendment expunged from the Constitution.

Far too often, Jewish men would rather "understand" their enemies than get even; they would rather, like Bill Clinton, "feel your pain" than dispense some of their own; they think revenge is a bad thing; they empathize with their archenemies because they think they, themselves, or, more likely, their nation must have done something wrong to have caused the enmity. If that sounds like a very feminine trait, it's probably because it is. In similar fashion, many of them, like Jeremiah Wright, believe that 9/11 wasn't simply an evil act perpetrated by Islamo fascists, but was instead retribution for America's transgressions. You know, the chickens coming home to roost scenario.

I could be mistaken, but I don't think so. How else would you explain why we Jews, as well-educated as we usually are, happen to be the only identifiable group in America - be it broken down by race, religion, gender, age or economics-- that inevitably takes sides with what it perceives to be the underdog, even when the underdogs (Black thugs, foreign-born Hispanics, Palestinians, death row inmates) openly despise them?

One of the most confounding aspects of the troubles in the Middle East is the way that so many American Jews have spoken up on behalf of Israel's sworn enemies. In my own circle, I find I am constantly having to defend Israel's right to defend herself. I suspect it is because Jews are so accustomed to siding with those they perceive to be the oppressed that they, like so many others, have fallen under the spell of the P.L.O.

In the minds of such people, violence is violence. To them, there is no difference between a suicide bomber and an Israeli soldier, no difference between blowing oneself up in order to murder and maim dozens of innocent bystanders and retaliating against terrorism. Cause and effect play no role in their moral judgments. So far as they're concerned, the cold-blooded murderer is no worse than his executioner. Steven Spielberg dramatized this nonsense in "Munich," when he made the case that there was a moral equivalency between the Palestinians responsible for the 1972 Olympic massacre and the Israeli agents who eliminated them. But, then, Mr. Spielberg is the same person who said that the eight hours he spent chatting with Fidel Castro were the most memorable hours of his life. I wonder if when he got home, he caught hell from Mrs. Spielberg for that remark.

Such people argue that the fact that Israel has had to defend herself against acts of aggression and terrorism for over 60 years doesn't excuse their building settlements as a buffer against their avowed enemies. In spite of all the wars waged against them, in spite of a world press that maligns them, in spite of Arab children raised on a diet of hate who want nothing more out of life than to kill Israelis, far too many American Jews refuse to acknowledge that Israel has no option to suicide other than to fight back.

Although the U.N. is constantly condemning Israel, while giving a pass to the terrorists who intentionally target Israeli women and children, and even though the enemy consistently uses its own civilians as camouflage, a study showed that for every 29 terrorists Israel has killed, only one Palestinian civilian has died as the result of collateral damage.

The world gave Yasser Arafat a Nobel Peace Prize, and when he died the L.A. Times called him a statesman, ignoring the fact that while he spoke peace in broken English, he incited blood lust in fluent Arabic. But, then, what else can one reasonably expect from the world? After all, if there's one thing that Israel has learned in its six decades of existence it is that, in spite of its being the only democracy in the Middle East, where every other country is a moral cesspool dominated by brutal dictators, other nations hate it solely because it's a Jewish state.

In a part of the world where ayatollahs, oil-rich sheiks and petty tyrants rule the roost, the United Nations consistently calls Israel on the carpet. The International Red Cross refuses to grant membership to Israel. CNN and the New York Times take turns defending Hamas and Hezbollah, bemoaning the fate of the poor, poor Palestinians. The fact that the Palestinians have been left to rot by their fellow Muslims for all these years, in spite of Arabs having nothing but real estate and oil money at their disposal, is inevitably besides the point.

Let me simply point out to the mathematically-challenged that considering the differential in our populations, each time 50 Israelis are blown up, it's the equivalent of America's suffering 3,000 fatalities. Just imagine having to deal not just with a 9/11, but a 3/11 and a 4/11 and a 5/11, ad nauseam.

Another problem with American Jews is that we are raised to think of ourselves as victims or at least potential victims. Considering the fact that we are often among the best-educated and most successful members of American society, it must seem odd to non-Jews to even imagine such a thing. What is easily overlooked, however, is that when a group of people have been oppressed for thousands of years, the sense of impending doom almost becomes part of their DNA. No matter how well things are going today, tomorrow you and your friends and all of your relatives could be on your way out. And the only question is whether it's merely out of the country or into the ovens.

As a result, Jews have an inclination to identify - some might say over-identify - with those they see as fellow underdogs. In America, those people would more often than not be Blacks, Hispanics and even criminals, which helps explain the large Jewish presence and financial stake in the ACLU. The pathetic irony is that those are three groups that are among the most virulently anti-Semitic in America. But it also explains why a great many Jews - particularly those who are young, secular and on college campuses - are such vocal partisans of Hamas and Hezbollah.

At times, it seems as if we exist in some surrealistic universe in which, with the notable exception of Jimmy Carter, American Christians are often more devoted to Israel's survival than American Jews are. At the same time, many Jews feel they have more to fear from fundamentalist Christians than from fundamentalist Islamics!

I know what you're thinking, ladies and gentlemen, but keep in mind I only said I'd try to explain it. I never said it would make sense.

It's a peculiar thing about Jews that we seem to trust our enemies more than we do our friends. Maybe that's because, historically, we at least had the comfort of knowing where we stood with those who openly despised us, but very often suffered betrayal from our alleged allies.

It would help explain why many of my older relatives, those who had been born in Czarist Russia and had experienced pogroms, believed in Stalin, and eagerly lapped up his propaganda. Because he was an enemy of their enemies, they foolishly mistook him for a friend. It's simplistic, but why else would so many seemingly well-informed American Jews have enlisted in the Communist Party, swelling the ranks of what Lenin referred to as "useful idiots"?

These days, the most consistently pro-Israel group of Americans, oddly enough, are evangelical Christians. A sane and rational person might assume that fact would be appreciated and applauded by us. By and large, however, that isn't the case. Many of my fellow Jews don't like or trust devout Christians. When I ask them why, they suddenly become history professors. To listen to them, you'd think the Inquisition had ended earlier this year. Frankly, when I hear them dredging up ancient animosities, I'm surprised they haven't taken a page out of the Al Sharpton playbook and demanded reparations from Spain!

When I point out that Jews have enjoyed unprecedented freedom and prosperity in a Christian nation - namely, the United States - my friends insist that it's not Christian. At which point, I have to lie down and take a nap until the headache goes away.

Just because we're not a theocracy doesn't mean we aren't a Christian nation. When we say that Indonesia, for instance, is an Islamic nation and that India is Hindu and that Italy is Catholic, although none of them is a theocratic state, how can we deny that America, whose population is overwhelmingly Christian - and is only 2% Jewish - is Christian?! The fact of the matter is that America has a higher proportion of Christians than Israel, with its one million Arabs, has of Jews.

The problem between pro-Israel Jews and pro-Israel evangelicals is that the Christians believe that, come Judgment Day, Jews will have to convert to the true faith or be doomed for all eternity. Big deal. There are millions of people who believe that Elvis is alive, that James Dean will stage a comeback as soon as the scars heal, and even that the Cubs will go all the way this year!

I have no way of knowing if Christians are correct in believing that the Messiah is coming back a second time, or if Jews are right in thinking that Jesus was a first-rate prophet, but not quite up to raising the dead. Where matters of faith are concerned, I don't take sides.

As I've said, I'm not religiously oriented. However, I'm for anything that helps people behave decently and helps them cope with all the inevitable tragedies of life, up to and including death. In my experience, anyway, most religions in America perform those functions more often than not.

Unlike her enemies who hate Israel because it's a Jewish state, I do not support Israel for that reason. I am on its side because it is, one, a democracy in a part of the world where democracy is as alien as barbecued pork; two, it is a staunch ally of America; and, three, for over 60 years, although it has been besieged by terrorist states and fanatical killers, it has displayed remarkable restraint. It is a restraint that, I humbly confess, I could not duplicate in my wildest dreams.

So when I hear American Jews who, as often as not, are no more religious than I, dismiss Christian sympathizers, I say to them: "So you believe one thing about Jesus and they believe another. So what? Who cares? If it makes you happy, make a bet with an evangelical, and in a million years or whenever the great Hallelujah Day rolls around, one of you will owe the other one five bucks. In the meanwhile, in a world in which Israel's opponents out-number her supporters by at least five hundred-to-one, it's high time you learned to distinguish between friend and foe."

Besides, home, as we've all heard, is the place where they have to let you in. If that is the case, and if you're as fearful as you claim that your Christian neighbors may some day turn on you, isn't it in your best interest to make certain that your one safe haven continues to exist?

I suspect that some of the antipathy that American Jews feel towards Israel is because the view from here is of a rugged people who not only don't share their phobia where guns are concerned, but actually know how to use them.

The question is why so many Jews are so vehemently opposed to decent, law-abiding citizens owning guns? After all, most people - unlike Hollywood celebrities - cannot afford to surround themselves with armed bodyguards. And as dedicated as the police may be to protect and serve, they're usually not around at the very moment your life is being threatened. Besides, if liberals had their way and the Second Amendment was repealed, the only people in America with guns would be cops, criminals and the military. Interestingly, of those three particular groups, criminals are the ones liberals hate and fear the least.

Part of the reason that we Jews are so squeamish around firearms is that, traditionally, we're not that great with hardware tools. So, I suspect, a lot of us think we'll wind up shooting ourselves if there's a gun lying around. It's almost as if we think the revolvers are little anti-Semites who are just waiting for the opportunity to shoot us in the back.

The other thing is that even though America is the most tolerant nation on earth, Jews tend to think if terrible things happened to their ancestors in 15th Century Spain and 19th Century Russia and 20th Century Nazi Germany, it can and will happen here. It's a form of paranoia. But it's a very strange form. For as we all know, this is a nation of 300 million. So, wouldn't you think a minority numbering a mere five million, and in constant fear of pogroms, would spend as much time as possible down at the firing range?

It's no secret that George Soros and Hollywood's Jewish population are some of the biggest contributors to left-wing candidates and causes. They are also major financial supporters of the ACLU. They also hold leadership positions in the organization, and most of the legal staff is filled with secular Jews. Which reminds me, most generalizations about the way American Jews vote and think are not true of the Orthodox community. In that way, it's similar to the dichotomy in Hollywood, where actors, directors, writers, producers and studio executives, tend to be left-wingers, while the below the line personnel - "the people we fly over" in left-wing parlance - stuntmen, gaffers, grips, make-up artists, costumers, tend to be conservatives.

One of my main objections to the ACLU is their insistence that "separation of church and state" exists somewhere in the Constitution. They have been at it for so long and so persistently that there are even judges who seem to believe it.

For years now, they have used this lie as a cudgel with which to bash away at Christian symbols and traditions.

I never thought I'd live to see the day that Christmas would become a dirty word. You think it hasn't? Then why is it that people are being prevented from saying it in polite society for fear that it will offend?

Schools are being forced to replace "Christmas vacation" with "winter break" in their printed schedules. At some major retail chains, the word is verboten, replaced as a matter of policy by the generic Happy Holidays. Carols, even instrumental versions, are banned in certain locales. A few years ago, a major postal delivery service not only made their drivers doff their Santa caps, but ordered them not to decorate their trucks with Christmas wreaths.

How is it, one well might ask, that in a Christian nation this is happening? Although it seems a long time ago, it really wasn't, that people who came here from other countries made every attempt to fit in. Assimilation wasn't a threat to anyone, it was what the Statue of Liberty represented. E pluribus unum, one out of many, was our motto. The world's melting pot was our nickname. It didn't mean that any group of people had to check their customs, culture or cuisine, at the door. It did mean that they, and especially their children, learned English, and that they learned to live and let live. What's more, the goofy notion of dual-citizenship wouldn't have occurred to anyone.

That has changed, as you may have noticed. And to a great extent, I blame my fellow Jews. When it comes to pushing the multicultural, anti-Christian, agenda, you find Jewish judges, Jewish journalists, and the ACLU, at the forefront.

Because we were Jewish, even of the non-observant variety, Christmas was never celebrated by my family. But what was there not to like about the holiday? To begin with, it provided a welcome two-week break from school. The decorated trees were nice, the lights were beautiful, "It's a Wonderful Life" was a wonderful movie, and some of the greatest Christmas songs were even written by Jews.

But the dirty little secret in America is that, in spite of the occasional over-publicized rants by the likes of Mel Gibson and Michael Richards, anti-Semitism is no longer a problem in American society; instead, it's been replaced by a rampant anti-Christianity. For example, much of the hatred spewed towards George W. Bush had far less to do with his policies than it did with his religion. The Jews voice no concern when presidential candidates like Bill Clinton or John Kerry show up at Black Baptist churches or pose with Rev. Jesse Jackson, because they understand that's just politics. They only object to politicians attending church for religious purposes.

My fellow Jews only gave 26% of their vote to Bush in 2004, even though he was clearly one of the more pro-Israel presidents we've ever had in the Oval Office. Unlike Clinton, who had Yasser Arafat sleeping in the Lincoln Bedroom so often even Monica Lewinsky got jealous, Bush saw to it that the Palestinian butcher was persona non grata at the White House.

You may have noticed, though, that the ACLU is highly selective when it comes to religious intolerance. The same group of self-righteous shysters who, at the drop of a "Merry Christmas" will slap you with an injunction, will fight for the right of an American Indian to ingest peyote and a devout Islamic woman to be veiled on her driver's license.

I happen to despise bullies and bigots. I hate them when they represent the majority, but no less when, like secular Jews in America, they represent an infinitesimal minority.

I am getting the idea that too many Jews won't be happy until they pull off their own version of the Spanish Inquisition, forcing Christians to either deny their faith and convert to agnosticism or suffer the consequences.

I should point out that many of these people abhor Judaism every bit as much as they do Christianity. They're the ones who behave as if atheism were a calling. They're the nutcakes who go berserk if anyone even says, "In God we trust" or mentions that the Declaration of Independence refers to a Creator with a capital "C." By this time, I'm only surprised that they haven't begun a campaign to do away with Sunday as a day of rest. After all, it's only for religious reasons - Christian reasons - that Sunday, and not Tuesday or Wednesday, is so designated.

This is a Christian nation, my friends. And all of us are fortunate it is one, and that so many millions of Americans have seen it fit to live up to the highest precepts of their religion.

Speaking as a member of a minority group - and one of the smaller ones at that - I say it behooves those of us who don't accept Jesus Christ as our savior to show some gratitude to those who do, and to start respecting the values and traditions of the overwhelming majority of our fellow citizens, just as we keep insisting that they respect ours.

Finally, the problem is that if Christians complain that a minority is trying to bully the majority, they stand condemned as bigots. If I, a Jew, suggest that Christians should be free to celebrate one of their holier holidays in any fashion they like, and not have to feel guilty about it, I'm accused of being a self-hating anti-Semite. In short, nobody is allowed to be critical of Jews. Well, it so happens that while we Jews may be the Chosen People, that doesn't make us the perfect people. And, believe me, I'm not just talking about my relatives.

Many of us, Jews and Christians alike, have been annoyed with American Muslims because they seem to spend an inordinate amount of time whining about racial profiling at the airports, instead of condemning the world-wide butchery of Islamic fascists. Well, to me, the silence of American Jews when it comes to Christian-bashing has been equally deafening.

What truly astonishes me is the patience and good grace with which Christians have dealt with this attack on so many things they hold dear.

It is, I think, a tribute to their religion.

What makes me devoutly wish that we Jews would some day wake up and fly right is that we have so much political influence in spite of our small numbers. For instance, we represent a mere two percent of the population, but about four percent of the votes in every presidential election. We may not vote earlier than other groups, but we definitely vote more often. Moreover, our percentages are even further out of proportion when it comes to Washington, D.C. Although we haven't as yet elected a Jewish president, there are currently 31 congressmen and 13 senators who are

Jewish. And of those 44, only one representative, Virginia's Eric Cantor, is a Republican.

I can't help thinking of how different things could be if only we'd use our power for good.

CHAPTER SIX

Why Do 90% of Blacks
Vote Like 80% of Jews

Whenever I start thinking about all the damage that's been done to America by the social engineering Socialists, I have to remind myself that some of my best friends are left-wingers. That doesn't do much for my blood pressure, but at least it serves to remind me that they're not all as self-righteous as George Soros, as fatuous as Michael Moore, as smarmy as Jimmy Carter, as shrill as Nancy Pelosi, as hypocritical as John Murtha, John Kerry and Robert C. Byrd, or as deceptive as Barack Obama, the fellow who had the most left-wing voting record in the U.S. Senate and yet managed to convince tens of millions of people, who should have known better, that he was actually a card-carrying centrist.

I didn't include Jesse Jackson and Al Sharpton among the usual suspects because it's probably not fair to even refer to those two cheap race hustlers as Democrats. In truth, they're nothing but a couple of con men who'd probably be peddling the Brooklyn Bridge to foreign tourists if this "black spokesman" gig hadn't panned out so well.

The whole question of race is a dicey one. Pity the poor fool who wades into those troubled waters. Well, here goes. If a black person tells the truth - namely, that in 2009, 99% of Black problems are self-inflicted - he is, like Bill Cosby and Thomas Sowell, dismissed as an Uncle Tom. If a white person tells the truth - namely, that between crime, drugs and illegitimacy, no amount of government hand-outs will do anything but provide inner-city Blacks with a very expensive band-aid - he's condemned as a racist.

When Blacks say they wish to have a dialogue with whites, it only means that they want a forum at which to bash whites, while their victims provide a Greek chorus of mea culpas, provide the coffee and Danish, and drop a little something in the collection plate on their way out.

There is such a thing as white prejudice. No doubt about it. But it has nothing to do with race, and everything to do with character, culture and values. What Blacks refuse to acknowledge is that whites are intolerant of crime and the creeps who commit it, be they Black thugs or white trash.

The latter are those lowlifes who form Aryan gangs; tattoo themselves with skulls and swastikas; and produce, distribute and use methamphetamines. I don't know a single white person who isn't ashamed to be of the same race as these vicious cretins.

There is also white collar crime which is generally committed by creeps who wear suits and ties and carry attaché cases. Aside from their trophy wives and their accountants, I don't know a single white person who isn't ashamed to be of the same race as these custom-tailored, manicured villains.

But if a person such as Bill Cosby says he's ashamed of the promiscuity, drug use and illiteracy, that plague the Black underclass, he's called names. The real shame should be that millions of Black kids are fatherless; that their taste in music is for anything that's crude, lewd and loud; that their role models are too often basketball players who make more babies than baskets; whose language skills are embarrassingly abysmal; and that, although most of the street punks are peddling drugs for roughly the minimum wage, they regard it as a worthier, more manly pursuit than working at a 7-11 or, God forbid, going to church, school or a library.

Most whites in this country are not racist. Actually, what most whites are is cowardly. When we see Black kids with the top of their baggy pants drooping somewhere south of their butts, annoying people with their ear-splitting boom boxes, saying "they be" when they mean "they are," and we pretend that theirs is a different, but equally fine culture as our own, we're no better than those enablers who give money to drug addicts or booze to alcoholics.

When we finally stop patronizing loafers, louts and criminals, stop encouraging people who were born 120 years after the Emancipation Proclamation and 20 years after the passage of the Civil Rights Act, to pretend that their sloth and ignorance are the fault of white people, only then will Blacks come one step closer to having that colorblind society they claim they want.

After all that, I'd understand if you doubted me when I say that, as a group of people, there probably isn't one that I more greatly admire than American Blacks, so long as they're conservatives.

After all, it means they're not only intelligent, independent thinkers, but they have the spine to stand up to the ignoramuses who accuse them of acting white and calling them oreos or worse.

I'm not just referring to such people as Thomas Sowell, Bill Cosby, Walter Williams, Shelby Steele, and Ward Connerly, but to the 10% who refuse to take their marching orders from the likes of Al Sharpton, Jesse Jackson, Maxine Waters, Louis Farrakhan, Jeremiah Wright and the tawdry members of the Black Congressional Caucus. I'm referring to the 10% of Blacks who have the gumption to actually cast their votes for the candidate who's not dealing the race card from the bottom of the deck.

In short, I'm not talking about Oprah Winfrey. Up until last year's primaries, I regarded her as someone who had used a great deal of ambition to achieve a gigantic amount of success. The few times I saw her show, I found it nonaddictive. But she was certainly more tolerable than the harpies who infest "The View," and I liked the fact that she encouraged her audience to occasionally turn off the TV and read a book. Even if it would never in a million years be this particular book.

That all changed in 2008, when I read a rather astonishing item in the newspaper. It seemed that Ms. Winfrey had declared that the only presidential candidate who would be allowed on her show was the junior - the very junior - senator from Illinois. Now I could understand that, being a Democrat, she wouldn't want to roll out the red carpet for Giuliani, Romney, Huckabee, McCain or Thompson. But why carry water for Obama, but not Hillary Clinton or even John Edwards? From my vantage point, I couldn't at that stage see a scintilla of difference in their politics. They were all left-wingers, after all, who believed that raising taxes was the solution to all problems.

The only difference I could see was the only difference that I could literally see - namely, that Barack Obama had a darker complexion than the other two. Was the fact that Obama's sperm donor, a man who'd deserted his wife and little Barack at just about the time the umbilical cord was cut, sufficient reason for Oprah to give the guy her official blessing?

If a Mormon TV talk show host had refused to have any of the candidates on his show other than Mitt Romney or if Larry King banished everyone who wasn't Jewish from his domain, I'm dead certain he would have faced universal condemnation. So how is it that Oprah could have been that high-handed and nobody even said "Boo"?

From my vantage point, I would say that TV's empress is not only naked, but that she's a racist.

To suggest that there's a double standard where Blacks are concerned is to put it mildly. For example, when I first heard Blacks talking about reparations, I have to admit I started to laugh. Let's face it; it sounded exactly like the sort of get-rich-quick schemes that the Kingfish used to conjure up on "Amos 'n' Andy." And funny as he was, he wasn't half as wacky as John Conyers, Maxine Waters and Charles Rangel.

We all know there is so much white guilt floating around that if you could only transform it into electrical power, America would be freed of its dependence on fossil fuels. But, come on now. Reparations?

I recall wondering if I might be missing something. Were these people seriously demanding that damages should be paid 140 years after the end of slavery? What ever happened to the statute of limitations? What ever happened to common sense? And where do people four or five generations after the fact get off demanding pay-offs? People who weren't hurt demanding money from people who never hurt anyone? It sounded to me like a whole new definition of chutzpah. Or, if you prefer, like a plank in the Democratic platform.

The more I thought about it, the goofier it sounded. First of all, there's the question of where the money would come from. The answer, I suppose, is the same magical place from which all entitlements emanate - the pockets of the middle class taxpayers.

But surely we couldn't all be expected to kick in, could we? After all, surely Black Americans couldn't be required to ante up. But, then, neither could most white Americans, whose own ancestors, by and large, didn't arrive on these shores until long after the Civil War had settled the issue once and for all.

And, heaven knows, you couldn't very well demand reparations from those American Yankees whose forefathers not only ran the Underground Railroad, but perished by the hundreds of thousands in that bloodiest of wars. In fact, one could make a case that it's Blacks who owe a debt to the ancestors of those men who perished at Shiloh and Bull Run and Gettysburg.

Once you get done eliminating innocent parties, who's left to foot the bill? Mainly volunteers, I suspect. People like Boxer, Gore, Waxman, Kerry, and the Clintons, people in the business of feeling everybody's pain, would be free to pony up for the rest of us. The question would still remain: What do you do about Barack Obama? Would he only get to collect fifty cents on the dollar?

I'm sure when most people first heard about reparations, they dismissed it as just another of those race-baiting notions that seems to appear with the obnoxious regularity of death, taxes, and a Michelle Obama photo op. But when I thought about all the Yankee soldiers who died while preserving the Union and ending slavery, it occurred to me that there are millions of us who could line up for a piece of the reparation pie.

For instance, long after Blacks left the plantation, the Chinese were brought to America as cheap coolie laborers to lay railroad tracks. And once that job was over, they were treated like curs. By custom and by law, they were restricted to the worst jobs and the worst slums.

Let us not forget women. Once reparations catch on, the ladies will be front and center with their endless list of grievances regarding life as it's lived in a patriarchal society. You think picking cotton was bad? Try packing the kids off to school, picking up the dry cleaning, grocery shopping, driving the tots to their play dates, cooking, cleaning, and holding down a second job, all the while refraining from murdering the slob she's married to who insists on leaving his dirty socks on the floor!

Frankly, if this thing actually gets off the ground, I plan to submit my own claim. I'm short, you see, and in this country that's a far greater handicap than being Black, Chinese or female.

Finally, though, let me say that I agree with the brave Black New York Times reporter who, a few years ago, wrote that, as abominable as slavery was, he, personally, was grateful that it brought his ancestors to this country, enabling their great-great-great-great grandson to be born an American.

There are times when I find myself thinking that I am one of the few people in this country who was actually paying attention when Martin Luther King envisioned a society that judged people by their character and not by the color of their skin. But here it is nearly a half century later, and millions of us continue to accept, defend and rationalize bad behavior so long as it's Black behavior. When John Kerry said that he loved to listen to rap music, with its simple-minded rhymes and rhythm and its brutal and misogynistic lyrics, we knew he was a lying sack of manure. But every presidential candidate with a (D) after his name feels compelled to patronize the lowest common denominator in the Black community.

For instance, a few years ago, professional quarterback Michael Vick sponsored dogfights. He would drown, electrocute or bash in the heads of the losers. When I heard about his vile actions, it occurred to me that he was very lucky that team owners don't get to do the same to their underachieving quarterbacks.

But as repulsive as Michael Vick's actions were, what I heard and read in the aftermath struck me as being far worse. The dogfights themselves, and Vick's executions of the unfortunate canines, as vicious and sadistic as they were, involved only the Atlanta quarterback and a handful of his feebleminded lackeys. However, his defenders started crawling out from under rocks, parroting all sorts of appallingly ignorant nonsense. And I find that even more troubling.

By and large, the morons fell into one of three camps. There were those who want the rest of us to get over our outrage and be willing to give Vick another chance because we're all mere mortals, after all, and humans make mistakes. This argument falls apart as soon as you acknowledge that wearing brown shoes with a black suit is a mistake; guessing incorrectly on a true-or-false test is a mistake; torturing and killing dogs over and over again isn't a mistake or an error in judgment. It's a felony and, I'd venture, a mortal sin.

Another equally fatuous defense is that killing dogs is no big deal, considering that hunters are free to shoot just about every other animal under the sun. Even though I'm not a hunter, even I can readily see the difference. In spite of their having four legs and a tail, dogs are not exactly animals. Unlike elks and moose and wild boars, they are members of our families. Calling them man's best friend is only the slightest of exaggerations, and in the case of a great many men, not even that.

Some of the more ignorant Blacks defended Vick, insisting that the dogs were his and he should have been able to do whatever he wanted to them.

As was to be expected, the multi-culturalists in our midst weighed in with their own special brand of stupidity. So far as these pinheads are concerned, white Americans are never supposed to be judgmental of what others do. So, for instance, if Black and Latino teenagers choose to spray paint your fence, that's their culture, and who are we to deny them their artistic freedom? Or, for that matter, who are we to say that the music of Bach, Beethoven and Brahms, is in any way superior to the noise which we have come to know as rap and hip-hop?

Likewise, how dare we sit in judgment of Mr. Vick? After all, there are places on earth where dogs aren't pets, but, instead, are a major source of protein. To which I can only respond that there are also hellholes where, canines being a scarce commodity, they make do with people.

The whole concept of tolerance has been turned topsy-turvy in contemporary America. Perhaps it's because our Baby Boomer journalists and academicians have contended for so many years that America is the source of all evil that millions of our young people have come to be accepting of any culture just so long as it's not their own. Even if it happens to be one that sanctions honor killings, beheadings, female mutilations, suicide bombings, or, in Vick's case, the massacre of dogs.

At least Michael Vick went to prison. But when it comes to Blacks, far too often they get away with stuff just because they're allowed, even encouraged, to claim victimhood. In O.J.'s case, what he got away with was murder.

But isn't it high time that Blacks had to finally stop insisting it's discrimination whenever things don't go exactly as they like?

A prime example of this sort of nonsense took place a few years ago at Ball State. In the wake of allegations that basketball coach Ronny Thompson had violated a number of NCAA rules, including illegal recruitment, he demanded additional money, alleging that he left the university because of racial hostility. Talk about chutzpah! Now I don't happen to live in Muncie, Indiana, but if there's one thing I do know it's that basketball is a religion in that state and, whether the coach is black, white, green or beige, any guy with a 9-22 record is going to find himself in a hostile environment.

Heck, if Ball State was so racially intolerant, they wouldn't have given the ingrate a job in the first place and they sure wouldn't have hired Billy Taylor, who just happens to be Black, to replace him!

This brings us to Tennie Pierce. Mr. Pierce had been a fireman here in Los Angeles for many years when one night he sat down to dinner in the firehouse and was served what he assumed was spaghetti and meatballs, but was in reality spaghetti and dog food. He promptly got in touch with a law firm and sued the city for about fifty trillion dollars. His lawyers finally agreed to a settlement of roughly $1.5 million.

While I have no idea what his meal tasted like, I figure that so long as it didn't contain poison or ground glass, he was rewarded far in excess to his pain and suffering. If I'd been on the city council, I'd have offered Mr. Pierce dinner for two at an Italian restaurant of his choice.

I'm not being cavalier about this because Mr. Pierce is Black, but because what we all knew from the start is that he was the biggest prankster of all. For a long time, he had been the prime instigator of practical jokes at the fire station. I happen to despise practical jokes. It's bad enough that they tend to be petty and stupid, but the victim then has to pretend that he thought they were clever and original, or he runs the risk that the ignoramuses who were involved will label him a spoilsport who is entirely devoid of the humor gene.

But the very idea that this fathead could indulge in similar horseplay for years on end and then turn around and collect a small fortune for no other reason than that he's Black, and is therefore entitled, strikes me as a prime example of reverse racism.

Because I have often shared my honest feelings, both positive but also negative, about Black Americans, I have had more honest discussions with Blacks than have most whites, who feel they must pussyfoot around such a hot button topic.

Not too long ago, I was being interviewed on the radio by a Black woman. Early on, she attacked me for having suggested that most racists in America are Black, not white.

I wasn't surprised that she disagreed with me, but I couldn't believe my ears when she actually said that the brouhaha some years ago over Janet Jackson's bared breast proved that white America is a racist society. I asked her if she'd been unaware of the stink raised over Britney Spears smooching with Madonna. And that display took place on a late night music awards show that had nothing like the audience or the number of young viewers that the Super Bowl commanded.

Sometimes, it's easy to get the idea that many Black Americans are unaware that there are nearly 260 million of us who, without being Black, garner our share of grief and misery. It goes with being human beings, and has nothing to do with pigmentation.

Even the high and mighty aren't above the fray. Go back a few decades and you have the spectacle of Richard Nixon's having to resign from the highest office in the land. Or consider V.P. Dan Quayle, who suffered far more public humiliation than Ms. Jackson simply because, one, he forgot how to spell "potato," and, two, he voiced a legitimate concern that TV's Murphy Brown was setting a bad example for America's youth by having a child out of wedlock.

People ridiculed Quayle by pointing out that Ms. Brown was a fictional character. But, then, who ever claimed a fictional character couldn't influence the highly impressionable? Look at Huck Finn and Scarlet O'Hara, the Three Musketeers, Rocky Balboa, Harry Potter, Superman, and Hillary Clinton.

When Al Campanis and Trent Lott misspoke on the subject of Blacks, they were immediately banished to Lower Slobovia. However, lambasting whites is a surefire path to success for many upwardly mobile Black American race hustlers.

When Pat Robertson dared run for the presidency, the liberal media castigated him for blurring the division between church and state. But nary a discouraging word was voiced when reverends Jackson and Sharpton tossed their hats in the ring. And while we're on the subject, do those two palookas ever bother attending church, let alone ever actually function as ministers?

When I suggested to the radio hostess that the biggest problems for Blacks in this country were self-inflicted, and that whites were not responsible for a 70% illegitimacy rate, for turf wars over drugs, and for the alarming drop-out rate among high school and college students, she said I simply wouldn't understand - that it was a Black thing!

The fact is, most Blacks who are raped, robbed and murdered, are the victims, not of white bigots or white cops, but of Black thugs.

But some people find it easier to play the race card, to pretend every time Black celebrities are arrested, it's because rotten white society is out to get them. Funny how that works, though. The same society that arrested O.J. Simpson had first given him a free college education and then handed him millions of dollars to play football, make movies, and run through airports in TV commercials.

The very same society that arrested Michael Jackson, Mike Tyson, Michael Vick and Kobe Bryant, first made them kazillionaires.

It's the same society that has made icons of Oprah Winfrey, Bill Cosby, Michael Jordan, Denzel Washington, Halle Berry, Tiger Woods, Quincy Jones, Alice Walker, Beyonce Knowles, Toni Morrison, LeBron James, Shaquille O'Neal, Colin Powell, Will Smith, Condoleezza Rice and, let us not forget, Barack and Michelle Obama.

If this were a racist society, believe me, we would not know any of those names. Those people would be working in the fields or doing time in the gulags or they'd be dead. That's the way it works in racist societies.

I do not happen to believe that most white Americans are bigots. I think, by and large, we judge Blacks exactly the way that Dr. King suggested - by their character and their intelligence and their ability. It's the same way we judge each other.

However, we don't have a lot of sympathy for those who claim to be victims of racial oppression. We can't stomach those who wallow in self-pity, demanding everything from reparations to college degrees as birthrights.

We have no patience with those who blame their lack of ambition in school or the work place on people they don't even know. And we certainly have no use for the creeps who spawn all those millions of children, condemning them to be raised in fatherless homes, simultaneously condemning the rest of us to live with the violent, illiterate thugs so many of them will inevitably grow up to be. And who then, for good measure, blame white society when these punks eventually wind up in jail.

Needless to say, the lady on the radio took strong exception to my words.

I simply couldn't get through to her. It must be a white thing.

A few weeks ago, I was listening to a radio talk show when a Black man called in to take Barack Obama to task for suggesting that Black men were sloughing off their responsibilities as fathers. The caller didn't deny recent data that indicated that 70% of Black babies were being born to unwed mothers. Instead, he said that this dire situation wasn't the fault of irresponsible young men and women, but, instead, was the logical result of rampant racism in our country. He claimed that Black American males simply can't find jobs, and that's the reason they don't support their families.

I waited for the talk show host to set him straight, but it never happened. So I guess, as is so often the case in this cowardly, politically correct, age, I'll have to do it myself.

First of all, if I had been hosting the show, I probably would have laughed in the caller's face. Which may very well explain why I'm not hosting a radio talk show.

The notion that in 2009, anyone can seriously suggest that it is Whitey's fault that millions of Black men are abrogating their responsibility to get married and help raise their children would be laughable if the results weren't so tragic both for the Black community and for America at large.

How is it, I would have challenged the caller, that his grandparents and their grandparents managed to get married and bring up their youngsters in spite of Jim Crow laws, separate-but-definitely-unequal schools and rampant racism that kept them in menial jobs, but that all these years later, in spite of decades of Affirmative Action, government-enforced equal opportunity in the workplace and quota systems that benefit minorities, Black men lack the ability to do the same? And how is it that people all over the world who are much poorer than American Blacks manage to pull it off?

It's obvious that millions of Black men simply prefer shirking their responsibilities, while simultaneously insisting that they're the victims of white society. They make a huge deal of demanding respect, of insisting they're men and not boys, but all the while millions of them do precious little to earn anybody's respect or to prove that they are anything but irresponsible brats.

How can I be so certain that I'm right and that the angry caller wasn't? Simple. After all, how can it be possible that all these millions of Black men are unable to support their babies, but millions of single Black women somehow manage?

To suggest that I am not enamored of the president is putting it mildly. Quite frankly, I do not understand why the media went into the tank for this guy. I mean, inasmuch as nearly all of them are liberals, I wasn't surprised that they had, as my friend Bernard Goldberg put it, a slobbering love affair with Obama when he squared off with John McCain. But the media had become smitten long before that. For years, after all, they had courted Hillary Clinton, dubbing her the smartest woman in America, sending her flowers and bon bons, and then, after she said "Yes" to their proposal, dumped her. Like a groom who suddenly decides he's gay, the media ditched her at the altar and ran off with the best man.

Or if not the best man, at least the man who was 50% blacker than Hillary.

At one point in the primary, it appeared that Hillary might actually have a chance to turn things around, but it was at that point that Barack Obama gave a speech that his disciples compared favorably to the Gettysburg Address and the Sermon on the Mount, but which I thought came a lot closer to Richard Nixon's "Checkers" speech, a desperate attempt to keep himself from being relegated to the trash heap of history.

Coming in the wake, as it did, of all we had come to know about Rev. Jeremiah Wright, I thought Obama's speech was far too little and much too late. Say, 20 years too late.

Frankly, I'm surprised that so many people, and not just liberals, were so willing to give Obama a pass. It's one thing, after all, for this half-white fellow to join the Trinity United Church of (a Black) Christ in order to use it as a launching pad into Chicago's scummy political scene. That's just playing the game. But when one not only sticks around for two decades, but has the creep perform your wedding ceremony and baptize your daughters, and you then bring those children into church to listen to this demagogue damn our country and vilify white Christians, I really didn't understand why everyone wasn't as disgusted as I was with Mr. Obama.

The junior senator from Illinois first campaigned on the premise that he was the one person who could put racial differences behind us, but when it was discovered that he was joined at the hip with Louis Farrakhan's best friend, insisted he was ready to engage in an honest dialogue on race. But of course he wasn't. He simply regurgitated the same old dump-on-Whitey bilge that Jesse Jackson, Charles Rangel, Maxine Waters and Al Sharpton, have been spewing out for so many long and profitable years.

It was back in 1964 when the Civil Rights Act was passed. In the intervening decades, this country has spent billions of dollars to compensate people who hadn't suffered from Jim Crow laws for the simple reason that they hadn't even been born yet. Be that as it may, the government continues to fund Operation Head Start, continues to use Affirmative Action as a means by which to leap-frog underachieving Black students over, in most cases, better-qualified Asian students; continues to favor Black-owned businesses with low interest loans; and, under Obama, continues to funnel billions of tax dollars to such predominately black left-wing gangs as ACORN and the SEIU. But it's never enough and God knows there's no end in sight.

You'd like an honest dialogue about race relations, Mr. Obama? As Jack Nicholson's Col. Jessup yelled at Tom Cruise's Lt. Kaffee in "A Few Good Men": "You want the truth? You can't handle the truth!"

The truth is, in America, anyone with brains, grit and self-discipline, can rise to unimaginable heights. But of course, a guy with a racist agenda, a con man like Jeremiah Wright, won't tell you that. No, instead he used his bully pulpit to insist that we honkies cooked up the HIV virus as a means to exterminate Black people. Believe me, if we had extermination in mind, we wouldn't have come up with anything that fancy. Why would we invent a disease that would infect whites as well as Blacks? And we surely wouldn't be blowing billions of tax dollars to combat the disease in Africa.

If we were a racist society, Oprah Winfrey, your fairy godmother, certainly wouldn't be a billionaire; she'd be fetching someone's mint julep. And Colin Powell and Condoleezza Rice wouldn't grow up to be secretaries of state; they'd be sweeping out the stables. And Will Smith and Denzel Washington wouldn't be movie stars; they'd be in the fields picking cotton.

I don't claim to speak for all white Americans, only for myself. But, personally, I think it stinks that there's even a single Black American who has the gall to blame white Americans for the troubles that continue to plague Black communities in 2009. I mean, how is a high illegitimacy rate the fault of white people? How is the fact that young Black men are more likely to wind up with a rap sheet than with a college degree our fault? Too many Blacks, in and out of politics, get away with claiming that whites are the only racists in America because only whites have political power. But how is it that we all agree that the Ku Klux Klan is a racist organization although, aside from Robert Byrd (D), no Klan member holds high elective office? And how is it that, in this allegedly racist society, there are any number of Black congressmen, governors, mayors, police chiefs and even a Black United States president?

By the way, how is it that if whites are the racists, there is far more Black-on-white crime than white-on-Black? Far, far more. It's not even close.

This isn't to suggest that we whites are blameless. Some of us are innocent, but surely not the members of the Democratic party. You'll never hear one of their politicians utter an unpleasant truth about Black underachievement. They're quite happy to pay off Black ministers at election time to extend their blessings and their pulpits to any hack with a (D) after his name. Their favorite pastime, though, is tossing tax dollars away on Black so-called entitlements, otherwise known as bribes. After all, it's not their money and they wind up with 90% of the plantation votes in their pocket.

I, myself, wouldn't mind at all voting for a Black president. In fact, it wasn't that long ago that I was quite prepared to vote for General Colin Powell when it appeared he was a conservative and might make a run for the White House. And, frankly, I think a cabinet filled with people such as Shelby Steele, Walter Williams, Ward Connerly and Thomas Sowell, would be as good as it gets.

The sad irony of Obama's candidacy was that so many white Americans were convinced that by voting for a Black racist they were proving how wonderfully tolerant they were. All they really proved is how childish and naive some people are, whatever their age.

By sitting in that pew for 20 long years, soaking up Rev. Wright's poison, Obama convinced me he was as big a race hustler as Al Sharpton or Jesse Jackson. The only real difference I was aware of was that he didn't shout, try to sound like Algonquin J. Calhoun or insist on giving speeches that rhyme.

Oh, how I long for the good old days when the worst thing that anyone could say about Barack Hussein Obama is that, down deep, he might really be a Muslim!

If I hear one more person point out that Obama is the president and that it's our duty to support him, I just might run amok. For one thing, I resent being reminded that he actually won the election and that it's not all a bad dream from which I'll awaken as soon as the alarm clock rings. For another, there was a very good reason that I voted for John McCain, and it certainly had nothing to do with my having great expectations of the man, and everything to do with my conviction that Obama was a left-wing ideologue.

I'm afraid I now have to reevaluate him. He's even worse that I feared. It's been one disaster after another. His appointments have been a series of embarrassments. His hard sell of the Pelosi-Reid trillion dollar earmark makes him look like the worst sort of fear-monger. And, considering the fact that he was sold to us as eloquent and a fellow who could think on his feet, his over-use of a teleprompter reminded me of the Wizard of Oz, the con man behind the curtain. I guess you can take the man out of Chicago, but you can't take Chicago out of the man.

Frankly, I don't know why anybody continues to hold Obama in high esteem. Maybe it's like those women who marry charming fellows only to discover after the vows have been exchanged that he's a wife-beater. In spite of the black eyes and split lips, the ladies are just too embarrassed to call the cops and have their friends and relatives discover what a dunderhead they've been.

The way Obama has been jetting around on Air Force One, which costs the taxpayers a bloody fortune every time it lifts off the tarmac, you'd think the environmentalists would be reading him the riot act. But as we've learned with Al Gore and Robert Kennedy, Jr., so long as you're a liberal, you only have to say the right things about fossil fuels, you don't actually have to believe them. Even when he and Michelle took separate jets to Copenhagen to lobby on behalf of Chicago's most corrupt elements for the 2016 Olympics, liberals bit their tongues.

The question that keeps begging to be asked is whether Obama ever says anything with honest conviction. Even when he championed the so-called stimulus bill, he indulged in double talk. Obama swore that it would create or save four million jobs. Now I can't swear to be an expert in Obama-speak, but to me that sounded like he would get to claim, if at some time in the future there were four million Americans still gainfully employed, that he had lived up to his word.

What truly astonishes me isn't that the Democrats, along with three feeble-minded Republicans named Specter, Collins and Snowe, voted for the trillion dollar pork package, even though nobody had the time to wade through its eleven hundred pages. After all, even without knowing the details, they knew that the actual purpose of the legislation was to suck up even more money and power for themselves, thus completing the job begun 75 years earlier by FDR. What I found profoundly depressing was that, according to a poll at the time, a majority of Americans approved its passage even though they were convinced that it would hurt, not help, the economy. Perhaps the politicians are entitled to regard us as contemptuously as they do.

Then along came Obamacare, which would pretty much give the federal bureaucrats the power to determine how much money and effort would be expended on behalf of the elderly. If you thought HMOs were bad, you ain't seen nothing yet. When I heard about it, I was instantly reminded of a 1973 movie called "Soylent Green," which starred Charlton Heston and Edward G. Robinson. Mr. Heston's character spent most of the movie trying to discover what the mysterious and strangely ominous Soylent Green Corporation did. He found out in the end that they turned old people into protein wafers.

As if Obama isn't annoying enough, the way he is constantly jutting his chin skyward as if in homage to Benito Mussolini, he saddles us with an attorney general who calls white Americans cowards because, to his way of thinking, we don't engage in frank conversations about racial matters.

I get the impression that Eric Holder is confused about the nature of his job. He is only the government's chief lawyer. Being the political scold is, in the immortal words of his boss, above his pay scale.

It seems that while Holder grants that these days the workplace is integrated, he is troubled that there's "not much significant interaction between whites and blacks in social settings. On Saturdays and Sundays,

America in the year 2009 does not, in some ways, differ significantly from the country that existed some 50 years ago."

This is the arrogant twit who, in spite of playing a part in Bill Clinton's pardoning of Marc Rich and commuting the sentences of 16 Puerto Rico terrorists and a handful of Arab troublemakers, got the job for no other reason than that he's Black. He wants frank talk? Fine. That's why I'm here.One, most white Americans don't spend a lot of time dwelling on anyone's race. They're much too busy trying to make a living and raising their kids. Two, in case you were out of town, in 2008, white people elected the first Black president. What's more, a great many of them did it for no better reason than his race. Three, most people, Black and white, spend their weekends with their families, who, even now, tend to be of their own race. Four, many Americans belong to churches open to all denominations, even though Holder's boss attended an all-Black church for 20 years. I have no idea what sort of church, if any, Mr. Holder attends, but if spending quality time with white people is so important to him, that might be a good place to start.

Five, does our new attorney general spend much time with Asians or Hispanics, or is it only whites he yearns to hang with? Six, does this mean that he intends to start inviting lots of white people over to the house for weekend bar-be-cues and sleepovers? And has he run this plan by Mrs. Holder?

As I recall, Barack Obama insisted he was going to be the first post-racial president. Perhaps sitting down and talking turkey with this turkey he selected to be the nation's attorney general would be the appropriate place to begin.

Some people have wondered why I, who take so much interest in politics and politicians, have never run for public office. Aside from not wishing to spend a lot of time with politicians, the only job that would appeal to me is the top one. I mean, who wants to be one of 435 congressmen and have to listen to Nancy Pelosi day in and day out or be one of 100 senators and try to stay awake while Harry Reid, Robert Byrd or Barbara Boxer, droned on?

As for being president, I'm afraid the deck is stacked against me. It's not that I'm Jewish or a conservative, but that I'm bald, short and have a beard. The fact is it's been over 50 years since we last elected a bald president, and Eisenhower had the advantage of twice running against bald Adlai Stevenson. In nearly every presidential election, the taller candidate wins. And, for good measure, the last man with facial hair to be president was William Howard Taft, who only had a mustache, and that election was in 1908. The last man with a beard to be elected was James Garfield, in

1880, and he was shot and killed shortly after he was elected. Even I can see the writing on the wall.

Just possibly the reason we wind up with so many oafs in the Oval Office is because, down deep, it's far more important to us that they be tall, clean shaven and with a full head of hair, than that they be honest, honorable and patriotic.

Finally, lest I be accused of only picking on left-wingers, let me confess that I recently sent an e-mail to Sean Hannity. Although I think dumping Alan Colmes was a smart move, I let him know that I thought the "Hate Hannity Hotline" videos on his TV show were a ridiculous waste of time. After all, if I wanted to listen to a bunch of loudmouth, left-wing ignoramuses sounding off, I wouldn't be tuned to Fox, I'd be watching MSNBC.

Before concluding this chapter, I have one final bone to pick on the subject, and it involves, of all things, our national anthem.

Admittedly, "The Star-Spangled Banner" lacks a certain something, musically speaking. But over the years, singers ranging from my aunt Sarah to Richard Tucker have been able to do it justice, merely by singing it simply and sincerely. But at some point during the past dozen years or so, certain Black female singers have decided that the only way to perform it was as if they were auditioning to provide orgasms for a porno soundtrack. The words should come from the heart, not the groin.

Maybe I'm being too harsh. Perhaps these song birds don't intend any disrespect to the anthem. Perhaps they simply don't understand that patriotism means loving your country, not having sex with it.

CHAPTER SEVEN

Hollywood Would Rather Make
Trouble Than Movies

When I titled my first book "Conservatives Are From Mars, Liberals Are From San Francisco," I could just as easily have pointed out that liberals are from Hollywood. It really is a different planet from the one most of us live on.

To begin with, it is populated with high school drop-outs and drama majors making millions of dollars a year, convinced they should decide how the rest of us think, live and vote. What you must never forget about these pampered pets is that the first lesson they learned in acting class was to get in touch with their feelings. Those self-absorbing exercises only served to diminish whatever thought processes they might have possessed. The end result is that, at their best, they can mimic emotions and action, but have an impossible time trying to suggest they are thinking about anything at all, except for the size of their trailers and their back-end points.

Never forget that the things we see on the screen are shadows. The real articles are people who spend their lives wearing other people's clothes, mouthing other people's lines, and being told how to walk and talk by directors. They should come with warning labels stating that, for all their fame and fortune, they are as bright as department store mannequins.

One thing you have to give Hollywood celebrities credit for is their monumental gall. I mean, Barbara Streisand insults conservatives more often than she bathes, knowing full well it won't harm her CD sales. Julia Roberts announces that if you look up Republican in the dictionary, you'll find it right after reptiles, and yet she continues selling movie tickets, even though nearly half of the electorate cast their ballots for John McCain.

You'll notice that show biz liberals are very outspoken, just so long as they're addressing the choir. But you rarely see them placing themselves in a situation where they have to debate the issues. Have you ever once seen Michael Moore addressing any group that didn't consist of either American college students or French film snobs? No, neither have I.

Some years ago, long before Alzheimers set in, Charlton Heston offered to debate Ms. Streisand on the subject of gun ownership, all the money collected to go to the charity of her choice. Naturally, the debate never took place.

Alfre Woodard's inane contention that her colleagues in SAG are "informed, articulate and compassionate," aside, the sheep of Hollywood are more likely to question the deaths of James Dean, Marilyn Monroe and Elvis Presley, than they are to seriously question a single plank of the Democratic platform. And, being the self-righteous boors they are, they never see any contradiction between the populist pap they parrot and the way they actually live their lives.

I have had a love/hate relationship with the entertainment industry for my entire life. It began in my childhood with radio and continued on with movies and TV. I even owe my love of reading to motion pictures. I had been an indifferent reader during most of my childhood, making do with a few visits to Oz and the occasional "Dr. Dolittle." But when I was 11, an older brother took me along to the movies to see a reissue of "The Grapes of Wrath." It impressed me so much that when we got home and I saw a book with the same title on the shelf, I asked if there was a connection. When I was told there was, I immediately took the book down and began reading it. Perhaps I was hoping the book had a happy ending.

As time went on, I spent 14 years as a movie reviewer. That's probably when the hate portion of the relationship began. By the time I called it quits, I was no longer a fan. Understand, I could still enjoy the movies of the 30s and 40s, and, to a lesser degree, even those of the 50s. But a person can only sit through so many really lame comedies starring either Jerry Lewis or Peter Sellers before waving a white flag and negotiating terms of surrender.

The 60s, the decade during which I did most of my reviewing, was notable for very young, very untalented, essentially illiterate British and American directors who gave new meaning to self-indulgence.

As if the movies weren't bad enough, as plot and character gave way to annoying camera angles and improvised dialogue, the movies kept getting longer and longer. The explanation at the time was that because TV was providing people with the equivalent of B-movies for free, the day of the double feature was over. So, in order for the audience to feel it was getting its money's worth, running lengths had to be expanded. That almost sounded believable, but it was really a lot of hooey. The reason that movies kept getting longer was because of the inflated egos of the directors and the stars. With the passing of the studio moguls, it was they who filled the power vacuum. Their attitude was that if they deigned to make a movie, it automatically became a major theatrical event - and nothing conveys importance quite so much as an epic running time.

For all his various shortcomings as a moviemaker, Woody Allen is the only star or director who consistently turns out short movies. For that reason alone, I can even forgive him "Small Time Crooks," "Manhattan Murder Mystery" and "The Curse of the Jade Scorpion." Well, almost.

Back when I was reviewing, I decided one December, after sitting through the usual year- end glut of Oscar hopefuls that I would write a rave about the next movie I saw just so long as it ran less than two hours. As luck would have it, the next movie turned out to be the vile "Where's Poppa?" which ran a scant 82 minutes, proving that when a movie is truly putrid, it can fool you into thinking you've been sitting there for three or four grueling days.

But things could be worse. Instead of reviewing movies back then, I could be doing it today. The mere thought makes my blood run cold. Frankly, it's a wonder to me that there are grown-ups willing to spend their lives in dark theaters just so they can come out and assure us that once again our worst cinematic fears have been realized.

With nearly every movie costing upwards of a hundred million dollars to produce, nobody is willing to take a chance on something even halfway original. Instead, they either churn out a lousy sequel to a lousy movie or they re-make something that was done far better in the past, such as "Alfie," "Bad News Bears," "The Manchurian Candidate" and "Charlie and the Chocolate Factory." Worse yet, they re-cycle old TV shows, simultaneously producing rotten movies and trampling on our nostalgia for such fare as "The Avengers," "Sgt. Bilko," "Bewitched" and "The Honeymooners."

When you factor in the cost of tickets and popcorn, even if you don't have to pay for parking and a babysitter, and even if you're willing to overlook the sticky theater floors and the clucks who forget to turn off their cell phones and those who forget to turn off their mouths, there is no good reason for any sensible person doing a damn thing to subsidize Hollywood's pampered children.

Isn't it bad enough that unless you happen to be a knee-jerk leftist, they dismiss you as a stupid redneck? As they laugh all the way to the bank, who exactly do you think they're laughing at?

So, the next time you even think about forking over all that money at the local Bijou to see yet another movie in which a ball of flame almost, but not quite, barbecues the hero, treat yourself instead to a lobster dinner. Even if you wind up with a mild case of heartburn, it will be well worth it. At least you won't hate yourself in the morning.

When I read a while ago that Robin Wright was divorcing Sean Penn after several years of marriage, I was hoping she would attribute the split not to the usual irreconcilable differences, but to irreconcilable differences of opinion. I mean, if I were the judge and Mrs. Penn testified that she'd finally had her fill of Sean's going on like a besotted teenager about how cool Hugo Chavez is, I'd be happy to give her custody of the kids and 100% of the community property, including the Oscars he should never have won for his hammy over-the-top performances in "Mystic River" and "Milk."

Speaking of Oscars, there's a great deal wrong with them, even aside from the fact that the Academy voters actually handed one over to the bozos who wrote the song, "It's Hard Out There for a Pimp." For starters, there's the fact that they are hardly ever awarded to comedies or to those who write or star in them. On rare occasions, someone such as Kevin Kline or Marisa Tomei picks one up in a supporting role. But, as a rule, if you want to win an Oscar, your best bet is to appear in an overlong, overwrought drama as a mute, a cripple or a prostitute.

But as bad as the Academy Awards are, the biggest scam of all are the Golden Globes. At least most of the members of the Motion Picture Academy either work in the movie industry or used to work in the industry. But the folks who hand out the Golden Globes are 80-odd part-time foreign journalists. In the old days, when I was working for a production company, the joke was that if you cared about getting a nomination, you invited these underpaid wretches to a party and fed them pigs-in-a-blanket. If you actually cared about winning, you'd go whole hog and feed them jumbo shrimp in cocktail sauce.

Many Americans have complained that the only message to be found in Hollywood product these days is that George W. Bush and Dick Cheney were dictators, that the CIA is a combination of the Gestapo and the KGB, and that those who serve in the U.S. military do so only because it enables them to rape, pillage and murder, to their hearts' content. But I wonder if the subliminal message that comes through when audiences around the world watch this swill isn't the opposite of what the Hollywood crowd intended. I believe if I were watching one of these stinkers in most foreign nations, I would be thinking, "What a great and free country America must be that these ungrateful louts are allowed to make movies so critical of the government. Over here, they wouldn't be paid millions of dollars and treated like royalty. Over here, they'd be lined up against a wall and shot."

Although, as a rule, those people who star in movies are more obnoxious than their colleagues in television - perhaps because we're not inviting them into our homes - the folks on TV tend to be even whinier.

The question that comes to mind is when appearing on the tube went from being a well-paid privilege to being an inalienable right.

So far as I'm aware, it first became an issue when "Murder She Wrote," a CBS staple from 1984 to 1996, was canceled. The phenomenon may have pre-dated that event, but that's when I became aware of the sea change. Prior to that, diehard fans were naturally disappointed whenever one of their favorite shows bit the dust, but it was understood that nothing went on forever.

However, in 1996, Angela Lansbury went ballistic over her show's demise, even though it had already made her enormously wealthy. As I recall, Ms. Lansbury felt that CBS had not treated her and the show with the proper reverence. She didn't seem to realize that a pink slip is a pink slip, and should not be confused with a condolence card. In any case, I felt that someone should have pointed out to the lady that CBS is a corporation and not a friend of the family - although God knows this particular corporation had been enormously generous to her family, most of whom had wound up on the show's payroll - and that a 13-year run is about as reverential as TV ever gets.

Since then, every time a show gets axed because of poor ratings or lousy demographics or because the star is so deeply into drugs that she can't read a cue card, we have come to expect the likes of Ellen Degeneres, Jane Seymour and Brett Butler, to accuse cold-hearted corporate robots of having it in for them. The fact of the matter is that any TV network would be only too happy to hire Osama bin Laden to host a game show if they could only work out a deal. There is a reason, after all, they call it the bottom line.

Will we ever forget the media frenzy over Ted Koppel's possible cancellation and the spectacle of Bill Maher's carrying on over the axing of "Politically Incorrect" as if it was another of those notorious right wing conspiracies? The plain fact of the matter is that nobody had been tuning in "Nightline" for years, except to see if Koppel had finally found a decent barber. As for Maher, I personally don't know anyone who hadn't grown tired of his incessant, adolescent gushing over the sheer wonderfulness of marijuana. So, while his post 9/11` comments about the cowardice of the American military may have cost him an advertiser or two, did he really expect that his talk show, which was neither entertaining nor enlightening, was entitled to an eternal slot on the schedule?

From whence comes this bizarre sense of entitlement? And how is it that modestly talented people who have been made ridiculously rich and famous feel compelled to bite the hands that have fed them so well? What ever happened to simple, old-fashioned gratitude? More to the point, why do any of us hop aboard their ugly little, ego-powered, bandwagons?

And, finally, I'd like to know if Angela Lansbury ever sent Christmas cards and birthday gifts and little love notes to CBS during any of those 13 years they were going together.

Because California, and Hollywood in particular, have been the punch line for so many jokes over the years, I suspect that people who don't live out here assume we can't possibly be that wacky. They don't know the half of it.

In order for you to better understand what conservatives in this neck of the woods have to deal with, I'll relate a few typical incidents. The first took place several years ago. My wife and I were invited to a dinner party by the widow of a screenwriter who'd been my longtime tennis partner. We were one of six couples. Which meant that, counting the hostess, there were 13 of us sitting around after dinner. I recall thinking at the time that this is how superstitions come to be perpetuated.

All the men in the group were in show business. As we were all either writers, directors or producers, it was probably inevitable that somebody would bring up Charlton Heston's name, and in a negative manner. At that time, after all, Mr. Heston had just become the president and spokesman for the NRA, and was garnering a great deal of national attention.

Although I had never met Mr. Heston, we had exchanged a number of congenial notes. So when one of the guys at the party made an insulting remark about him, I naturally took umbrage. But knowing that my wife is always nervous about my ability to turn a minor skirmish into a full-fledged war, all I said in Heston's defense was, "Well, whether or not you agree with him, you have to admit he's got guts."

The way the other guests reacted, you'd have thought I'd said something along the lines of, "For all his faults, you have to admit that Hitler dressed well and had very nice table manners." They were simply outraged.

As I wanted to be certain I hadn't been misunderstood, I added, "I'm not saying you have to agree with Heston's point of view. All I'm saying is that, as a working actor, it takes a great deal of courage to be openly conservative in a town where most of the people in a position to hire him are obviously liberals."

In the end, I could not get a single person, aside from my wife, to acknowledge that, whether or not you agreed with the man's politics, you had to grant that he had the courage of his convictions.

That evening provided me with one of my more enlightening epiphanies. I had long been aware that left-wingers were on the wrong side of every issue I cared about, but dealing with those 11 weasels confirmed that they lacked even the modicum of honesty required to give a decent man his due.

The next incident took place more recently. The Writers Guild of America hosted a reunion lunch for all of the "MASH" writers. There were two large tables filled with us old duffs. Over coffee, one of the fellows at my table announced that he had recently canceled his subscription to the L.A. Times. That grabbed my attention, and I said, "Really, Gene? I always thought you were a liberal."

"What makes you think I'm not?"

"Well, I'm a conservative, so it would make sense for me to cancel that rag. But why did you?"

"Because the Times has gotten too damn conservative!"

Two interesting things then took place. First my jaw hit the floor. Next, the writer who had been seated between us for the entire lunch turned to glower at me, and said, "You're really a conservative?"

As soon as I admitted I was, he got up and walked away so quickly, you might have thought I'd just acknowledged being a leper.

But his glower was nothing compared to the sneer I was getting from Gene Reynolds. "How can you be a conservative?"

I wasn't sure if what confused him the most was how I could possibly be a conservative if I was Jewish or a humorist or a former "MASH" writer or simply dare to be in his immediate proximity. But all I said was, "It's easy. I think conservatives are right and liberals are wrong."

"Wrong about what?"

"Well, Iraq, for one thing. I believe we were right to invade, to topple Saddam Hussein, and to stick around and make certain the bad guys didn't win. I'm sure even you wouldn't want to see the Islamics using Iraqi oil revenue to fund worldwide terrorism."

"And how long do you think we should stay there?"

"As long as it takes. For crying out loud, we still have troops in Korea half a century later. Heck, it's been over 60 years since the end of World War II and we still maintain a military presence in Germany and Japan. What's the big rush to get out of Iraq?"

"In case you haven't noticed, we've lost 4,000 soldiers over there!"

"Nobody regrets that more than I do, but I'll remind you that we used to lose more than that in a single battle. The difference is that in those days, we didn't have a bunch of people like you insisting that our soldiers had died for no good reason. The fact is, the men and women we conservatives call heroes, people like you, John Kerry and others on the left, call dupes."

With that, he pointed his finger in my face and announced, with eyes blazing and spittle flying in my direction, "You're George Bush!"

"And you, Gene, are an idiot."

"Don't you dare call me an idiot! I didn't call you names."

"Of course you did. When you call me George Bush, we both know that's your idea of the ultimate obscenity. Compared to that, calling you an idiot is almost a compliment."

What made Gene Reynolds' outrage over my lack of decorum so amusing is that I knew something that he didn't know I knew. Back in 2001, you see, shortly after the presidential inauguration, a friend of mine and his wife were invited to a Hollywood cocktail party. By the time they arrived, most of the other guests had gathered in the living room. As the two of them entered, one of the guests proudly announced, "Well, I, personally, don't know a single asshole who voted for George Bush." At which point, my friend said, "Well, you do now."

The fellow who felt entitled to make that public announcement in a room with ladies and maybe even a few conservatives present was none other than Gene Reynolds.

I used to believe that one of the reasons that a lot of the male movie stars of the 30s and 40s drank so much was out of guilt that they were making more money in a week than most Americans earned in a year, and that even in the middle of the Great Depression they were living like royalty. But I also suspected that they turned to alcohol partly out of shame because they were engaged in what would generally have been regarded as a passive, feminine occupation - playing dress up, being told what to do and how to do it by male directors, standing by while rugged stunt men did all the heavy lifting and, maybe worst of all, wearing makeup all the livelong day.

Then, on top of that, they had to answer to a bunch of real life tough guys, studio bosses such as Darryl Zanuck, Harry Cohn, Jack Warner and Louis B. Mayer, who told them how to live, whom to date and even when and if they could get married.

Is it any wonder that so many of them, including Humphrey Bogart, William Holden, Sonny Tufts, Robert Walker, John Barrymore, Dana Andrews, Gig Young and Bing Crosby, tried to find their refuge and possibly their lost manhood in a bottle of booze?

On the plus side, it may also help explain why, honest patriotism aside, when World War II rolled around, so many of the major stars - Jimmy Stewart, Robert Montgomery, Tyrone Power, Clark Gable - walked away from huge contracts to enlist in the military. Back then, even the stars who didn't or couldn't get into the service because of age, marital status or physical liabilities, made propaganda films, joined USO troupes, toured the country selling U.S. war bonds and regularly visited military hospitals.

Hollywood is such a different place these days that it might as well exist in a whole other galaxy.

Now, you have the likes of Sean Penn paying his respects to Saddam Hussein and Hugo Chavez, and taking bows for his courage. You have everyone from Tim Robbins to Billy Crystal slandering conservatives and insisting that America is a far greater threat to democracy than China or Iran.

Far from feeling slightly guilty about their wealth and their life styles, these spoiled brats insist it's our country that should be guilt-ridden. They have raised hypocrisy, if not their movies, to the level of an art form.

Even if you overlook their hatred of President Bush and their disdain of the U.S. military during a time of war, there's the matter of their taking Al Gore's global warming warning to their collective bosoms. Now, it's one thing for me, a devout non-believer to pooh-pooh the threat to polar bears and to go on my merry way. But wouldn't you think that some-one who regarded Mr. Gore as the new messiah would question his sincerity when he gads about in private jets and lives in a mansion? I think you would if you yourself were the least bit sincere, and not just another derriere-kissing sycophant. But when, like George Clooney and Leonardo DiCaprio, you also spend half your life in Lear jets and limos, and live in a series of homes the size of Buckingham Palace, the deal is that nobody ever asks an embarrassing question or points out an inconvenient truth. Instead, you hold banquets and present one another with awards that contain the word "environment."

The plain truth is that if guys like DiCaprio, Clooney and Robert Redford, were women, they'd be called bimbos.

For years, I argued against the very existence of the National Endowment of the Arts. If an artist can't be self-sustaining in a capitalist country as large and as rich as America, he should get into another line of work. It's certainly not the business of the politicians and the bureaucrats, whom you might notice aren't spending their own money, to support him and his artistic pipedreams. Of course, as you may have noticed, the NEA no longer even pretends to be anything but a propaganda-producing tool of the Obama administration.

If 300 million of us have decided we don't wish to underwrite inferior work, where do a handful of senators and congressmen get off wasting millions of our tax dollars to keep these dilettantes in beer and skittles?

Understand, I'm a live-and-let-live kind of guy, and I have no problem with the private sector squandering its own money any way it likes. Heck, if the trustees of the MacArthur Foundation see fit to bestow $300,000 grants on a bunch of weirdos who write Eskimo poetry or build sand castles, that's their affair. Still, I can't imagine why they'd rather give all that money to some beatnik who makes giraffes out of pipe cleaners, and will probably blow the dough on cheap hooch and wild women, when they could just as easily give it to me, knowing that I will use it to invest in gold and buy tax-free municipal bonds.

Almost every time you read about a community going berserk over an art exhibit that is either sheer pornography or re-creates the Christmas creche using animal blood and human excrement, you can rest assured it's your tax dollars at work.

A few years ago, I read about a controversial artwork that, for once, wasn't underwritten by the feds. On that occasion, it was only the good citizens of Livermore, California, who got taken to the cleaners. And if it happened there, it can surely happen in your own hometown. So if you notice your councilmen suddenly sporting berets and floppy bowties, and dropping a lot of French words into their conversation, hang on to your wallets and run for the hills.

It seems the city fathers had $40,000 lying around, so, instead of spending it on books, they decided to commission a ceramic mural to grace the exterior of their new library. For some reason, they decided that the perfect artist was someone named Maria Alquilar. I'm not certain why, of all the artists in America who would kill for a $40,000 pay-day, she was selected. Only a cynical old poop would hazard a guess that her selection, as was the case with Sonia Sotomayor, may have had more to do with Ms. Alquilar's race and gender than with her natural talent. Whatever the reason, it obviously had nothing to do with her spelling ability.

For when the 16-foot-wide work was unveiled, 11 of the 175 famous names had been misspelled! They included the likes of Einstein, Shakespeare, Van Gogh and Michelangelo. On the bright side, Ms. Alquilar got 164 of them right.

In her own defense, the lady said, "The importance of this work is that it is supposed to unite people ... The mistakes wouldn't even register with a true artisan. The people that are into humanities, they are not looking at the words. In her mind, the words register correctly."

The city council, clearly not into the humanities, subsequently voted to pay the artist an additional $6,000 plus expenses, to fly cross country from her new studio in Miami to correct her spelling errors.

Now do you see why it's such a stupid idea to allow public servants to dabble in the arts? A private citizen would know better than to fork over the entire $40,000 before the job was finished. You or I certainly wouldn't pay even more money so that Ms. Alquilar could repair the damage. She'd do it or we'd sue her ass in small claims court! But, then, you and I don't go around commissioning art; we know there's already plenty of the stuff lying around, and without spelling mistakes.

Hell, I'd sue Alquilar just for being so damn snotty, and trying to turn illiteracy into a virtue.

I suppose, to be fair about it, she did get most of the names right. So one could look at the big picture - or ceramic mural, as it were - and ask whether the glass is half full or half empty.

Speaking of that particular glass, I have long wondered who came up with that line, which so neatly defines the distinction between pessimism and optimism. I suspect it might have been the very same fellow who first moved the couch out of the living room and into the office so that he could write it off as a business expense, Sigmund Freud. Or, as Ms. Alquilar might put it - and very likely did on the Livermore mural - Sigman Fried.

One of the questions I get a lot is: Why have movies gotten so bad? Of course it's next to impossible to reach a consensus when it comes to judging movies. Still, if reasonable people can agree that "Casablanca," "The Maltese Falcon," "The Best Years of Our Lives," "Destry Rides Again," "Gone With the Wind," "Citizen Kane," "The Shop Around the Corner," "The Wizard of Oz," "Gunga Din," and "It's a Wonderful Life," all of them produced between 1939 and 1946, are much better than any 10 movies made over the past few decades, it's a question worth considering.

A while ago, I was a member of a panel that discussed movies. At one point, the moderator asked us to compare today's actors with those in the past. All the others surprised me by voting for the current crop. Even while granting there is some excellent talent around these days, as a group I honestly don't think there's any comparison.

Part of the handicap that today's movie stars labor under in this post-studio era is that the hey-day of the character actor has come and gone. In years gone by, even if the star was just another pretty face, he or she would be propped up by the likes of Charles Bickford, Fay Bainter, Peter Lorre, Thomas Mitchell, Charles Coburn, Beulah Bondi, Claude Rains, Frank Morgan, Alice Brady, Basil Rathbone, Helen Broderick, Lionel Barrymore,

Eve Arden, William Demerest, Thomas Gomez, Sydney Greenstreet and Edward Everett Horton and, so, the audience never felt short-changed.

In the 30s and 40s, actors who wound up on the big screen had generally had years of seasoning on Broadway, in vaudeville and on the English stage. In addition to which, radio was in vogue, so they usually had distinctive voices. Today, not only can't I distinguish between one actor's voice and another, I doubt if the actors, themselves, can do much better.

Which reminds me that it once occurred to me that Hollywood actresses are so pumped full of plastic that I wondered if even their dogs could pick them out of a crowd.

At times, you find yourself thinking that nothing ever changes, and then, one day, you look around and you feel like Rip Van Winkle waking from his nap. Over night, it seems, the whole world has gone topsy-turvy.

For instance, when I was a youngster, I didn't know anybody whose parents had gotten divorced. Even though none of my friends or relatives were Catholics, the whole idea of divorce was so alien that when a cousin of mine split up with his wife, everybody in the family had to take the equivalent of a blood oath not to tell my grandmother. To this day, I don't have the slightest idea what story they concocted to explain Beverly's disappearance. For all I know, they may have implied that my cousin had severed their relationship with an axe. Anything, after all, was less shameful than divorce.

These days, not only has divorce become rather commonplace, but among Hollywood's role models, having children out of wedlock is considered tres chic. Unlike some people, I don't entirely blame the fictional Murphy Brown for setting a bad example. But she certainly didn't help things.

What I fail to understand is how it is that couples in long-running relationships, especially those couples with children such as Goldie Hawn and Kurt Russell, Susan Sarandon and Tim Robbins, Johnny Depp and Vanessa Paradis - couples who give every indication of growing old together - decide not to make it legal.

Are they that terrified of not appearing hip? Are they afraid that after 10 or 20 years of living together, the marriage ceremony will make the magic vanish? Or have they managed to convince themselves that, without the vows and the rings and the toaster ovens, they're proving that they're staying together because they choose to, and not just because they don't want to risk ever finding themselves on a first-name basis with a gaggle of divorce lawyers?

Or maybe, even after the babies started showing up, they still weren't sure it was really for keeps. After that, not being married just became something of a habit. And what with their friends and press agents telling them how cool they were, they didn't dare risk ruining their reputation.

Being a traditionalist myself, I'm hoping that down the road, after their various sons and daughters have grown up and left the nest, Goldie and Kurt, Susan and Tim, Johnny and Vanessa, will all finally tie the knot, explaining as they do so: "We just stayed single for the sake of the kids."

But silly as it may sound, I think the worst thing that happened to the movies was the 1960s. That was the first decade in the history of the world in which parents wanted to grow up to be just like their children, thus turning the natural order of things on its head.

Over night, or so it seemed, adults began looking to their kids to be their role models. In frighteningly large numbers, American grown-ups were asking the squirts to tell them what was hip and cool. Adults lived in constant dread that their children would regard their taste in movies and music as square!

It was the time when demographics became the most important word in the lexicon of mass media. No longer was it enough that millions upon millions of people bought a certain magazine or watched a certain TV show. They had to be the right people. They had to be urbanites between the ages of 16 and 35. People you wouldn't trust to pick out your necktie suddenly became America's taste-makers when it came to popular culture. And, like most people, what they were mainly interested in were people just like themselves.

It led in 1971 to the cancellation of such top-rated TV shows as "Red Skelton," "The Beverly Hillbillies," "Lawrence Welk," and "Green Acres," shows that appealed to older, rural-dwelling viewers. At what might be considered the high end, the culmination of this particular mind-set was "Friends," a show starring six actors in their 30s pretending to be characters in their 20s, all of whom spoke and behaved like teenagers. At the low end are the cheaply-produced, mindless, so-called reality shows.

While it's easy to blame the folks that produce TV and movies, we shouldn't give a pass to the audience. If they are so easily satisfied that they'll watch virtually anything on TV and actually pay good money to see "Halloween XXVII" and "Spider Man: The Golden Years," you can't entirely blame the people who supply the stuff.

Still, it is worth noting that the movies used to turn out leading men the likes of Humphrey Bogart, John Wayne, Gary Cooper, Clark Gable, Spencer Tracy, Jimmy Cagney, William Holden, Gregory Peck, John Garfield, Jimmy Stewart, Richard Conte, Charles Bronson and Cary Grant. Compare them to the likes of Tom Cruise, Matt Damon, Mark Wahlberg, Tobey Maguire, Jim Carrey, Jack Black, Leonardo DiCaprio, Will Ferrell and Adam Sandler. Even though the youngest in the crowd is in his mid-30s and half of them are in their 40s, they all seem like their biggest concern is getting carded when they go to buy brewskis for frat house beer bashes.

Perhaps, as my fellow panelists seemed to agree, it's just me. But, frankly, I think we've gone from having leading men to having leading boys.

This brings us to a subject that's long been close to my heart. Namely, the Hollywood blacklist. I was acquainted with some of the people who had lost employment or at least potential employment years ago because of their politics. Among them were Al Levitt, Jean Butler, Dalton Trumbo, Jeff Corey, Paul Jarrico and Ollie Crawford. The last two were even friends of mine. But I always thought they were muddle-headed when it came to politics.

I didn't think they were evil, but it bugged me that, even years later, they found it so difficult to accept that Joseph Stalin and the Soviet Union were evil, and that Alger Hiss and Julius Rosenberg had actually committed treason.

Left-wingers, to this day, refer to the late 40s and early 50s as the time of witch-hunts. A funny thing, though, is that the hunting of witches is not such a bad thing if you've got a coven of them causing trouble. Which is exactly what the Communists were doing in the 30s, 40s and 50s. And while I don't think the idiots in Hollywood were anywhere near as dangerous as the Reds in the State Department or at Los Alamos, they could be counted on to do what they could to further the Soviet's agenda, even if it was only to tithe America's sworn enemy.

But one should realize that, besides school children and members of the Mafia, the only people who take seriously the injunction against "snitching" are the left-wing morons who inhabit Hollywood, a community famous for having raised betrayal to the level of an art form.

When whining about anything that puts them in a bad light, left-wingers always accuse others of promoting McCarthyism. They started saying it back in the days of the Hollywood blacklist, but they can't even get that right. Joseph McCarthy was a U.S. senator and had nothing to do with Hollywood. It was the House Un-American Activities Committee (HUAC) that conducted the star-studded hearings in Los Angeles. But I guess HUACism doesn't have quite the same panache.

From my point of view, the worst thing about HUAC wasn't that a few people had their careers derailed, at least temporarily, but that it trivialized the Communist menace. John Garfield, Larry Parks, Gale Sondergard and Ring Lardner, Jr., did not pose a danger to America, and by focusing their attention on going after celebrities who would garner them headlines, people like Karl Mundt, J. Parnell Thomas, John Wood and Richard Nixon, did America no favors.

I would say the same - apologies to Ann Coulter - about Sen. McCarthy and his aides, Roy Cohen and G. David Schine. Perhaps McCarthy's biggest drawback was that he looked and sounded like the fellow Central Casting would send over to Warner's in the 30s to play the leader of a lynch mob. I'm not suggesting that looks are everything, but when the public face of anti-Communism has the voice and demeanor of a barroom bully, and looks exactly like the Herblock caricature come to life, it doesn't help the cause and it made him an easy target for people like Joseph Welch and Edward R. Murrow.

The congressmen who came to Hollywood, not only weren't trolling for Russian spies, but they even stooped to working hand-in-hand with a sleazy publication called "Red Channels," which purported to identify actors, writers and entertainers, who were Communists, subversives and fellow travelers. "Red Channels" was the brainchild of an opportunistic grocery chain owner named John G. Keenan, who found there was more fun and profit in extortion than in selling turnips and cans of corn. On more than one occasion, "Red Channels" got the names wrong. But even when they got the names right, sometimes the folks named had done nothing worse than voice opposition to Nazi Germany prior to America's entering World War II.

Still, not every victim of the blacklist was what was then called a premature anti-fascist. Most of the Reds in Hollywood took their marching orders from a screenwriter named John Howard Lawson. Jack Lawson, a man born to run a gulag, was head of the Communist Party in this town. The Party members prided themselves on being pro-democracy. They showed it by contributing sizeable portions of their Paramount, Universal, Warners, MGM, Columbia, RKO and 20th Century Fox salaries to Joseph Stalin and the Soviet Politburo.

When screenwriter Albert Maltz, like Lawson, one of the Hollywood Ten, dared to write an article for the New Masses, stating that a writer's main responsibility was to his art and not to the Party, Lawson led an intervention of Maltz's friends and colleagues. For several hours, they verbally bludgeoned him in his own living room. The result was that he caved in and wrote a second article for the magazine in which he essentially pleaded temporary insanity.

These days, there is another blacklist taking place, but they're calling it a graylist because the victims are scriptwriters who made the stupid career decision of allowing themselves to become gray-haired or, in some distinguished cases, even bald.

Back in 1999, a class action suit was initiated by about 150 of us. Today, there are over 600 aging writers who are plaintiffs suing the various studios, networks and major talent agencies, for conspiring to blacklist WGA members on no other basis than their age.

Some people might find it ironic that Hollywood's liberals, who are still inflamed over a blacklist that took place 60 years ago, not only condone it in their hometown, but practice it every single day of their lives.

For those of us involved in the lawsuit, it's been an interesting decade. Those among us who don't play golf find it helps fill the time. The lawyers for the other side have done everything in their power to delay a court judgment. The masochists among us particularly enjoyed the interrogatories. Not only did they want us to recall the date of every meeting we ever had with any of the defendants, but what was said, by whom, if we got the assignments and, if so, when was the script shot, when did it air and how much were we paid. By this time, some of us have a hard time recalling what we had for lunch.

It's quite obvious that the defendants figure time is on their side, that all they have to do is wait us out and we'll start dropping like flies, like very old flies. Fat chance! What they haven't taken into account is that the lawsuit is providing some of us with the will to live that we might not otherwise have.

Not to sound too cynical, but when I saw Abe Polonsky leading a picket line composed of unrepentant Commies outside the Academy Awards in 1999, and saw Ed Harris, Amy Madigan, Nick Nolte, and a few other Tinseltown pinheads, sitting on their hands and sneering when 90-year-old Elia Kazan came on stage to collect his honorary Oscar, it merely reminded me once again how hypocritical, rude and self-righteous the liberals in this town can be.

In spite of "A Tree Grows in Brooklyn," "Boomerang!" "Gentleman's Agreement," "A Streetcar Named Desire," "Viva Zapata!," "East of Eden" and "On the Waterfront," Hollywood's political elitists couldn't get over the fact that 50 years earlier Kazan had, as they say, named names. What's more, he made no secret of the fact that he was proud to have named the names of those he regarded as the enemies of his adopted country.

The truth is that long before the Reds got it in the neck for pledging allegiance to the Soviet Union, conservatives were persona non grata at many of the studios. In the 60s, I met and interviewed Morrie Ryskind. For those of you unfamiliar with the name, he had shared the Pulitzer Prize for "Of Thee I Sing," had been Oscar-nominated for "Stage Door" and "My Man Godfrey," and had also written "Penny Serenade" and a slew of Marx Brothers movies, including "Animal Crackers" and "A Night at the Opera." In spite of having far more impressive credits than any of the pinheads collectively known as the "Hollywood 10," he had not had a screen credit in several years simply because he was regarded as a political reactionary.

The "Hollywood 10" were also known as the Unfriendly 10, which once led my old friend, Billy Wilder, to remark, "Only two of the 10 had talent; the others were just unfriendly."

Finally, as we all know, the patron saint of Hollywood, a town dedicated to back-stabbing and betrayal, is Lucretia Borgia, and the fact of the matter is that the bottom feeders have no real objection to naming names. It's only when they're the names of left-wingers that there's a problem. Had Kazan named fascists or, better yet, card-carrying Republicans, the motion picture community would have erected a statue of the man at the corner of Hollywood and Vine, and, for good measure, changed the name of its major award from the Oscar to the Elia

CHAPTER EIGHT

Sex, Sex and More Sex

When you realize how fixated Americans are on sex, it's a wonder we have time for anything else.

It has permeated our movies, television, advertising and even our politics.

Although the peccadilloes of FDR and John Kennedy were kept under wraps until they were dead, sex proved the undoing of Gary Hart's political career, fatally quashed Ted Kennedy's presidential aspirations and even got Barney Frank censured by his congressional colleagues.

Every so often, there's a national debate over America's number one pastime. Is it baseball, football, or basketball? I contend that it's none of them. Our favorite spectator sport is sex!

For instance, consider that for millions of us, the computer age with its magnificent superhighway of information translates into a multi-billion dollar pornography industry. I mean, let's face facts - when people objected so strenuously to the portions of the Patriot Act that permit the feds to eavesdrop on our computers, what do you think it is that made them so darn nervous? That the world would discover that they've been checking up on the annual rainfall in Outer Mongolia or tracking down Millard Fillmore's middle name?

Sometimes, I swear people are so daffy when it comes to things even slightly sexual that I almost feel like donning a beret, lighting up a stinky cigarette, and snorting through my nose.

I'll mention just a few things, and you decide whether or not we're a nation of goofballs. First, there's the fact that Paris Hilton, a woman of rather ordinary looks and no discernible talent, became famous simply because a video of her having sex with some guy became public property.

Next, there's the annual swimsuit issue of Sports Illustrated. Every week, SI is jam-packed with extremely well-written and well-photographed articles dealing with the world of athletics. Then once a year, they devote a cover and a few pages to photos of pretty girls modeling bikinis, and you get the idea the end of the world is nigh. Now keep in mind that Playboy has been displaying even prettier girls in and out of bikinis for over 50 years. Still, every year, as predictably as the swallows returning to

Capistrano, you can count on pundits endlessly kicking the topic around in newspapers and on talk shows. What's more, if I could collect twenty-five bucks for every Sunday sermon in which some minister pondered whether this marked the end of western civilization, I could run out and buy a new car.

At least the women in Sports Illustrated are gorgeous and voluptuous. They are, after all, hired specifically for their good looks. But a few years ago, we were all witnesses to something that should have served as a wake-up call. A woman's soccer team had just won a big match. One of the stars, Brandi Chastain, celebrated the victory by pulling off her blouse and running around the field. If you recall, she wasn't naked. She was wearing a sports bra, which in the world of lingerie is comparable to your grandmother's bloomers. What's more, Ms. Chastain, a fine soccer player and probably a very nice person, is as flat as an ironing board. But the way that America carried on, you'd have thought that the woman had pulled a Lady Godiva and gone horseback riding nude, at high noon, through the center of town.

Why, you ask, is this so important? Simply because it behooves us all not to supply the French with artillery with which they can mock us. Which, when you get right down to it, is the only sort of artillery the French ever actually use.

Back when Bill Clinton was leaving his mark on history by leaving his mark on Monica Lewinsky's dress, one of the most aggravating aspects of the entire shabby episode was having our nation being patronized by the European media. As usual, the snidest commentary came to us courtesy of the Parisians.

Our alleged lack of sophistication is like food and drink to them. They couldn't stop snickering over our bourgeois value system. After all, the French premier had a mistress. What real man didn't? It's to be expected. Only people as backward as Americans would make a fuss over something so natural. All the while, the French ignored the fact that Clinton had committed perjury, which many of us took far more seriously than whether he had cheated on Hillary. Feeling as we did about his wife, that struck many of us as perfectly reasonable behavior.

As silly as heterosexuals are when it comes to matters sexual, homosexuals are even goofier. Speaking as an outsider, I simply don't understand how a group of people can seemingly base their entire identification on their sexual proclivities, rather than on, say, their nationality, religion or even profession. When heterosexuals, such as Hugh Hefner, put so much emphasis on their penises, most people find it ludicrous. But when gays do it, the rest of us are supposed to find it admirable, even courageous and uplifting. In California, even as I write this, a bill has just been signed by the governor to make May 22nd "Harvey Milk Day." Why not Rock Hudson Day? At least his death made millions aware of the fact that even someone they liked and thought they knew could die of AIDS, and not just drug addicts and people who frequented homosexual bath houses! Or, better yet, why not a day dedicated to Charles Nelson Reilly or Paul Lynde? At least they were funny.

I realize that many people, after several years of unrelenting gay propaganda in the media, have been brainwashed into believing that anyone who opposes same-sex marriages is the worst kind of bigot. They have cleverly insisted that it is akin to being opposed to bi-racial unions. That, of course, is sheer sophistry. The marriage of a man and a woman of different races is akin to marriage between a man and a woman of different religions or different nationalities. Marriage between two men or two women, on the other hand, is the end result of political correctness carried to its ludicrous extreme.

It is fascinating how completely the heterosexual world has come to accept homosexuality as a norm. Back in the 1890s, Oscar Wilde sued the Marquis of Queensberry, the father of Wilde's male lover, for daring to call him a sodomite. Three days into the ill-advised libel suit, Wilde's lawyers decided to call it off when it became all too apparent that the Marquis was going to be able to prove his case.

At that point, Wilde was arrested on the charge of gross indecency. During his subsequent trial, Wilde was asked to explain what the Marquis' son, Lord Alfred Douglas, had been referring to when he wrote to Wilde of the love that dares not speak its name. "It is beautiful," replied Wilde, who was notorious for picking up sailors, servants and young male prostitutes, "it is fine, it is the noblest form of affection. It is intellectual, and it repeatedly exists between an older and a younger man, when the older man has intellect, and the younger man has all the joy, hope and glamour of life before him."

The trial ended with, you should excuse the expression, a hung jury. There was then a second trial and Wilde was found guilty and sentenced to two years at hard labor. Apparently, the jury didn't regard Wilde, who was in his mid-30s when he took up with Lord Douglas, as sufficiently avuncular to buy his old graybeard defense.

It's strange from our vantage point to realize there was a time before same-sex marriages and gay pride parades when homosexuality was the love that dared not speak its name.

These days, it's the love that never shuts up.

I can understand that gays don't want to go back into the closet, but

I can't, for the life of me, understand what those gay pride parades are all about. Inasmuch as it all comes down to indulging in anal intercourse, what exactly is the source of all this pride?

And just when did liberals decide that homosexuals get the final word when it comes to matters of morals, values or anything else, for that matter?

It's bad enough that any number of self-righteous academics kept military recruiters off college campuses, pretending that their objection stemmed from the Army's don't ask/don't tell policy, and not simply because left-wingers hate anything and everything that smacks of patriotism.

In much the same way, those on the Left have led a crusade against the Boy Scouts of America because, so they say, they oppose the policy of not allowing homosexuals to be Scout leaders and take young boys into the woods on camping trips. Sensible people regard that as a sensible policy. It's not meant to suggest that every gay man is a pedophile, but simply recognizing that a lot of pedophiles are gay men. Just as every Muslim is not a terrorist, just about every terrorist these days is a Muslim. So, why should parents take any unnecessary chances with their most precious possessions just so homosexuals won't have their feelings hurt?

Liberals don't really care about homosexuals, by the way, unless they themselves happen to be gay. The truth is liberals rarely serve in the military now that service is voluntary and they don't usually let their kids join the Boy Scouts, not because they're offended by the aforementioned policy, but because the group fosters traditional values and faith-based patriotic ideals.

If you want a perfect example of liberal hypocrisy, consider the beauty pageant when a repulsive little freak who calls himself, in homage to Paris Hilton, Perez Hilton (born Mario Lavenderia), who had no business even being on stage at a competition involving beautiful women, got to ask Miss California, Carrie Prejean, how she felt about same-sex marriages. Her honest answer probably cost her the victory, while earning the respect of most fair-minded and decent Americans. What I find so telling about the incident was that in California, the reason that the same-sex marriage measure was defeated on the November, 2008, ballot was because 70% of Blacks voted that way. But the gays only demonstrated outside Catholic and Mormon churches and businesses. Furthermore, I guarantee that if Miss Prejean had been Black, instead of a blue-eyed blonde, Mr. Hilton wouldn't have dared open his ugly little yap.

It's also worth noting that President Obama gave the exact same answer to the exact same question during the campaign, and yet the gays voted overwhelmingly for him. Which certainly suggests that, thanks to the insane asylums being relatively empty these days, honesty can cost you a tiara, but not the presidency.

Recently, I noticed a similarity between atheists and homosexuals that hadn't occurred to me before. It has to do with the way they wage their wars. Basically, they erect straw men, put words in their straw mouths, and then engage in battle with these creatures they've cobbled together with spit and glue.

It just seems to me that it's high time we began setting the record straight. To begin with, there is no such thing as homophobia. A phobia is defined as a fear or anxiety that exceeds normal proportions. Concocting the word was simply a rather sly way of suggesting that it is heterosexuals who are deviant. The other lie that is parroted with some frequency is that those who don't fully support the gay agenda are most likely latent homosexuals, which is supposed to suggest, I assume, that lurking inside every heterosexual male is an interior decorator screaming to get out and do something about those damn drapes.

Odd, isn't it, that you never hear about latent heterosexuals?

Even the ancient Greeks, to whom modern-day gays enjoy comparing themselves, never engaged in anything quite as bizarre as same-sex marriages.

The proof that heterosexual men aren't sitting around fantasizing being seduced by Boy George or Richard Chamberlain is that every heterosexual man I know much prefers having his cavity worked on by a dentist than by a proctologist.

Homosexuals like to picture themselves as the innocent victims of the oppressive majority. The recent unpleasantness in California on behalf of same-sex marriages doesn't happen to be a response to laws depriving gays of any rights or privileges to which they are otherwise entitled. They are as free as they've always been to marry members of the opposite sex. For several thousand years, everyone has understood marriage to mean the sacred union of a man and a woman.

I have asked on more than one occasion if the institution of marriage is to be turned on its head to accommodate the ludicrous demands of a very small number of people, on what moral or legal basis does society then deny fathers and daughters, mothers and sons, or, say, your cousin Phyllis and a dozen Elvis impersonators, from tying the knot? If the parties merely need to be consenting adults, on what basis could you prevent Hugh Hefner and his bevy of blonde companions from pledging their troth before man and God? I have yet to receive a response.

One other point should be made. In spite of all the rioting and all the whining in the wake of Proposition 8, only a few thousand same-sex marriages have taken place in Massachusetts, Connecticut or even here in California, where it was permitted for a while. And most of those marriages involved lesbians. Yet the way their male counterparts have been carrying on, you'd have thought the gay bars had all been padlocked.

This brings us to atheists and their own brand of hypocrisy and lies. It's silly enough when they feel they can use logic to disprove the existence of God. But it's worse when in voicing their angry opposition to organized religion, they begin sounding exactly like the religious zealots they claim to despise.

Still, it's when they begin blaming all the evils of the world on religion that my own sense of reason and logic kick in. Inevitably, they bring up the Spanish Inquisition, as if this were 1478. Ask them to make a slightly more contemporary case and they'll bring up Nazi Germany with a "gotcha" gleam in their eye. While it's true that Germany had been a traditionally Christian nation, Hitler was neither German nor Christian. He and his followers were pagans. The Germans didn't march, torture and murder under the cross of Jesus Christ, but under the swastika of Adolf Hitler.

Whenever atheists blame religion for causing most of the world's mass murders, they merely prove that they're not only bigots, but ignoramuses. While nobody knows exactly how many millions of innocent people have been butchered in the past 90 years, we do know that the vast majority died at the hands of Stalin, Hitler, Castro, Mao and Pol Pot, atheists all.

The only exception to that rule, of course, are those who have been gassed, beheaded and blown up, by the Muslim faithful. And yet Islam, interestingly enough, is the one religion that doesn't seem to enrage atheists! Could the reason possibly be that, for all their huffing and puffing about how awful all religions are, even the atheists understand that Jewish and Christian martyrs will die for their beliefs, whereas Islamics will kill you for theirs?

Unlike many of my fellow conservatives, I am not in favor of a constitutional amendment declaring that marriage be limited to a man and a woman. It's not that I regard the Constitution as sacrosanct. I mean, for crying out loud, this is a document that already has two amendments that deal strictly with booze! So, even though I oppose same-sex marriages on purely rational grounds, the reason I don't become absolutely hysterical at the notion of gays and lesbians tying the knot is because, goofy as it is, I am a Pollyanna at heart and I try to see the glass as half or even two-thirds full.

For openers, being libertarian at heart, I am in favor of people doing pretty much whatever they like so long as they don't include me in their plans. For another thing, I've already concluded that all those extra ceremonies can only be a boon for our ailing economy. When it comes to spreading the wealth around, nothing short of hosting a Super Bowl primes the money pump quite like a spree of marriages. Even poor people splurge like drunken sailors when marrying off a daughter. Get a couple of lesbians pledging their troth and you get to double the amount lavished on flowers, champagne, canapes, bridal gowns, musicians, silver service gifts, honeymoons and trousseaus. And eventually and inevitably, there'll be the accountants, the furniture movers and the divorce attorneys, carving out their own sizeable slices of the wedding cake.

Still, one does wonder what sort of practical advice parents feel called upon to offer on those special pre-nuptial occasions. Do doting mothers tell their daughters about the birds and the birds, while well-meaning, but slightly stammering, dads give their sons the lowdown on the bees and the bees?

I can only hope that these young folks know what they'll be letting themselves in for. As they may have heard, but never before had reason to heed, living together is about as much like being married as being a community organizer is like being president of the United States. Suddenly, they'll have to learn a whole new vocabulary. Expressions such as "Just for that, smarty pants, you can sleep on the couch," "I'd love to, but I've got this terrible headache" and "That's the last straw - I'm going home to father!" will become all too commonplace.

Nevertheless, I know I don't speak for the majority. Most Americans, although they favor civil unions, are opposed to same-sex marriages. The fact is, a great many married Americans wished they, themselves, were involved in civil unions, rather than the frequent uncivil variety.

Basically, the opposition to gay marriages comes down to tradition. The truth is, those opposed to tampering with the institution are not hypocritical ogres. They simply feel that for centuries, marriage has meant the joining of a man and a woman in holy matrimony, and they see no good reason to change the status quo.

As usual, I, the single greatest compromiser since the glory days of Henry Clay, have come up with an obvious solution. The real hang-up, so far as I can see, is the word itself. Heterosexuals wish, rightly or wrongly, to maintain their copyright on "marriage." Fine and dandy, I say. So, instead, let the unions between gays and lesbians be called "carriages." Under my plan, the carriage trade would have all the legal and financial rights as their married brethren. The sole distinction between the two alliances would be a single consonant. What could be fairer than that?

Frankly, I can't imagine anybody objecting to my plan. It would give gays and lesbians everything they want, with the possible exception of something to be cranky about.

And while I can see people of my political bent initially digging in their heels, I would hope that they would quickly come to their senses. For, as we all know, married folks tend to vote Republican more often than not. So, why shouldn't we assume the same would hold true for carried people?

Living in L.A., as I do, I don't have wonderful choices when it comes to my local newspapers. There's the parochial Daily News, which focuses its attention on the San Fernando Valley. Which is fine, if you happen to be more interested in the war on potholes than the war on Islamic terrorism.

The alternative rag is the L.A. Times. They slant the news so far to the left, the words almost slide off the page. A person could easily jump to the conclusion that the entire editorial board cut their teeth on Pravda and the Daily Worker. Instead of parroting the party line for Stalin or Khrushchev, they now carry the water for the likes of Barack Obama, Nancy Pelosi and Harry Reid.

Speaking of the Senate's Majority Leader, wouldn't you think that instead of simply announcing a while back that America had lost the war in Iraq, thus simultaneously lending aid and comfort to Al Qaeda and pulling the rug out from under our troops, Reid would have made it a sporting proposition? I mean, even if his scummy behavior didn't put you in mind of Benedict Arnold, Marshal Henri Petain and Vidkun Quisling, wouldn't you think that the man who owes his seat in the U.S. Senate to Nevada's gambling interests, would at least have said, "The odds are seven-to-five that we've lost the war in Iraq"?

The Times is so politically correct that a hiring memo that was made public a few years ago indicated that the paper not only wanted to make certain that racial minorities be moved to the head of the line, but that gays and lesbians should also be given job preference.

And yet, I must confess I was taken aback a while ago when I opened the sports section to find an article by Times writer Mike Penner, 49, which began: "I am a transsexual sports writer. It has taken more than 40 years, a million tears and hundreds of hours of soul-wrenching therapy for me to work up the courage to type those words."

Mr. Penner went on to state that he'd be taking a two-week vacation, and when he returned he'd be Ms. Christine Daniels.

As forthcoming as he was, he neglected to mention how he intended to spend the fortnight. Although one might presume he was going in for the sort of surgery I'd rather not think about, it's possible he'd merely spend the time shopping for a new wardrobe. He also failed to mention why he was changing not only his first name, but his last. I also wanted to know how his wife took the news and whether they have children, who will have to remember to buy two gifts on Mother's Day.

I even tried to imagine how my own wife would react to such news, but all I could come up with were gales of laughter, followed by a deadly serious "Don't you even look at my shoes!"

According to the Times, most of the response from readers was overwhelmingly positive. I'm not sure if that means they're extremely compassionate human beings or just plain nutty.

For my part, being of a suspicious nature, I found myself wondering if Mike Penner was working a scam. After all, the Times, which has lost hundreds of thousands of subscribers since 2000, has been firing staff at a rate that must be nightmarish for those fortunate few still drawing a paycheck. So, what if this is just a clever career move? What if Mr. Penner is no more a transsexual than Alec Baldwin is, but figured if he claimed to be one, the PC bosses down at 2nd and Spring Street would never dare cut him, you should excuse the expression, from the paper.

A year-and-a-half later, Christine reverted, without giving an explanation, to once again being plain old Mike. So, apparently, he was more a transvestite than a transgender - and the only thing that got altered was his wardrobe.

CHAPTER NINE

It's Not Your Country Just
Because You Say It Is

A couple of years ago, I attended a conference headed up by the great Ward Connerly. Over the two days, a great many issues were discussed by the group. The participants weren't exactly a cross section of the general public, consisting, as the gathering did, of lawyers, academics, successful businessmen, and me.

Although there were divided opinions on all issues, the one that created the most heat and, I suspect, the least light was the matter of illegal immigrants. You couldn't even get everybody to agree it was a problem. For those who favored open borders, "undocumented workers" was the term of choice. In the end, it all came down to the same old liberal/conservative argument.

Those whose attitude can best be summed up as "the more the merrier" accuse the opposition of being racist. Those on the other side argue that a nation without borders is not a nation at all, but merely a state of mind.

Just last week, I was arguing the issue with a friend. I pointed out that every other country in the world guards its borders, and that definitely includes Mexico, which protects its southern border while violating our own on a daily basis. He said he didn't care what other countries did. He believed that America, being America, should have a welcome mat out for anyone who wants to enter. He simply didn't want to slam the door in the face of poor people.

I told him he was a hypocrite. After all, I knew for a fact that he had locks on the windows and doors of his home. Why shouldn't poor people be allowed to enter his dwelling and set up housekeeping in his living room? By what right should he have greater authority over his property than the nation has over its own?

I live in Los Angeles, haven to hundreds of thousands of illegal immigrants. It is also the place that Cardinal Mahony, defender of pedophile priests, calls home. Any time a local politician suggests that illegals are coarsening the quality of life in our community while crowding our schools and overwhelming our health care resources, Mahony, a Latino in spite of his last name, can be counted on to label the man a racist. Like an actor responding to his cue, Mahony will insist that these are all hard-working Mexicans who are only looking to share in the American dream. But does anyone really believe that Mahony or any of his cohorts in the Catholic hierarchy, all of them looking to fill church pews, would give a damn how hard-working those border sneaks were if they happened to be Mormons or Lutherans?

Those who condemn us, the anti-illegal crowd, as racists are always contending we wouldn't be so anxious to defend our borders if those were Swedes coming across. The truth is, illegals are illegal, and I don't happen to care what nationality they are. I simply have a bone to pick with anybody whose first act on American soil is to break the law. There are, after all, millions of people all over the world waiting their turn to emigrate legally. When you get right down to it, it's those who constantly argue on behalf of Latinos for no other reason than their race who are the real racists.

To put this problem in some perspective, a conservative estimate of illegal Hispanics in America is 12 million. But not this conservative. I'm guessing it's closer to twice that many. But even if it were 12 million, in order to match that number, not only would every single Swede have to pack up and sneak over, but they'd have to bring a few million Norwegians along with them.

Instead of honestly debating the issue, liberals prefer to quote Emma Lazarus on the subject. "Give me your tired, your poor,/Your huddled masses yearning to be breathe free,/The wretched refuse of your teeming shore..." That works fine in the context of legal immigration. But the last time I looked, there was nothing in there that said, "Let those fortunate enough to share our borders sneak in ahead of everybody else. They don't have to play by the same rules as Poles and Kenyans and Koreans. So long as they speak Spanish, they get a free pass."

And let us keep in mind that what Miss Lazarus was writing was a little poem, not national policy.

Out here in Southern California, a local Spanish-language TV station caused a stink by putting up several billboards reaching out to potential viewers in the city they dubbed "Los Angeles, Mexico." Predictably, as soon as outraged Gringos complained, they were accused of being racists.

How is it, I keep asking myself, that it's only the biggest racists in America who are given carte blanche to condemn others for being what they are themselves?

Who but a racist would conclude that America's sovereignty is merely a minor inconvenience they are free to ignore for no other reason than that they are members of la raza, and are therefore entitled? I mean, it's not as if the folks sneaking across our border are, like so many other people around the world, trying to escape bloody tyrants or religious intolerance. They simply want the opportunity to make a better living. Well, who doesn't? But that's no reason to give them special treatment.

Among other entitlements, we were given to understand, are schooling, medical attention, and a higher minimum wage. In addition, they believe they should be allowed to vote in our elections as well as Mexico's, even if they know less English than I know Greek.

The reason I'm so skeptical about that estimate of 12 million illegals is because that's the number I've heard bandied about for several years. For that number to be even close to accurate, it would mean, one, that the border has been securely sealed for all that time, which we and the Minutemen know is absurd, and, two, it presumes that they haven't had babies in the U.S. I also do not accept that a baby born to parents who are here illegally is a citizen. Section One of the 14th Amendment declares: "All persons born or naturalized in the United States, and subject to the jurisdiction thereof, are citizens of the United States and of the state wherein they reside." The Amendment, passed in 1868, was intended to guarantee the rights of freed slaves, not to provide a technical loophole for illegal aliens.

After all, in no other instance is a person allowed to benefit from the commission of a crime. How is it that sneaking into America and having an anchor baby is the single exception to that rule?

It's no secret why former President Vicente Fox went so far as to provide illegals with tips on how best to avoid detection by our border patrol. At my local post office, most of the people in line with me are here illegally, but if only 12 million of them mail only twenty dollars a week to their relatives south of the border, it amounts to twelve billion dollars a year. That's a hell of a lot of pesos. Is it any wonder that Mexico is in no rush to turn off the golden faucet?

What confounds me, though, is that, instead of displaying some amount of gratitude for our taking millions of unemployed Mexicans and any number of criminals off their hands, they tweak our nose by refusing to extradite cop killers and serial rapists because Mexico, which has raised police and political corruption to levels reminiscent of Chicago in the 1920s, doesn't happen to approve of capital punishment! However, that policy doesn't prevent the federales and the drug dealers from exchanging gunfire in the streets on a daily basis.

Some of my fellow conservatives don't believe in foreign aid. It so happens that I do. But I don't believe in offering up our tax dollars with no strings attached. For instance, however much we currently give Mexico, I suggest we deduct a large amount for every illegal we catch and an even larger amount for every killer who finds sanctuary south of the border. And, furthermore, when we catch one of them committing felonies on our turf, we should deduct the cost of his trial and incarceration from all future charitable donations.

Finally, it's not racism when you resent people sneaking into your country simply because, by reason of geographical proximity, they're able to get away with it. In fact, that's why the idea of simply deporting illegals has never made any sense to me. It's not like sending scofflaws back to Europe or Asia. Our border, after all, is basically nothing but a line in the sand.

If you actually believe that Mexicans are entitled to be here simply because they want to be here, it's you who are a racist. Furthermore, I'd like to know where you live so I can sneak into your house and help myself to whatever I find lying around.

And, remember, no fair calling the cops.

Here in Los Angeles, Mayor Antonio Villaraigosa has been portrayed as a wonderful role model because he'd been a high school drop-out and gang member who cleaned up his act and gone to college. But inasmuch as he had the distinction of failing the bar exam four or five times before taking the easy way out and becoming a politician, I'm not sure I'd want him role-modeling my kid. Although he has stated that he won't be running for governor in 2010, I see no reason to take him at his word. How can he not be tempted once he fully realizes he'll only need to beat out a couple of gringos named Jerry Brown and Gavin Newsom?

On the downside, the mayor's marriage broke up a few years ago when his wife found out he'd been canoodling with a Latina newscaster who'd apparently advanced her career by getting close, extremely close, to several of her sources. But, interestingly enough, San Francisco's Mayor Gavin Newsom also got himself wrapped up in a sex scandal when it came out that he'd been having an affair with the wife of his campaign manager, Alex Turk, who also happened to be his best friend.

Jerry Brown, 71, on the other hand, had avoided making tawdry headlines by pretty much avoiding women during the 50 years since he left the Catholic seminary where he'd been studying for the priesthood. Actually, Brown seemed to have turned Gloria Steinem's quip about women needing men like a fish needs a bicycle on it's head. However, in 2005, in his late 60s, just like Ms. Steinem, he, too, finally got hitched. It's funny how these old folks suddenly decide one day to rush out and buy bicycles, when one might have assumed they were too old to ride.

The one thing all three potential candidates agree on is that illegal immigrants are good for California and good for America. Which is just one of the reasons I will be voting for any Republican who steps forward to replace Arnold Schwarzenegger.

I understand that there are many Americans who disagree with me when it comes to illegal aliens. These would include the folks who own farms, restaurants and hotels; clothing manufacturers, the Catholic Church; and, naturally, the ACLU.

We are assured that there are plenty of jobs for unskilled laborers willing to work for minimum wage or less. We are all supposed to be happy about it because it means our lettuce will get picked, our dishes will get bussed and washed, and the savings will be passed along to us, the consumers.

That's wrong on a couple of counts. First off, I, personally, don't like the 21st century version of slavery much more than I liked the 19th century variety.

For another thing, anybody who tells you that the millions of illegals in this country are paying their own way is simultaneously selling you a bill of goods and trying to send you off on a guilt trip. Most illegals are day laborers working for cash, menials working for about eight bucks-an-hour, unemployed and/or criminals. Considering that none of them is earning enough to pay income taxes, how on earth can anybody claim they're not costing the middle class a fortune in health care, schooling, welfare and incarceration?

Furthermore, even though it's in bad taste to mention it, it's a fact that birth control is not one of their major priorities. So, not only is their first act on American soil illegal entry, but their second is quite often giving birth to a baby who suddenly has all the rights and privileges guaranteed by the Constitution.

Mexico keeps insisting that Mexicans should have dual citizenship, a concept that has never made sense to me. It sounds an awful lot like polygamy. What astounds me is that nobody ever seems to ask why, if it's such a wonderful idea, Mexico doesn't offer it to Hondurans and Guatemalans. Instead, the federales are lined up on Mexico's southern border. That's not to suggest nobody comes across. Bribes are still the Mexican equivalent of visas and passports. But even then, the ultimate destination of the Central Americans had better be Arizona or California, not Acapulco or Chihuahua.

I even hear that there's nothing that can be done about the problem, although conservatives at least, unlike the liberals, will admit there is a problem. Attempting to put a good face on it, they blather on about decent, hard-working people seeking better lives. They ask, hypothetically, what could possibly be done at this late date when there are all these millions of illegal aliens in the U.S.

Well-meaning people wring their hands. They say we can't deport millions of people. We can't break up families. Many of the children, after all, are natural-born citizens. It's not as if we could construct a 1,500 mile long 40-foot wall. (Actually we could, but that's not my solution.)

First off, deportation is a lousy idea even if we had the means to round up that many people. After all, if they snuck in once, there's no reason to think they won't do it again. So, we don't arrest every illegal worker in America; instead, we arrest every employer who hires an illegal. We fine them and we send their sorry butts to the cooler. Next, we do not grant automatic citizenship to babies born to illegals. In short, we do whatever needs to be done to take the "welcome" off our welcome mat. People have been wiping their feet on it long enough.

Sooner, rather than later, the message would be received south of the border that Uncle Sam is no longer going to be played for a sucker.

Am I heartless? I think not. I'm not forgetting the millions of people around the world on immigration lists who are playing by the rules, waiting their chance to emigrate legally to America. Allowing, even encouraging, a bunch of scofflaws to butt in ahead of them just because they don't have an ocean to cross is immoral. And before you whip out the racist tar brush, keep in mind that many of these people on waiting lists are waiting in Asia, Africa and the Caribbean.

If the price of all this is that a head of lettuce will cost an extra nickel or burgers will cost a tad more, I think we could live with it.

Of course there is one other option. We could annex Mexico, making it our 51st state. With all its oil and natural resources, I'm sure we could make it financially feasible. At the very least, I think we'd all feel a lot better about having Americans, not foreigners, on our dole.

With all those Democrats running things in Washington, I assume amnesty will soon be declared. And, voila! the problem of illegal aliens will vanish with the morning dew.

Then, for their next trick, they'll do away with robbery, rape and murder, by simply decriminalizing them too.

While I acknowledge that Democrats are a lost cause on this issue, as they are on all the others, for Republicans, it's not even smart politics. Back in 2002, I was telling everyone that, in spite of the polls and President Bush's inexplicable refusal to campaign on his behalf, Bill Simon could defeat Gray Davis in California's gubernatorial race if only he made border closure the main plank in his platform. Instead, he skirted the issue and lost by a scant four percent. Had he heeded my advice, not only would he have defeated Davis, but we Californians would have been spared a recall election which put Schwarzenegger in the governor's mansion. As I'm sure you know, the Terminator is a Republican in name only. He turned out to be Maria Shriver with muscles and an Austrian accent!

Even Republicans, if you can call people like John McCain a Republican, pushed for the amnesty bill in 2008 and ballyhooed the work program, claiming it would bring together employers seeking workers with Mexican workers eager to do those jobs that Americans don't want. The problem is that there is no such job...so long as the job pays a decent wage. But so long as you allow illegals to stream across our porous borders, there's no compelling reason for the folks who own farms, hotels and restaurants, to pay anything over the basic minimum. Besides, once they're in America, most of those people don't want to work in the fields.

Which leads me to ask this obvious question: With something like fifteen or twenty million illegal aliens already in the United States, how is it we don't already have sufficient numbers to change our sheets, bus our tables and pick our lettuce? At what point are we finally prepared to say, "Enough already"?

There is simply no upside to turning a blind eye to the problem. After all, the risk to our own national security aside, the flood of aliens, has already helped destroy the quality of life in every place they've settled. Which, by this late date, is clear across this country.

It would not only be horribly ironic, but the worst kind of pyrrhic victory if we managed to gain sovereignty for Iraq while we simultaneously surrendered our own.

CHAPTER TEN

Liberals: The Other White Meat

I used to be what I thought was a liberal. If, at that time, anyone had asked me to explain myself, I would have said that I opposed Jim Crow laws, that I believed workers were entitled to make a decent wage and work in a safe environment, and that American citizens shouldn't be discriminated against because of their race, religion or national origin.

I quit being a liberal because I didn't believe that members of particular minority groups deserved advantages denied to others; that illegal aliens weren't entitled to anything but a swift kick to the backside; that being a devout Christian didn't make you a bad person; and that capitalism was a system that worked, while Communism not only didn't work, but, wherever it was tried, morphed into a tyrannical regime.

I honestly don't know why there are so many liberals today and I certainly can't imagine why they have such a lousy agenda. I have come up with a theory, however. Here in California, roughly 30 years ago, because of budget cuts, a great many people were released from insane asylums. They wound up living in the streets, which explains the large number of homeless people, even though liberals would have you believe that those are normal people who simply lost their jobs along the way. In truth, the great majority of those living alfresco are drug addicts, alcoholics and the terminally delusional.

Even after the state became more solvent, it became impossible to get these poor souls back into institutions where they could be fed, clothed and given their meds, because the ACLU lawyers fought for their inalienable right to starve, freeze and use the sidewalks of your city as their combination bedroom, den and toilet.

Inevitably, they also got to vote. As a result, the likes of Barbara Boxer, Dianne Feinstein, Gray Davis, Willie Brown, Arnold Schwarzenegger, Antonio Villaraigosa, Gavin Newsom and Jerry Brown, wound up winning all the major elections. The sad truth is, you'd have to be drunk, on drugs or crazy to vote for those people.

I have to suspect that a similar scenario took place all over the country. How else to explain that so many Americans actually believe that Barack Obama's policies will save our economy? I'm not even a Christian, but I find it bizarre that people who pooh-pooh the idea that Christ raised the dead or walked on water are totally convinced that a guy who's tossing trillions of freshly printed dollars into the air is a financial miracle worker. Talk about blind faith!

It makes me wonder if these same people, were they facing personal bankruptcy, would think that the answer to their own financial difficulties would be to give their wife an American Express card and drop her off at Tiffany's.

If liberals aren't simply insane, they surely must be hypocrites. Why else would they insist that spending eight years bashing President Bush and comparing him, Dick Cheney and Donald Rumsfeld, to the Nazi High Command was patriotic, but merely questioning President Obama's qualifications, judgment and policies, makes one a racist?

Also, how is it that when, between 2000 and 2006, when the GOP had control of the Oval Office, the House and the Senate, on those rare occasions they didn't do the bidding of Ted Kennedy, John Murtha or Charles Schumer, they were condemned as divisive? However, when Obama and his left-wing cronies rushed through a trillion dollar stimulus package and a pork-filled budget over Republican objections, nobody in their crowd cried "Foul!" or insisted on reaching across the aisle for a group hug and a few choruses of "Kumbaya"?

Before anybody bothers sending an e-mail reminding me that three Republican senators voted with the Democrats on the stimulus bill, I haven't forgotten. But, let's face it - the two ladies from Maine are merely the east coast version of Boxer and Feinstein. As for Arlen Specter, who switched from being a Republican nobody trusted to being a Democrat nobody trusts, I suspect that along the way, he'll switch to the Extraterrestrial Party if he decides that's his last best hope of winning re-election.

I know that people such as Sen. Specter and Sen. Jeffords would have us believe that they switched parties because of their principles, but I would prefer it if they only said such silly things in the hope of making me laugh. That's because I love to laugh, but I hate being taken for a fool. I mean, really, Jim Jeffords wakes up one day when he's 67 years old and Specter opens his eyes at the age of 79 and suddenly decides that the GOP isn't as conservative as they'd like, so the solution is to link left arms with the likes of Nancy Pelosi, Harry Reid, Chris Dodd, Henry Waxman and Barney Frank?

Speaking of Frank, when he told a woman at his town hall meeting that arguing with her would be like arguing with his dining room table, I could hardly believe my ears; when, as a rule, it's Barack Obama's ears I can't believe. Actually, I, for one, would pay good money to see Barney

Frank debate his dining room table. What's more, I'd give odds and take the table.

Something else that makes me wonder if, in a nicer, kinder world, liberals wouldn't be housed in a warm place where they'd be kept safely away from sharp objects, heavy machinery and voting booths, is their notion of what constitutes torture. In my world, cutting off Daniel Pearl's head, throwing Anne Frank in an oven or having to listen to Chris Matthews prattle on, is torture. But by no means is it playing loud music, keeping people awake, making them share space with a caterpillar or even dousing them with water, in order to get them to cough up information that might prevent another 9/11.

Only a liberal could confuse actual torture with college hazing. I suspect there are members of fraternities who could share more harrowing tales than the Islamics with their Korans, their three squares and their personal prayer mats at Gitmo.

Another difference that seems to escape liberals is that it's torture when the only purpose is to cause pain, not when it's done in order to pry vital information from terrorists.

Those leftists who trashed George W. Bush for most of this past decade claim they weren't being rude or unpatriotic, but were simply speaking truth to power. That has a nice ring to it, so I think I'll give it a shot.

To begin with, Secretary of Defense Robert Gates insists that Guantanamo has to be shut down because its very name is a source of embarrassment for America throughout the world. Well, I happen to think the world is an embarrassment and is therefore in no position to cast stones or insults. But the obvious solution in any case is not to shut down Gitmo, especially when it will cost $80 million to do so and when nobody has the slightest idea where to move the terrorists, but to simply change the name of the facility. We could call it any number of things, ranging from Club Paradise to Fantasy Island. Or we could take our lead from the pop singer, Prince, and simply change it to the Prison Formerly Known as Guantanamo.

Next, I would like President Obama to quit chastising his predecessor while at the same time carrying forth his policies. Understand, I approve of many of those policies, which kept America safe for eight years. But saying one thing while doing another may fool some of the people some of the time, and fool Chris Matthews and Keith Olbermann all of the time, but it doesn't make Obama look superior to the ex-president; it merely makes him look petty and deceitful.

Furthermore, I would suggest that Barack Obama quit telling us that everything he says and does garners us great respect in the world community. The majority of that community is made up of lunatics and gangsters, and most Americans don't want to gain the love and admiration of North Korea, Syria, Iran, China, Pakistan, Afghanistan, Turkey, Yemen, Somalia, Russia or Indonesia. It would be nice, though, if they were at least a little bit afraid of us.

If I had the president's ear, I would beg him not to be a sucker, and not to believe for a second that, in spite of his Nobel Peace Prize, international villains will succumb to his much-publicized charm. They will applaud his speeches, particularly those in which he denigrates America, and return his smiles, and they'll happily pick his pocket and stab him in the back. I would try to make him realize that the world's political leaders are just like Chicago's, except that some of them have nuclear bombs at their disposal.

Speaking of which, I sincerely hope that when Obama goes in for his annual check-up, the doctors at Bethesda won't forget to do a brain scan, for surely something must be seriously wrong with a man who seems so much more concerned with a Jew building a house in Israel than with Muslims building a nuclear bomb in Iran.

And by this time, when other national leaders have proven to be impervious to his over-hyped charms, snubbing him when he requested their assistance in Afghanistan and again when he begged them to take the Gitmo prisoners off our hands, he merely comes off as a lot of hot air. The last straw was having the Olympic Games committee in Copenhagen spurn him in favor of Rio. Brazil, for heaven's sake, didn't even have to fly in Oprah Winfrey in order to take home the gold.

It's easy, I would tell the president, to mouth all the usual platitudes and be lauded by the various hand puppets and hand maidens at CNN, MSNBC and the New York Times, but being politically correct is, unfortunately, not the same thing as being correct politically.

Certain people of the leftist persuasion are always trying to convince the rest of us that Europe is superior to America and, quite frankly, I'm getting sick and tired of it. We even hear that certain Supreme Court justices are less interested in what the Constitution says, or common sense would dictate, than in how their decisions will be viewed on the other side of the Atlantic.

Whenever the Europeans do something, no matter how cowardly or corrupt, their champions in our country can be counted on to put the best possible face on it. With one Socialist country after another perched on the brink of bankruptcy, they continue to ballyhoo their failed policies as if they were all paid flacks.

What is particularly peculiar is that these are the very same people who dislike white American males of European descent, but who can't stop gushing about white European males. Go figure.

These numbskulls insisted that Bush was a puppet of the Saudis, but ignored the fact that they begged him not to invade Iraq. That's the kind of puppet that only Stephen King could dream up. Without missing a step, they claimed that we were only invading Iraq in order to capture its oil fields. Odd, though, that they didn't seem to notice that we didn't confiscate Kuwait's oil fields after driving out Saddam Hussein in '91. Instead, they hailed France, Germany and Russia for refusing to depose Hussein, ignoring the sweetheart deals these countries had with the oil broker of Baghdad.

One of the favorite lies the leftists like to parrot is that the U.S. is an imperialistic power. Wouldn't even the dumbest of them have figured out that if we were, we'd have far-flung colonies to show for it? At the very least, wouldn't we have invaded Cuba by this time and sent Castro packing, the way that America's cigar smokers have long demanded?

The truth is, Europe is a hodgepodge of second-rate powers who don't trust each other, and with good reason. A few of them are so fearful of their own Muslim populations that they actually feel they have to line up with Hezbollah and Al-Qaeda against Israel. Of course, being as anti-Semitic as so many Europeans are, they'd probably swing that way in any case.

These loony Americans also tend to side with the Islamic fascists against the only democracy in the Middle East. So in spite of the fact that the Muslims represent the antithesis of everything that liberals theoretically espouse - free speech, equal rights for women, separation of state and religion, the rule of law, free elections - our lefties consistently side with the followers of Mohammed.

They also argue that if only America would get out of the Middle East, Islamic terrorism would come to an end. Once again they choose to ignore the facts, namely that the terrorist acts were being committed long before we rescued Kuwait. They also choose to ignore the fact that terrorist bombings in India, Spain, Bali, Africa, England, Japan, the Philippines, etc., etc., have nothing to do with the United States. Likewise, the slaughter of Christians in Lebanon and other parts of the world has nothing to do with us. Or with Israel, for that matter. It has everything to do with their blind hatred of what is laughingly referred to as the civilized world.

Of course these American leftists never get upset about suicide bombings in Israel or the anti-Semitic ravings of Iran's Mahmud Ahmadinejad. It's only when Israel defends itself against the lunatics who have sworn to exterminate the Jews that these moral midgets work themselves into a proper frenzy.

Quite frankly, not only don't I admire European values, such as they are, but I can't think of a single European tradition I'd want us to adopt. I don't want to run naked through the snow like the Finns, I don't want to have dinner at 11 p.m. like the Spaniards, and I sure don't want to wave a white flag every time a car backfires like the French!

I spend an inordinate amount of time trying to make sense of the world. Which is probably all the proof anyone needs to prove that I'm certifiably loony. Even though I know that one of the most obvious symptoms of insanity is to keep doing the same thing over and over again in the foolish belief that the end result will be different this time, I can't help myself.

For instance, a question that constantly plagues me is: why are there still people who long to see Communism prevail? Even back in the 1930s, when America was suffering through the Great Depression, very few American leftists packed their bags and moved to the Soviet Union. They certainly paid lip service to the so-called worker's paradise, the Communist Eden, trying to peddle it to the masses, but they, themselves, the Soviet's "useful idiots," chose to remain here, in Chicago and New York, Philadelphia and Detroit. A few of them went over there, but they didn't stay long. All in all, they seemed to think it was a nice place to visit, but they didn't want to die there. So why do so many people continue to promote the vile system?

Perhaps, way back in the old days when Marx and Engels were kicking ideas around, people could be excused for seeing something nice in their theories. But ever since then, wherever societies have attempted to turn theory into reality, the earth has been bathed in blood, whether it was in Russia, China, East Germany, Cambodia, Cuba, Venezuela, Hungary or North Korea; brutal tyrannies, each and every one. In none of those countries, not too surprisingly, has art, literature or science, flourished. Aside from various forms of torture, these regions have contributed absolutely nothing to mankind, and yet the yahoos of the Left continue their incessant cheerleading.

Such extremely successful capitalists as Oliver Stone, Steven Spielberg, Sean Penn and Michael Moore, pay court to Fidel Castro, in spite of the fact that Castro censors the Cuban press, persecutes homosexuals, imprisons AIDS victims, and executes his political foes. But, then, what else would you expect in a world in which Che Guevara posters continue to sell in the millions?

Speaking of millions, even I was shocked to read that, according to

Forbes, Cuba's dictator is richer than England's queen. I knew it was good to be king, but apparently it's even better being a left-wing tyrant.

If you're of a certain age, you may recall that years ago, during the Cold War, there was a major controversy revolving around the introduction of fluoride into America's water supply. Those in favor claimed it would strengthen our teeth and help us ward off cavities. Those on the other side insisted it was all a Commie plot. I can't recall exactly what it was the anti-fluoride crowd worried about. But if they suspected that, while toughening up our teeth, it would simultaneously weaken our national resolve and turn us into a bunch of weak-kneed, chicken-hearted, liberals, who insist we run from any fight we can't win in five minutes, they just may have been on to something.

Lately, it seems every time I turn around I hear about some politician or bureaucrat who is absolutely indispensable. As often as not, these people are talking about themselves. And, frankly, if this keeps up, I'm going to have to stop turning around.

The first of these braggarts was New York's Mayor Michael Bloomberg. In demanding that the city council do away with term limits, Bloomberg insisted that, thanks to the financial crisis, New York needed him, and him alone, at the helm.

When people say these kinds of things, we assume they're either a banana republic dictator or an inmate at an asylum with his hand tucked in his jacket, claiming to be Napoleon.

In spite of the fact that he was a tax-cheat for several years, Tim Geithner, according to Barack Obama, was the only guy in America who could be trusted to be Secretary of the Treasury, the man whose duties include running the IRS. As I see it, after years of overlooking his own taxes, does it really make sense that he is now charged with overseeing everybody else's? I guess this comes under the heading of "It Takes a Thief."

Next, we have William Lynn III, President Obama's choice to be deputy Defense secretary, in spite of the fact that Obama had vowed to make his administration a lobbyist-free zone. Mr. Lynn just happened to have been a major lobbyist on behalf of a major defense contractor, the Raytheon Co.

Now I have nothing personal against Bloomberg, Geithner or Lynn. For all I know, they may be nice guys and maybe even competent. But the notion of being indispensable rubs me the wrong way. Americans such as, say, Aaron Copland, Andrew Wyeth and Tennessee Williams, can be called indispensable to a certain degree because if they'd never been born, "Rodeo" would never have been composed, "Christina's World" never been painted, and "The Glass Menagerie" never been written. But when it comes to mayors, cabinet members and deputy Defense secretaries, I refuse to believe that in a nation this large, we can't find three other fellows who could do the job, and probably for a lot less money.

Speaking of money, I think Illinois Governor Rod Blagojevich may have been on to something. Understand, I don't like him any better than you do. But the way I see it, he had a Senate seat to fill and he figured he might as well make a few bucks off it. And, really, when you get right down to cases, whoever was going to wind up being the junior senator from Illinois, be it Roland Burris, Jesse Jackson, Jr., Valerie Jarrett or Oprah Winfrey, was going to be a knee-jerk liberal. So what's the big deal if Blagojevich was going to wind up being able to afford box seats at Wrigley Field, a new Lexus and a haircut?

Until the enactment of the 17th Amendment in 1913, U.S. senators were appointed, not elected by the voters of the state. Frankly, I wouldn't mind seeing governors selecting all of them. When you look at a lineup that includes Pat Leahy, John Kerry, Olympia Snowe, Dick Durbin, Robert Byrd and Harry Reid, you know they couldn't do any worse than the electorate. And if the seats got auctioned off for a million or two bucks, it would be a lot cheaper than it is now. To run for the U.S. Senate in my state costs tens of millions of dollars, and we still wind up with the likes of Dianne Feinstein, she of the thin skin, and Barbara Boxer, she of the tiny brain.

Considering my generally low opinion of politicians, including those in the GOP, you might wonder why I'm even registered as a Republican. For one thing, Democrats must never be in a position to appoint judges. But the biggest difference between the two parties is the two groups of voters. By and large, Republican voters are more patriotic, more mature, more logical and far more honorable. If only the politicians measured up to the civilians in the party, a lot of us could quit holding our noses when we entered the voting booth.

Those on the Left actually believe that those of us who don't see Barack Obama in the same flattering light they do must be racists. I'm certain they won't believe me when I say that I don't know any Republicans who dislike or distrust him because of his race, but it happens to be the truth. How is it that left-wingers figure we're racists for not adoring Obama, but don't regard themselves as racists when they bellow their hatred of Clarence Thomas, Walter Williams, Thomas Sowell, Shelby Steele, Condi Rice, Alan Keyes, Michael Steele and Ward Connerly?

Politics aside, the reason a lot of Republicans are turned off by the president is because they find him arrogant. The way he is constantly tilting his head, as if posing for a statue or a Roman coin, reminds many of us of Benito Mussolini in his heyday. He, too, was forever jutting his chin skyward. What's with these guys, anyway, always trying to get their jawbones above their foreheads?

Speaking of former rulers reminds me that several centuries ago, it is said that King Canute grew so weary of listening to his butt-kissing courtiers proclaiming his greatness that he went down to the ocean, sat in a chair, and commanded the tide to stop. He didn't expect it to, and not only didn't it stop in its tracks, but it got his shoes wet. Being a religious man, it was his intention to prove that he was a mere mortal, and that although he was a king, he was not the King of Kings. On the other hand, one has the feeling that Obama would expect the earth to stop spinning if he simply sent a memo to Rahm Emanuel.

Conservative pundits keep lecturing us about treating Barack Obama with respect, instead of following the example of those nasty liberals who, not satisfied with trashing George W. Bush for eight long years, are still at it. As if we were a bunch of brats misbehaving in church, we are constantly admonished to always respect the office. To which, I say, hooey!

So far as I'm concerned, respecting the office of the president has nothing to do with loving America and everything to do with the man occupying the White House. The way I see it, it makes no sense to respect the man whom I believe is single-handedly destroying the country simply because he won a beauty contest in November of 2008.

What truly confounds me is the blind faith that liberals have in the federal government, at least during those years when left-wingers are running the show in Washington. What, I constantly ask myself, is wrong with these people that they're dying to have the feds in charge of their health care? After all, these are the same bureaucratic dunderheads who mailed out at least 10,000 of those $250 stimulus checks to dead people. Just in case you were wondering, it didn't stimulate even one of them back to life.

However, maybe it wasn't a $2.5 million goof, after all. Maybe it was simply Obama's way of rewarding 10,000 of Chicago's most loyal voters for past services to the party.

Earlier this past year, Colin Powell took umbrage at Dick Cheney and Rush Limbaugh for suggesting he's not a real Republican. Frankly, I'm shocked that he continues to insist he is one. I, for one, began doubting it years ago, when, as Secretary of State, he publicly opposed George Bush over the invasion of Iraq. When in 2008, he timed his endorsement of Barack Obama to do the most damage to John McCain, I naturally assumed Mr. Powell had finally gotten around to changing his registration. After all, if you can't support McCain, who was about as close to being a Democrat as a GOP candidate could be, what Republican could Mr. Powell possibly get behind? Abe Lincoln?

I kept asking myself why, after supporting the most left-wing presidential candidate since Henry Wallace, the man would insist on calling himself a Republican. Frankly, I'm stumped. But, human nature being what it is, it must obviously work to Powell's advantage. Well, at my age, I need every possible edge I can get. Therefore, I am now announcing that I'm a Democrat. Understand, I am opposed to the bail-outs and to the monstrous debt Obama is running up. I am opposed to the feds taking over car companies, banks and lending institutions, and determining executive salaries. I am opposed to Barack Obama's cavalier attitude towards Iran's nuclear program; his kowtowing to Arab princes, ACORN and the UAW; his fund-raising activities on behalf of Harry Reid's re-election campaign; his endorsement of a expanded AmeriCorps; and to his belief that "compassion" is a prerequisite for a Supreme Court justice. I am also opposed to his bringing Cuban-style health care to the U.S. and to his waging class and race war in America.

What's more, I'm not too crazy about a guy who names the family dog after his own initials. I am curious, though, considering that Bo was a gift from Ted Kennedy, whether he drinks from a bowl or from a bottle.

Finally, at the risk of sounding too boastful, I'd like to say that I'm the best kind of Democrat. I'm the kind who votes for Republicans.

Trying to talk sense to liberals is a losing battle. In the 19th century, a clergyman named Charles Colton observed: "The soundest argument will produce no more conviction in an empty head than the most superficial declamation; as a feather and a guinea fall with equal velocity in a vacuum."

We have our pinheads to contend with and, obviously, Rev. Colton had his. Which reminds me, when my son first began crawling, for some reason the only gear he could manage was reverse. I don't know how commonplace a phenomenon that is, but I found it very amusing. He would get up a good head of steam, but no matter how hard he'd try to reach his destination, backwards he would scramble. It was many years ago and I rarely dwell on it, but the other day when I was thinking about Obama, Geithner, Sunstein, Axelrod, Jarrett, Holdren, various people named Jones and all the other folks in Washington who are in way over their pointy heads, it occurred to me that left-wingers put me in mind of little Max. They're always full of big plans, they're always going off in the wrong direction and, more often than not, their diapers need changing.

Oddly enough, those on the left are always telling us how smart they are. It all began, I believe, during FDR's first administration, when every left-wing kook who ever gave him a piece of advice or lit his cigarette or kissed his fanny was called a member of Roosevelts's brain trust. These days, those who would refer to themselves that way would include the likes of Chris Matthews, Janeane Garofalo, Keith Olbermann, Nancy Pelosi, Janet Napolitano, Harry Reid, Wanda Sykes, Chris Dodd, Rahm Emanuel, Bill Maher, Barney Frank, Sean Penn, Patrick Leahy, Hillary Clinton and now, no doubt, Arlen Specter. The irony is that the members of this particular brain trust have no brains and can't be trusted.

In conclusion, let me just admit that while I totally reject the idea of the indispensable man, I am entirely open to the notion of the indispensable dog. The dog I have in mind isn't our own Maltese, the philosopher Duke, who first barked, "I sleep; therefore I am." Rather, it's a distant relative of his, the Maltese known as Sumo.

It seems that Sumo, who has been treated for depression, once bit his master, the former French president, Jacques Chirac, otherwise known as Saddam Hussein's lap dog.

Mrs. Chirac said that Sumo bit her husband for no apparent reason. Ha! The woman probably also believes the dog was depressed for no apparent reason.

As a rule, Malteses are jovial, light-hearted, happy-go-lucky little fellows. If Sumo is depressed, I suspect it's only because he has had to share living space with the insufferable Monsieur Chirac, the jackal who supplied Iran with a French-built nuclear reactor and high grade uranium back in the 1970s, but carried on some quarter century later as if he were George W. Bush's moral superior when he refused to take part in the Iraq invasion for no other reason than that France had been bought off with cheap oil. Which of us wouldn't have bitten him?

For the longest time, I thought that the main difference between those on the Left and those on the Right was that whereas conservatives believed that liberals were wrong on the issues, liberals were convinced that conservatives were just plain evil.

I still believe that to be the case, but I've also become aware that, in addition, leftists regard those on the other side as stupid. My basis for that is that they like nothing better than to stereotype us all as creationists while they wrap themselves up all snugly and warm in Charles Darwin's theory of evolution.

Just to get my cards on the table, I am not religious. I don't take either Testament as gospel. But that doesn't mean I think those who do are ignorant or even a lower form of animal life. By and large, I think that religious people - yes, even born-again Christians and creationists - are often better people than those who aren't. By better, I mean more kindly, more decent, better friends, better neighbors, better parents.

So many people who know even less science than I do, and who have never bothered reading any of Darwin's books, base their defense of his theory on Stanley Kramer's truly awful movie about the Scopes trial, "Inherit the Wind."

Representing enlightenment, as Clarence Darrow, Kramer cast Hollywood's avuncular Spencer Tracy. As William Jennings Bryan, he miscast Fredric March, and then had him sweat and spray spittle for two solid hours. It was, by the way, the only time that the two fine actors, who had each starred in a version of "Dr. Jekyll and Mr. Hyde," worked together. With the notoriously heavy-handed Kramer at the helm, Darrow naturally came off like Jekyll, while Bryan came off as Hyde.

It's true that Bryan was a loquacious fellow who'd never use one word when there were thirty or forty lying around just going to waste. Darrow, however, was the criminal defense attorney who, for an enormous fee, used his legal skills to make certain that the vile Leopold and Loeb weren't executed for the cold-blooded murder of young Bobby Franks. Between those two, I'd take my chances with Bryan. Better a bore than a man with innocent blood on his hands.

The fact of the matter is that it doesn't make much difference if Darwin was right or wrong. Really, how would it affect your life if his beliefs could be proven one way or the other? Unless you're one of the very small number of academics involved in evolutionary biology, it wouldn't make a scintilla of difference in your daily life. Even Darwin couldn't explain how everything began in the first place, his theories only dealt with the manner in which things evolved from some unexplainable point of origin. So if creationists choose to believe that God set everything in motion, and that belief makes them happy, there's nothing in Darwin to refute their theory!

The truth, so far as I can see, is that liberals only love Darwin because they hate those who don't swallow him whole. It makes them feel smart, as if they were somehow scientists themselves, logical and intellectually superior, even if they can't tell the difference between a Bunsen burner and a tiki torch.

So while the snobs on the Left lump all conservatives in with those they regard as ignorant, simple-minded, anonymous oafs, conservatives aim their barbs at the leaders of the opposition - Ivy League-educated twerps like Kerry and Kennedy, Pelosi and Dean, Reid and Leahy, Clinton and Clinton, Boxer and Feinstein, Biden and Byrd. The truth now, would you follow any of those dirty dozen into a war? Me, I wouldn't even follow them to the buffet table.

For what it's worth, Mr. Darwin's beloved wife was a religious woman who took the Bible literally, and they got along just fine.

Over the years, so many people have asked me how I've managed to maintain friendships with liberals that I had considered writing a book on the subject. Unfortunately, I haven't figured out how to expand my one and only rule, which is to limit discourse to sports, movies and the weather, to book length.

I have already gone on record to suggest mother of 14, Nadya Suleman, should be committed to an asylum, and that Dr. Michael Kamrava who, at taxpayer expense, performed the in vitro procedure, should be committed to the county lockup. But that still leaves those 14 innocent children to be considered. Perhaps because I kept hearing that Ms. Suleman was obsessed with Angelina Jolie, a solution occurred to me. Instead of adopting a kid here, a kid there, wouldn't it make more sense if Ms. Jolie went whole hog and adopted the entire litter?

In a book devoted to excoriating liberals, it might strike some folks as odd that I'd include John McCain. If that's the case, they just haven't been paying attention. Not only did Sen. McCain push through the McCain-Feingold Bill and try to sneak through the McCain-Kennedy Amnesty Bill of 2008, but when he was running for president, he was far kinder and more respectful to Barack Obama than he was to his own running-mate, Sarah Palin. I know he has already announced that he'll be running for re-election to the Senate in 2010, but, along with a great many other people, I'm wondering who the Republican candidate will be.

The majority of the 535 senators and congressmen voted to pass the Pelosi and Reid Pig Trough Bill of 2009, which will not only burden our grandchildren with a big fat I.O.U., but should finish the job begun by FDR of turning America into a socialistic state. What is particularly noteworthy about all this is that we are moving further and further to the left at the same time that Europe, which has been suffering from the economic malaise of socialism, has been moving to the right, electing one conservative after another.

Isn't it strange that left-wingers, who always love to pay lip service to Santayana's line about those who don't learn from history being doomed to repeat it, never seem to learn a damn thing? FDR, the patron saint of the secular left, kept the Great Depression going long after it might have been ended if only he and his beloved Brain Trust hadn't been more interested in promoting a leftist agenda and making American voters dependent on the federal government than in solving the economic crisis. Talk about history repeating itself!

Although I usually rail against the blatant hypocrisy of Al Gore whenever I touch upon the monumental con game known as man-made global warming (aka climate change), I would be remiss if I didn't focus some attention on his cohort, Robert Kennedy, Jr. For the longest time, I had been aware that Kennedy, like most left-wingers, was a sterling of example of "Do As I Say, Not As I Do," traveled by private jet as he flew hither and yon scolding the rest of us for driving to the supermarket.

What I had not been aware of until recently is that he's been arrested twice. I'm sure he wouldn't mind discussing, probably even boasting about, his arrest in 2001, when he was guilty of trespassing at Camp Garcia, the U.S. Navy facility in Puerto Rico. In that instance, he and a few of his fellow ecological fruitcakes were demonstrating against the Navy firing guns on the test range. No doubt the noise was interfering with the sleep or mating habits of some plague-bearing insect.

The arrest I have in mind was the one in 1983 that took place at the Rapid City, South Dakota, Airport, when he was nabbed, at the age of 29, for possession of heroin. Being a Kennedy, he got off with two years probation and several hundred hours of community service. He chose to perform his service with the Riverkeeper, an organization dedicated to suing alleged polluters of the Hudson River. As soon as his community service term ended, Kennedy was hired as the Riverkeeper's chief prosecuting attorney. And thus a high-priced environmentalist activist was born. You have to hand it to those Kennedys. Whether it's somehow turning what might have been a manslaughter conviction into a half century in the U.S. Senate or a heroin habit into a career, those boys sure know how to turn lemons into lemonade.

In trying to see an upside to the current financial crisis, I'm afraid the best I could come up with is that a lot of parents can no longer afford to blow their hard-earned dollars financing their children's indoctrination by an army of left-wing professors. Frankly, it's always perplexed me when well-meaning adults blithely send their impressionable kids off to be force-fed four years of lies, such as the perils of global warming; the notion that America's hog farmers, according to Robert Kennedy, Jr., being a far greater threat to the nation than Osama bin Laden and his terrorism network; that all countries are equally good, except, of course, America and Israel; and that all religions deserve equal respect, except, of course, for Christianity and Judaism.

I think we conservatives sometimes go slightly overboard when we attack liberals. That's not to say they don't deserve attacking. But your run-of-the-mill lib is usually just a well-meaning dunderhead, but not actually satanic. We can certainly agree that they're wrong about nearly everything, from bilingual education and capital punishment to affirmative action and the United Nations. The poor saps can't even decide how many people it takes to raise a child; except when they're trying to make a case for unmarried women and gay couples, they insist it takes an entire village!

But, having known a large number of liberals, I feel I can vouch - at least in most cases - for their good intentions. They really do believe that there isn't a problem in America, ranging from illiteracy to illegal aliens, that can't be solved by throwing tax dollars and good intentions at it.

The reason that we on the right tend to despise, rather than pity, mush-minded liberals is because they don't see the need to separate themselves from the truly demented members of the radical left.

You know who they are. They're the unbathed goonies you used to see marching in the streets carrying signs equating George Bush or Tony Blair or Dick Cheney or Uncle Sam with Hitler. Oddly enough, they never seem to equate actual living dictators with der fuhrer.

They are the same mob that takes to the street every time the industrialized nations have an economic conference. God only knows what it is that sets them off. Possibly it's the sight of so many people who are neat, clean and well-groomed. For all I know, or am able to make out from their bizarre array of picket signs, they just might take clean fingernails as a personal affront.

TV enjoys covering their demonstrations for the same reason TV loves major fires, earthquakes, tidal waves and lurid murder trials. It's because TV is all eyes and stomach and has no soul.

By covering the demonstrations, TV over-emphasizes their importance and, naturally, the rest of the media falls into line. For instance, some years ago, TV reported that 100,000 people were in the streets protesting President Bush's state visit to England. What nobody seemed to bother remarking on was the irrefutable fact that roughly 8,000,000 Londoners weren't carrying picket signs; they were at work or they were home having dinner and watching the riffraff on the telly.

The bottom line is that radicals everywhere are always far more likely to march in the streets than conservatives because they are far more likely to play hooky from school and far less likely to have jobs and responsibilities.

Then, for good measure, when conservatives do demonstrate at Tea Parties or in the nation's capitol, the media either ignores them, underestimates their numbers or refers to them as violent mobs, fascists and astroturfers.

There is, however, one group of radicals who are gainfully employed. Far too gainfully, in my opinion. I refer to college professors; specifically those in the humanities.

Their radicalism is fired by their boundless arrogance. They really do believe they're the smartest people around. Like politicians, they probably believe this because they are paid a ton of money to do a job that doesn't require any heavy lifting.

They remind me of an old radio show called "Duffy's Tavern." Each time the phone rang, Archie the bartender would answer it with, "Duffy's Tavern, where the elite meet to eat." The audience at home, knowing what a collection of lowlifes constituted the tavern's clientele, would chuckle knowingly. That is exactly how many of us feel about academics. The Wizard of Oz convinced the brainless Scarecrow that he was brilliant by presenting him with a diploma. The same trick works on our professors. If they know anything at all, which in some cases is highly debatable, it's their one small special area. So, yes, they may know more than the ordinary bear when it comes to French poetry of the 19th century or the events leading up to the signing of the Magna Charta or every practical joke ever played on Arthur Schopenhauer, but so what? Who would you rather have living next door - a nice guy who can fix your plumbing or some boring pedant who can explain why a haiku contains 17 syllables and not 16?

It figures that the human brain would begin to mutate in mysterious and dangerous ways after years and years of delivering the same dreary lectures to the same apathetic students. Moreover, I contend that something is bound to snap in the human mind when a person has barely strayed off school grounds since the age of six!

The only professors who actually get out in the world are archaeologists. But, of course, they're scientists. Unlike their colleagues, when they have a hunch about something, they go off and dig a hole in the ground. After they've dug around for a year or two, they either uncover the lost city they expected to find or they wrap up their shovels, admit they were mistaken, and call it a day.

But in the humanities, professors are never required to admit they're wrong. At worst, it becomes a matter of two scholars squaring off over whether, say, Shakespeare or Bacon wrote "Hamlet." They will then spend the rest of their overly compensated lives trying to make their case.

Students in the humanities are not only captive, but they can be punished with bad grades if they voice a heretical thought. So, hearing nary a discouraging word, the profs wind up spending their entire careers spouting claptrap to a bunch of highly impressionable 18-year-olds.

But even professors are human. And when the choice is between either boring students to death rambling on endlessly about pre-Columbian musical instruments or mouthing off about the evils of America, capitalism, and the kids' stupid, materialistic parents, it's really no contest.

Let's face it, if you're trying to seduce the cute blonde coed in the second row, who would you choose to be - Mister Chips or Che Guevara?

What you have are tenured rams propagandizing undergrad sheep. Which is why when they answer the phone, they should be required to say, "Harvard (or Princeton or Columbia or Cal Berkeley), where the elite meet to bleat."

My friend Pat Sajak recently made an excellent point. He said that inasmuch as he doesn't take global warming to heart, he sees no good reason to alter his life style. However, he wonders why those who are insisting they can feel the rising ocean lapping at their ankles don't take drastic action to alter theirs.

He's right, of course. I mean, assuming you are one of those people who actually has faith in U.N. reports and really believes that man controls the earth's thermostat, wouldn't you have to shape up? I mean, wouldn't you think these worrywarts would all begin riding bicycles and start wearing their snow suits to bed? It's damn hard taking their "The End is Near" placards seriously when they're driving their Hummers to and from the demonstrations. And did you all notice what a god-awful mess Obama's people left behind when they went home after his inauguration? These self-righteous slobs claim they're worried sick about the environment, but not worried enough to clean up their candy wrappers.

Consider Al Gore, the man who could give Chicken Little lessons in panic and hysteria. As ominous as global warming is, it obviously hasn't done anything to spoil his appetite. And why, when he isn't shrieking into a microphone, doesn't he look terrified? If you thought that, say, a giant meteor was hurtling at the earth or a dozen nuclear bombs were set to explode, would you be grinning and saying "Cheese" to every camera pointed in your direction? The thing about liberals is that they're always telling the rest of us how to live and then, oh so conveniently, ignoring their own advice. Take such professional busybodies as Arianna Huffington and Bobby Kennedy, Jr., for instance. She excoriates people who drive SUVs while she and her two tots live in a mansion that I can guarantee sucks up BTUs at a rate that would make your head spin. As for Mr. Kennedy, he spends his life screaming about what the rest of us are doing to destroy the ozone layer, but nevertheless is constantly gadding about on private jets.

Let us not forget that other holier-than-thou character, Michael Moore, who has also sworn off commercial airlines in favor of corporate aircraft.

Of course, that brings us to her royal highness, Nancy Pelosi, non-stop Speaker of the House. First off, she insisted on an upgrade to a larger military jet than the one her predecessor had. She wanted one with a private bedroom, a kitchen, and room for her entire family - second cousins included - on a jet that was capable of flying non-stop from Washington, D.C. to San Francisco.

When some people began to question the need she had for this airborne palace, she insisted that rabble-rousers were only raising a stink because she was a woman. Poor dear! She had no sooner lifted that marble ceiling all by her wonderful self, and here it came crashing down on her tiara!

Personally, I think she should have the largest plane the military has available. As I see it, they'd need a jumbo jet just to get Pelosi's ego airborne.

What's interesting about global warming is how quickly the Left added it to their manifesto, right along with pacifism, affirmative action, bi-lingual education, unilateral disarmament, open borders, the so-called Fairness Doctrine and outlawing gun ownership. What makes global warming such a joke is the way that the same liberals who know even less about climatology than I know about 18th century Irish clog-dancing are trying to pass themselves off as science experts. As the late Michael Crichton pointed out, when folks start talking about consensus among scientists, they're talking politics, not science. Nobody goes around claiming there's a consensus of experts when it comes to the laws of thermodynamics or asks the U.N. to decide if the law of gravity is even legal. Only with global warming are we supposed to put it to a vote, and then, as in Iran, abide by the results of a fixed election.

Let a scientist suggest that man plays a very puny role when it comes to determining the earth's climate, and you can count on Al Gore's goon squads trying to bully him into silence, and even questioning his right to teach or to conduct research.

When it's pointed out that in the 1970s, in a world very much like the one in which we now live, the same crowd was worried sick over the coming Ice Age, it's either dismissed as irrelevant or condemned as heresy.

The last time I argued with a left-winger about global warming, he actually said, "But what if we're right?"

What logic! What insight! I felt as if I were arguing with someone transported from the Dark Ages, someone convinced that the earth was flat. Even if you showed him photos taken from outer space, showing the curvature of the earth, he would still say, "But what if I'm right?"

Funny, isn't it, that these alarmists are always anxious to play the "what if" game when it comes to global warming, but not when it comes to global terrorism. Ask them, for example, what happens if we ignore Iran and its threat to nuke its enemies? Or what happens if we decide to quit policing the world and leave such matters strictly up to the U.N.? (After all, they did a bang-up job in Cambodia in the 1970s and have done equally fine work in Darfur.)

The reason it's so easy to despise liberals isn't simply because they're such blockheads, but because they are so hypocritical and self-righteous.

Understand, though, that I'm not suggesting they are entirely worthless. What I am suggesting is that we establish whether my suspicion is correct that they not only think like chickens and squawk like chickens, but actually taste like chicken. We could then raise them as livestock.

If I had a bigger ego, I could easily imagine that liberals say and do the things they say and do simply to perplex or annoy me. But I know I shouldn't take it personally. All sane and sensible people are equally dismayed.

For instance, Rep. Charles Rangel, chairman of the powerful House Ways and Means Committee, has been accused of failing to report income on a rental house he owns in a Dominican Republic resort, used one of his four rent-control New York apartments for campaign activities, mailed letters on official congressional stationery soliciting funds for an educational center to be named after himself, and used government property to store his Mercedes.

In response to the accusations, the congressman said, "I don't believe making mistakes means you have to give up your career." I agree. When a congressman makes these many "mistakes," he should go to jail.

Even the New York Times called Rangel an embarrassment. House Speaker Pelosi, who vowed to rid Capitol Hill of corruption - bringing to mind a picture of someone trying to drain the Pacific Ocean using a teaspoon - said that she "saw no reason why Mr. Rangel should step down." Of course not, Nancy. It's not as if he's a Republican.

When Rep. John Conyers was asked if he had actually read a certain bill before voting on it, he replied that he saw no point in wasting his time. After all, as he explained, you need a team of lawyers to make head or tail of those damn things. Just because he's a congressman doesn't mean he doesn't have better things to do.

Whatever you might say about Democrats, you can't deny that they're often good for a laugh. Back when he was the crack-smoking mayor, Marion Berry proudly announced, "Outside of killings, Washington, D.C., has one of the lowest crime rates in the country." Now that's what I call a half-full glass kind of guy.

Apparently nobody is immune to the financial meltdown. In return for endorsing Barack Obama, Hillary Clinton got him to promise to help pay off her campaign debt. Towards that end, Joe Biden sent e-mails to three million of Obama's donors, nagging them for contributions. What's more, he hit up those suckers twice on Hillary's behalf. Of course it's not for me to say how people spend their hard-earned money, but the last I heard, the Clintons were worth upwards of a hundred million dollars. Are they saving it all for a rainy day? Do these people even pay for their own lunches?

It's said that cynics know the cost of everything and the value of nothing. Look up "cynic" in the dictionary and you'll find a photo of the Clintons. Look up "happy" and you'll find a photo of Chelsea.

A while ago, I observed that sometimes it seemed as if the people most anxious to get married were homosexuals. But I was conned. We now see by the low number of same-sex marriages that have actually taken place that the entire campaign was more an excuse to whine about inequality than a sincere desire to tie the knot that motivated them to make an issue of the issue.

It's worth noting that Hollywood, as you would expect, is filled with people who believe fervently in same-sex marriages, but not so much in opposite-sex marriages. Even when there are kids involved. Just a few of the parent couples who have decided that marriage didn't fit in with their plans are Naomi Watts and Liev Schreiber, Halle Berry and Gabriel Aubry, Kurt Russell and Goldie Hawn, Tim Robbins and Susan Sarandon, Chris Noth and Tara Wilson, and, of course, Brad Pitt and Angelina Jolie. Of course by the time you read this, some of these people may be dumpers or dumpees, but you get the idea.

I must confess I got a kick out of Pitt's excuse for not proposing to the mother of his children. He said that until all the gays in America were given the right to marry, he wouldn't marry Angelina. I mean, I've heard of guys using wars, the economy and even the nuclear bomb, as an excuse not to march down the aisle, but this one takes the cake. Just not the wedding cake.

It occurred to me the other day that in spite of a bad back and his marriage vows, JFK chased everything in skirts; that Gary Hart allowed his libido to sink his political career; that even nerdy Jimmy Carter confessed to having lust in his heart, although nobody in recorded history has ever been so silly or sanctimonious as to suggest that lust resided anywhere above the belt; and that Bill Clinton, like a spooky version of Mr. Rogers, patiently explained to America's kids that oral sex isn't really sex.

With all that in mind, didn't it strike you as hypocritical for the Democrats to get up in arms over a married mother of five running for the vice-presidency? Didn't it seem at least slightly absurd that the only sexual activity that liberals frown upon is the sort that actually leads to babies being born to a married couple?

Speaking of sexual activity, I came across a very peculiar traffic sign last week. We in California have long become inured to the signs depicting a family of four illegal aliens - a father, mother and two children - scurrying across a road. The message, I suppose, is to ignore our basic instincts, and to slow down, not speed up, when we spot Mexican scofflaws sneaking into our country. The new sign I spotted is on Sunset Blvd., in West Hollywood, a community here in Los Angeles often referred to as Boys Town because it's home to even more gays per square mile than San Francisco. The sign announced that the location was a No Cruising Zone, and that anyone caught crossing the intersection more than twice in four hours would receive a citation. I assume "citation" means a traffic ticket and not a medal, but I could be wrong. I suspect, though, that any gay hustler could beat the rap by accusing the authorities of entrapment. I mean, with all the movie star wannabes lurking in West Hollywood, how could any of them be expected to resist the opportunity to be filmed, even on a traffic camera?

I'm certain that most people recall the photos of the American flags that were left for the trash collector after the Democratic convention in Denver. I happen to have two flags, one outside my front door and one in my heart, and I hate to think of an American flag being treated like garbage. It is, after all, the symbol of a nation that inspired my two sets of grandparents to travel several thousand miles so I could be fortunate enough to be born an American. Still, I wasn't as troubled by the photos as I would have been if they'd been trashed after the Republican convention. Liberals, after all, are always insisting that they're as patriotic as conservatives, but I don't believe it. If they were, they'd respect the military far more than they do, they wouldn't have nominated someone like Barack Obama and they certainly wouldn't keep insisting that America is despised around the world, while ignoring the fact that it's a badge of honor to be despised by the likes of Russia, China, Iran, Yemen, North Korea, Venezuela and the PLO. They would also acknowledge that there must be a darn good reason why millions of people who weren't as lucky as we were to be born in America, are literally, in some cases, dying to come here.

So, when I saw that the Democrats had treated the flags so shabbily,

I understood that to them the flags were only cheap props like the balloons, the bunting, the confetti and those corny Greek columns. The real problem wasn't that they trashed a few flags, but that they and Barack Hussein Obama keep trashing the country.

A friend of mine has come up with what I regard as a wonderful solution to the problem of leftist influence. She proposes that liberals be offered an incentive to leave America, as they are constantly threatening to do whenever it appears that a Republican might be elected president. The sum she came up with is a million dollars per person. That sounds like a lot until you realize that nowadays people casually toss around sums in the trillions when discussing federal budgets, deficits and the Obama date nights. Still, I think there is room for negotiation. The point is, these left-wing whiners would get a deal similar to the one the protagonist received in Edward Everett Hale's short story, "The Man Without a Country." Unlike Philip Nolan, though, they wouldn't be sentenced to spend the rest of their lives sailing the seas, but they would be denied the opportunity to ever again set foot on this sacred ground. Not even for a visit. Even if only a relatively small number of leftists accepted the deal, I, for one, would consider it money well spent.

Liberals have an impossible time defending their beliefs, which is why they rely on slogans and catch phrases, unfounded rumors and ad hominem attacks, on those who, like Sarah Palin, think clearly and live according to Judeo-Christian principles.

The brains and values of left-wingers have decomposed to the point where they actually believe that Keith Olbermann, Rosie O'Donnell and Chris Matthews make sense and that people like Whoopi Goldberg, Wanda Sykes, Al Franken, Joy Behar and Bill Maher, are funny. That is why I say that liberalism is an addiction - and why, as with other addictions, I'd like to see it kicked. Kicked good and hard.

I'll come right out and admit that I understand Islamic terrorists far better than I do American liberals. After all, once you realize that young Muslims are taught by their religious leaders that our nation is militarily powerful and technologically advanced because we cut a deal with Satan, you can see where they'd be upset with us. But what is the deal with liberals? How to explain their mushy heads? Was it something weird in their baby formula? Were they potty-trained when they were too young or, more likely, too old? Or is it simply something in their DNA? Are their chromosomes slightly out of whack, the way it is with homosexuals and the transgender crowd?

I'm serious. Why else would Americans so resent the United States having more influence in the world than, say, Luxembourg or Lichtenstein? Why do they seem to have no rooting interest in capitalism prevailing over all the other isms? Do they think that the reason they live so much better than the typical Russian or Turk is because they, themselves, are intellectually superior? Fat chance!

Why is it that liberals seem to believe that recycling cans is an important issue, but defeating terrorism isn't? Why do they put so much stock in the blathering of Al Gore and Michael Moore? Why do they regard secondhand smoke as a bigger menace than Mahmud Ahmadinejad? What is wrong with these people?

Why will the same folks who'd call a cop if someone set foot in their front yard be so unconcerned about millions of illegal aliens setting up camp in their country? And why will the same saps who work themselves into a tizzy if some small town sets up a Christmas tree in the public square defend a church's right to provide a sanctuary for foreign nationals who have no business being in our country?

Liberals wanted to see us cut and run from Iraq. That's because they enjoy seeing the American military lose. For them, Vietnam was positively rapturous. Their holy trinity consists of Jane Fonda, John Kerry and Walter Cronkite.

They kept insisting that Saddam Hussein had nothing to do with 9/11. What they refuse to acknowledge is that we are at war with Islamic fundamentalism. Hussein may have had nothing to do with the USS Cole or the first bombing of the Twin Towers or the attacks on our embassies and our Marine base. So what? Germany and Italy had nothing to do with Pearl Harbor. It's the mission that matters, not the venue. And our mission is to destroy Hamas and Al Qaeda and the Taliban and all the rest of the Islamic vermin. If they wish to fight us in Iraq or Afghanistan, so be it. Better to fight them there than in Atlanta or New York, Houston or Seattle.

I'm aware that liberals will tell you that the Islamics hate us because we're over there, violating their sacred turf. But if that were the case, why are they killing civilians in Holland and Bali, Indonesia and the Philippines, Russia and Spain?

If we're not at war with Muslim terrorism, why do I have to remove my shoes before I'm allowed to board a plane? And if we are at war, why can't airport security concentrate on Arabs of a certain age and quit behaving like a bunch of politically correct fatheads?

There's no getting around the fact that next to the liberals in the Senate, academia and the editorial boardrooms at CNN, MSNBC and the New York Times, the biggest left-wing dunces are to be found in Hollywood. This village is filled with a bunch of idiots who, when they're not busy getting drunk, shooting up and behaving like spoiled brats, can be found yammering about global warming and poverty in America. Oddly enough, those are two problems they could do something about. Assuming that carbon emissions actually have an effect on the earth's temperature, might it not be beneficial if these clucks stopped chugging around in Hummers and limos, stopped heating and cooling houses slightly larger than the palace at Versailles, and grounded their private jets for the foreseeable future?

As for poverty, the plain fact of the matter is that the only poor people these movie folks ever encounter are maids, gardeners, nannies and waiters. Well, if these overly pampered nincompoops were really serious about eliminating poverty in America, all they'd have to do is pay higher wages and leave bigger tips!

I happen to know of an extremely successful TV writer-producer. According to Forbes, he typically earns about $40 million-a-year. That works out to about $4,500-an-hour, including the hours when he's asleep. Well, it seems he needed a personal assistant. For those unfamiliar with the term, at least as it applies to Hollywood, the duties can consume 80 hours a week, and include everything from collecting dry cleaning, chauffeuring the wife and babysitting the kids to supplying drugs and sexual favors. The job paid the princely sum of $400-a-week! But this sanctimonious schmuck has a hissy fit anytime a Republican congressmen doesn't vote to raise the minimum wage.

I have friends who are liberals. I'm not bragging, you understand, merely stating for the record that I'm aware that they're not all hypocritical lunkheads, but I do have to keep repeating it to myself like a mantra, because otherwise the sheer weight of the evidence would bury me and my good intentions.

How is it, for instance, that they can bring themselves to parrot every moronic statement uttered by the likes of Gore, Reid, Schumer, Durbin and that noted plagiarist, Joe Biden? How is it that even the avowed feminists among them attack Sarah Palin for being tough as nails? Do they regard Nancy Pelosi, Hillary Clinton and Michelle Obama as warm and cuddly? Finally, how is it that so many of them got into line to plead for a child-rapist like Roman Polanski to walk free? Whoopi Goldberg, who apparently was paying attention when Bill Clinton parsed the word "is," even went so far as to insist that when Polanski got a 13-year-old child drunk, fed her qualudes and then sodomized her, it wasn't really rape.

Now, let us consider oil for a minute. If you were to believe the leading lights on the left, we can't drill our way out of the energy crisis. Oh, really? Just how do they think oil gets out of the ground and into their gas tank? Do all of them believe in the oil fairy? And what is it they have against drilling in Anwar and off our sea coast? If they claim that they're not simply against American capitalism and that their concerns are ecologically-based, they're liars and hypocrites. After all, whether or not America drills, Saudi Arabia, Venezuela, Iraq, Iran, Russia, Mexico, Brazil and Canada, are going to keep drilling. As the lefties keep reminding us, this is all one planet, Mother Earth.

Furthermore, as that other big mother, Mother Nature, with her tsunamis, earthquakes and hurricanes keeps reminding us, when it comes to raising havoc and making a really big mess, we mere mortals – even those slobs who attended Obama's coronation - are feeble and pathetic. As for global warming or climate change or whatever it is the numbskulls are fretting about this week, they should keep in mind that Ma Nature is a lady of many moods when it comes to the weather. At one point, ice covered Canada all the way down into what is now Nova Scotia, and it receded to the Arctic Circle without any help from the internal combustion engine.

The clearest proof that those lamebrains on the left will fall for anything that purports to be ecologically well-intentioned was a stunt carried off by those two notorious scamps, Penn and Teller. They hired a few earnest-looking young people to pass around petitions demanding that the government once and for all ban the use of H2O. Even I was surprised at the number of people who signed on, oblivious to the fact that they were demanding that water be outlawed.

We should all recall that the last time this same crowd actually got something banished from the planet it was DDT. Thanks to their humanistic concerns, malaria, which had nearly been eliminated, came back with a vengeance. And to date, millions of people, mainly children, have died painful deaths all across the globe.

I am constantly perplexed by the animosity liberals have to what they insist on calling big oil. Do they actually imagine that a small mom-and-pop outfit could get oil out of the ground and into a pipeline or aboard a tanker, move it thousands of miles, refine it and deliver it to your corner gas station? In any case, I at least know what big oil is. But what the heck is small oil? That grease spot on my driveway?

Another thing that gets on my nerves is the way that liberals are always telling us how smart they are. Jimmy Carter, they kept telling us, was a genius. Bill Clinton, they believed, was another Einstein. Hillary, according to them, is the smartest woman in America, and Barack Obama is not only brilliant, but, according to his running mate, very clean. Now, nobody stands in greater awe of brilliance than I do. Furthermore, I wouldn't be surprised if at this very moment, someone somewhere is coming up with an invention that will transform our lives the way the computer has, while somebody else is coming up with a cure for Alzheimer's or Parkinson's, while a third party, for all we know, is in a lab whipping up a contraceptive pill for men that will make Roe v. Wade as irrelevant as the Dred Scott decision. But whenever anybody describes a politician - even one whose politics I agree with - as a super intellect, I know that I'm dealing with some boob who has confused blind ambition and a massive ego with a great mind.

Some wag suggested that all politicians should be limited to two terms – one in office, the other in jail. Which, come to think of it, is just the way they do it in Illinois.

I mean, I know we have to have a president, but doesn't it disturb you when you stop and realize that whoever that person is actually believes he or she is the most qualified person in a country of 300 million people to make all the most important decisions affecting us and the rest of the world? Really, just how different are they from those poor deluded souls wandering around the asylums insisting they're Napoleon or Anastasia?

If at times, it is not easy to determine what a liberal is, it's because during presidential election campaigns, politicians who have been voting like liberals, talking like liberals and boasting about their liberal credentials, suddenly insist that they're really centrists as they go about trying to garner the votes of gullible Republicans and Independents. It's rather like Michelle Obama trying to convince us that she's just another stay-at-home mom who loves America and her kids, and in exactly that order, and who loves nothing better than getting dirt under her fingernails working in the White House vegetable garden.

Most of us on the right can spot a liberal a mile away, just as easily as experienced bird watchers can identify cuckoos, parrots and pigeons. But just in case you're not as proficient at recognizing the odd ducks that populate the left, allow me to be your guide through the wilderness.

In America, more than 80% of African-American and Jewish voters can be safely assumed to favor liberals in any and all elections. The reason that poor Blacks vote overwhelmingly for Democrats is because they have been told over and over again by plantation owners like Nancy Pelosi, John Kerry and the Clintons, that it's only through the federal government's largesse that they can manage to survive at all. I suppose even if an able-bodied person is told from childhood on that he lacks the ability to walk, let alone run, he will eventually come to believe he needs a wheelchair or at least a pair of crutches.

Middle-class, church-attending Blacks often owe their unnatural allegiance to the party of George Wallace, Strom Thurmond and Robert Byrd, because they listen to their ministers. Speaking of which, political bribes are usually frowned upon, except when the Democrats act as bagmen for the Black clergy. There is a reason, you understand, why white politicians get to spend so much time in Black churches at election time, in spite of their insistence that "separation of church and state" is writ large somewhere in the Constitution.

When it comes to Jews, the great majority of us are secular when it comes to religion, but religious when it comes to left-wing politics. It isn't a coincidence that Karl Marx and Leon Trotsky started out as Jews, and that all but one Jew currently serving in the House and Senate are left-wingers who, while disparaging Christian belief in Jesus as the messiah, have no problem whatsoever accepting Barack Obama in that role.

I happen to know a Jewish professor who lives in the Pacific Northwest. While he may not be typical, his mindset isn't all that different from many of my fellow Jews. When George Bush was running for re-election in 2004, Professor Sandy sent me an email in which he claimed that if Bush won, America would immediately begin building concentration camps for Jews, and he was glad he lived close to Canada and would be able to escape across the border.

Most liberals will tell you that they don't hate America, they merely hated George Bush. But when you ask them why they despised him so much, they start yammering about the invasion of Iraq, even though all the Democratic bigwigs spent the 1990s calling for regime change, and later voted for the invasion. The left also hated Bush because of the Patriot Act. They insisted that it cost us many of our basic freedoms. But I have yet to ask a liberal to name a single freedom he had under Clinton that he didn't have eight years later and received a coherent answer. Yet, even I can come up with one. Thanks to Jimmy Carter, who allowed the Islamic crazies to get a foothold in Iran by turning his back on the Shah, and Bill Clinton, who spared Osama bin Laden's life on more than one occasion, I no longer have the freedom to arrive at an airport half an hour before boarding and expect to make my flight.

There is a good reason, though, that liberals are liberals. By and large, they are people who never fully mature and who go through life, like sullen teenagers, resenting figures of authority - be they police officers, members of the military or teachers who believe in discipline and academic standards in the classroom - people, in short, who have rules and values. These folks started out by resenting their parents, assuming, that is, that their parents were responsible adults and not aging hippies, the sort of parents who set curfews and expected good grades, parents who objected to their offspring boozing, shacking up and using drugs.

For years, we have all heard Hollywood's most prominent left-wingers vow to leave America if we assorted racists, fascists and evil yokels, managed to elect a Republican president. And although Republicans have won five of the last eight presidential elections, and in spite of my standing offer to drive any and all of them to the airport, in all that time the only movie star who has left America except to make a movie or work on his tan is Johnny Depp, who moved to France. To their credit, Sean Penn and Robin Williams did the next best thing. They moved to San Francisco.

One of the most annoying things about liberals is that when nightmarish events don't take place as they predicted - be they concentration camps for Jews, cataclysmic hurricanes or rising sea levels - they never admit they were mistaken. They can't even bring themselves to acknowledge that global warming was a hoax concocted by Al Gore; instead, they merely start squawking like a barnyard full of Chicken Littles about the intentionally vague phenomenon known as climate change.

In the meantime, Nancy Pelosi turns off the lights in the House so that Congress can't vote for increased oil drilling. Then, to compound matters, she takes time off from her book tour to go on "Meet the Press" with liberal shill Tom Brokaw and explain that her personal financial investment in natural gas exploration was simply a means by which to wean Americans away from our dependence on hydrocarbons. Brokaw, either because he didn't know or, more likely, had no intention of embarrassing Madame Speaker, neglected to point out that natural gas is a hydrocarbon!

I find that whenever I write anything insulting about left-wingers in the context of taking them to task over some issue - be it their hysteria over global warming, their cut-and-run approach to Iraq, their laissez faire attitude when it comes to open borders - their response is invariably to attack me personally, never to defend their position.

By this time, I find it more amusing than annoying. There's something rather comforting about it. It's almost like a TV sit com where you know the characters so well that, even before they open their mouths, you're anticipating with great delight that Frank Burns is going to say something unbelievably stupid or Niles Crane is going to say something unbelievably snobbish.

But the thing I find hard to deal with is the remarkably high opinion of themselves that all liberals seem to have. I mean, almost without exception, they regard themselves as civil, sophisticated, and open-minded; in short, all the things that right-wingers aren't and can never hope to be. And yet it's always those open-minded free speech-loving liberals who boo and hiss on college campuses whenever conservatives such as Ann Coulter, David Horowitz, and Justice Clarence Thomas, are invited to speak. It's always those sophisticated liberals who throw pies at those they oppose,

142

and who giggle like school children when people such as Whoopi Goldberg make inane, off-color, remarks about Republicans.

It's the same folks who work themselves into an absolute dither when President Bush misspoke or stuck an extra syllable into "nuclear" who give standing ovations to the likes of those blithering nincompoops, Barbara Boxer and Robert Byrd, people whose every utterance sounds like the incoherent ramblings of a drunken lunatic.

That said, let me assure you I'm well aware that some liberals are very nice people. I count quite a few of them among my circle of friends. And, quite frankly, even I find that fact confounding. But, aside from the fact that I live in Los Angeles and therefore don't have much to choose from, I have come up with a theory that might help explain how this is possible. I think that, by some fluke of nature, a certain number of dogs and cats wind up being born as human beings. I happen to be an animal lover, and one of the things I love best about them is that they can't speak. At least they can't speak a language I understand. Yes, sort of like Senators Boxer and Byrd, now that you mention it.

As sweet and loyal as our pets are, these are animals who lick themselves, walk around naked as jaybirds, and poop in public. If they could speak, I suspect that I, for one, wouldn't care to hear what they had to say. Especially not about politics, for heaven's sake.

So it is, so long as we avoid serious topics, I'm able to endure liberals. Many of them, I can assure you, are as good-natured, fun-loving, and loyal, as my little four-legged pal, Duke.

And yet each has its drawback. With Duke, it's that he barks incessantly if anyone, including yours truly, approaches the front door. With liberals, it's the fact that they insist on voting. Better they should just meow.

Recently, I appeared on a San Francisco radio talk show. I had looked forward to discussing a wide range of topics with the host and his callers. That's why I had emailed a score of my essays to his producer. But I guess nobody bothered to read any of them. Instead, because the host simply introduced me as the author of "Conservatives Are From Mars, Liberals Are From San Francisco," virtually every caller for the entire hour wanted to know what I meant by conservative as opposed to Republican, and wondered why I insisted that, on most matters, I actually regard myself as a libertarian. Long before the hour was over, thanks to a notoriously low boredom threshold, my eyes had rolled back into my skull and I was gasping for oxygen.

Still, I blame myself for giving incomplete answers to a few of their questions. For instance, I claimed that whereas most people have come to expect the federal government to pay for everything, I feel that the feds should be limited pretty much to waging war and guarding our borders. When I was asked why I felt that way, I don't even recall what I replied. But what I should have said was that I am not an anarchist who is opposed to all forms of government, but the more localized government is, the more accountable it is to the people. For instance, it's fairly easy to remove incompetent mayors and corrupt councilmen, but go try to get rid of Charles Schumer or Patrick Leahy.

When asked if I really believed that if the federal government didn't tax us to death, people would actually take up the slack and give more to charity, I said people definitely would. But I should have gone further. I should have pointed out that, long before there was an income tax, Andrew Carnegie, a personal hero of mine, single-handedly created the public library system in America. Or I could have said that when I was earning good money in TV, I would pay for my mother-in-law to come out for annual visits from Nebraska. But when the jobs dried up, I was no longer able to fly her to L.A. It only stands to reason that the more money people have, the more generous they can afford to be.

Furthermore, it makes no sense to send our money to Washington, D.C., just so the politicians can dole it out as they see fit. For one thing, regular charity groups do a better job of it. Most of the money donated to legitimate charities goes to do what the donors intended. But a huge chunk of the money we send to Uncle Sam is skimmed off to finance bloated federal bureaucracies. When a charitable organization misbehaves, the executive director either ends up being fired or jailed.

When Americans are flush, they're the most generous people on earth. Look at the flood of dollars they sent to the survivors of 9/11 even though many of those people were already collecting on life insurance policies. Better yet, think of all the money we kicked in after the tsunami hit a part of the world where many, if not most of the people who were victimized, were Islamics who despise America! And of course, in the wake of Katrina, people all over the country were breaking open their piggy banks.

I'm afraid that too many of us have been bamboozled into buying into the notion that the folks in Washington should be encouraged in their attempts at social engineering. It shocks and saddens me that so many Americans see nothing wrong with the federal government encroaching into every area of our lives. For my part, I don't want the feds doling out small business loans, overseeing our schools, ruling on abortions, and I certainly don't want five idiots on the Supreme Court deciding that eminent domain gives local governments carte blanche to confiscate our homes and businesses in order to increase the tax base.

Understand, it has nothing to do with whether I agree with what the feds are doing, either. If it's wrong when I disagree with their behavior, it's no less wrong when I happen to be in concert. It has to do with the sort of country this is supposed to be. If I wanted Socialism, I would vote for Socialists or move to Sweden.

One of my callers, by the way, said she was all for a Socialistic government. I asked her why she thought that would be a good thing. She replied that people who had more would then have to share with people who had less. I said that I, along with the majority of people I knew, were in favor of sharing, but once it stopped being done on a voluntary basis, it was no longer sharing, it was Communism.

Frankly, I'm afraid that's where we're headed. I suppose it began back in the 30s when Roosevelt and Congress got together and created that alphabet soup of federal agencies. Ever since, Americans have grown more and more accustomed to Washington's usurping individual responsibility. As a result, we have become a nation of brats. We whine when the price of gas goes up, and accept it as our birthright when it goes down. It's as if we think we have a sacred right to pay the same price for fuel as our ancestors. In the meantime, without a squawk, we pay an arm and a leg for bottled water, $3.50 for a box of movie theater popcorn, and of course we keep right on buying cars the size of Sherman tanks.

Like teenagers, we expect Uncle Sam to pay for all the essentials, such as health care and housing, while we blithely blow our allowance on such pricey toys as over-sized TVs and cable service, cell phones, play stations, and $125 sneakers for the kids.

We even have the attention span of children. We get into a war, and immediately demand to know when it will be over - like little kids in the backseat incessantly asking if we're there yet. Can you imagine anybody inquiring of FDR, in 1943, if he had a timetable for withdrawing from North Africa or Italy or Corregidor?

Come to think of it, how is it that once Obama sat down in the Oval Office and took over the war in Afghanistan, those in the mainstream media never pointed out that the Afghanis hadn't attacked us on 9/11, never refer to the conflict as a quagmire and haven't once demanded to know his exit strategy?

I really don't like insulting liberals. It's a dirty job, but, as they say, somebody has to do it. The truth is, I have friends and relatives who are of that political persuasion, although, lately, some of them have started calling themselves progressives. Which is interesting because, back in 1948, when Henry Wallace, with the fervent backing of America's Communists, ran for president, he was the Progressive Party candidate.

Still, most of the liberals I know could be described as reasonably decent people. They try to raise their kids the right way, although they often send their tots off to private schools while denying vouchers to parents poorer than themselves. As a rule, though, I'd say they mean well.

But, sometimes, I swear, you could easily get the idea that they're from Mars, and are just down here for a visit. For openers, look at the cast of characters they rally around. I mean, imagine attending a party - let alone belonging to a party - that included the likes of John Kerry, Charles Schumer, Hillary Clinton, Michael Moore, Jimmy Carter, Patrick Leahy, Nancy Pelosi, Al Franken, Robert Byrd, Bob Beckel, Harry Reid, James Carville, Barbara Boxer, Henry Waxman and George Soros. Unless you had an affinity for humorless blowhards and hypocrites, you'd run screaming out of the house even before the soup was served.

One of the troubles with those on the left is that they don't react to crimes, even crimes of terrorism, the way normal people do. For instance, most of those who devote their careers to defending murderers, rapists and pedophiles, are of the leftist bent, as are the dues-paying members of the criminal-coddling ACLU. Furthermore, most of those deranged people who congregate outside prisons, holding candlelight vigils for serial killers about to meet their maker, are likewise liberals.

And the way they carry on over public displays of religion at Christmas and Easter, you'd think they were as terrified of crosses as Count Dracula.

While conservatives declare war on terrorism, liberals declare quagmires, and demand the announcement of deadlines for withdrawal that would merely serve to encourage Islamic fascists to bide their time.

Liberals always claim they support our troops even as they insisted the young men and women were fighting an unnecessary and illegal war in Iraq. What's more, they invariably take every opportunity to defile thousands of soldiers for the misdeeds of a few. It pretty much mirrors their attitude towards the police. Apparently, the mere sight of a uniform is enough to give these nervous Nellies a case of the vapors.

The same liberals who'd have a conniption fit if the government insisted that every felon in America be provided with a New or Old Testament carry on as if every Muslim terrorist incarcerated at Guantanamo is entitled to a pristine copy of the Koran under the terms of the Geneva Convention.

Liberals are convinced that the 3-strikes law is cruel and unusual punishment. They quail at the idea that a career criminal could go to jail for life for swiping a pizza or walking off with a six-pack of beer. The way they carry on, you'd think they were all criminal defense attorneys or even criminals. For one thing, only a small number of crimes are ever solved. For another, of those few, a sizeable number are plea-bargained down to misdemeanors. Taking all that into consideration, isn't it logical to assume that before anybody is convicted of two felonies, he has probably committed ten felonies or twenty or, more likely, fifty? And knowing that a third conviction might send him back to the cooler for life, wouldn't you think he'd make every effort to keep his nose clean? And if he lacks even that modicum of common sense or survival instinct, shouldn't we assume that he suffers from terminal stupidity, and shouldn't we lock him up not only for our own safety, but for his?

Sometimes, when I listen to the pro-U.N., one-world blather liberals spout, I feel a little like Dorothy in an updated version of "The Wizard of Oz". "Toto, forget Kansas. I don't think we're even in America."

And this time around, when the little mutt pulled the curtain aside, my guess is that the "great and powerful Oz," feverishly working the levers and the smoke machine, would turn out to be a red-faced nutjob who looked an awful lot like Howard Dean and sounded an awful lot like Barney Frank.

The way I see it, if you disagreed with Bush's actions in Iraq, that's your business. But when, like Harry Reid, you first announced that we'd lost the war, and followed that up by claiming the U.S. military had killed a million Iraqi citizens, knowing full well that you're lying through your teeth, it leaves me wondering why it is that one perverted politician is asked to resign for playing footsie in an airport men's room while another gets to continue being the majority leader of the U.S. Senate.

I happen to live in California - arguably the most liberal state in the Union - a state in which the likes of Barbara Boxer, Dianne Feinstein, Jerry Brown, and Nancy Pelosi, all hold high elective office, and Ed Asner, Martin Sheen, George Clooney, Julia Roberts, Sean Penn, Alec Baldwin, Barbara Streisand, and Susan Sarandon, seem to think they do. I'm not asking for your pity, though surely I deserve it. I merely mention my home state because it has provided me with such a perfect laboratory in which to study lefties in their natural habitat.

What first comes to mind isn't even their tedious cant, it's their hypocrisy. They will lecture one and all about global warming. They will disrupt the building of homes and offices, lest a species of snail be displaced. They will nest for months in some tree that a developer - the man who actually owns the tree - wishes to cut down or even move to a different location. They will conduct candlelight vigils if anyone even mentions the possibility of oil drilling in Alaska. However, nowhere on earth will you find more gas-guzzling SUV's on the road. The Hummers in Beverly Hills, alone, are enough to make an army tank commander salivate with envy.

In matters ecological, as in all else, it's always a case with liberals of do as I say, not as I do. You may have noticed that those on the far left have pictured Sarah Palin as the anti-Christ when it comes to ecology because she favors drilling for oil in the Yukon, but they never had a cross word for Saddam Hussein, even though his burning of the Kuwaiti oil fields ranks among the very worst ecological disasters in history.

Liberals are forever bemoaning the plight of the downtrodden, always eager to play the class card or the race card. However, as often as not, they're the ones who own the sweatshops and restaurants where the Hispanics toil for minimum wage. It's in their pricey homes where cleaning ladies and nannies from Guatemala and Honduras mop, vacuum and raise the children, while being paid under the table. Liberals are all for higher minimum wages and a thriving Social Security, just so long as it doesn't cost them an extra dime.

At the drop of a hat, liberals will deliver a speech on the glories of democracy. However, out here, when the citizens overwhelmingly vote for capital punishment or against subsidizing illegal aliens, liberals can always be counted on to rustle up an appeals judge eager to nullify the will of the people.

And isn't it strange that although it's those on the left who constantly claim they're the ones looking out for the poor, the oppressed, the disenfranchised, I've often heard liberals dismiss 250 million of their fellow Americans as "those people we fly over" when going from L.A. to New York. I swear I've never heard a similar remark from a conservative.

Furthermore, isn't it telling that the most poverty-stricken, slumridden cities in America, including Detroit, New Orleans, Philadelphia, St. Louis, Cleveland and Newark, tend to be those municipalities that haven't elected a Republican mayor in the past half century?

A couple of years ago, I received an email from a man I didn't know, in response to a piece I'd written lauding President Bush for preventing a recurrence of 9/11. Not satisfied with merely attacking me as a know-nothing, he proceeded to argue that Bush had only won the election in 2000 because he carried "so many rural states." Clearly, in his universe, only urbanites are real Americans. So, while liberals will sing folk songs celebrating the wonderful folks who build the bridges, till the soil and run the railroads, they just don't want them voting.

Liberals pat themselves on the back for being the only truly color-blind people in society. Yet they're the ones crusading for Affirmative Action, insisting that certain segments of the population be given special status for no other reason than their color. The same people who grew up believing, with good reason, that quotas were reprehensible when they were used to keep Jews out of certain schools made a moral U-turn somewhere along the way and decided that they were just fine when they only worked to the disadvantage of Asian students.

Liberals always brag that theirs is the party of inclusion, proudly boasting that they're home to the likes of Maxine Waters, Al Sharpton and Jesse Jackson - three people most us wouldn't even want to have over for dinner. Waters is the woman, after all, who not only argued for eubonics being taught in inner-city schools, but insisted that crack cocaine was a conspiracy concocted by the C.I.A. to undermine the Black community; and this was long after the newspaper that had published the "scoop" came clean, admitting they'd been taken in by a vile hoax!

Sharpton is the weasel who rode to media prominence by claiming a Black girl had been raped by New York cops. He never recanted, even after the girl confessed she had trumped up the story after spending a weekend shacked up with her teenage boyfriend, to avoid being disciplined by her mother!

Jesse Jackson started out lying about Martin Luther King's dying in his arms, and went on to distinguish himself by calling New York "Hymietown," siring an illegitimate child, raising corporate extortion to an art form, and cavorting with any dictator who'd make a hefty donation to his Rainbow Coalition.

On the other hand, when you hear liberals badmouthing the likes of Clarence Thomas, Thomas Sowell, Michael Steele, Walter Williams, Larry Elder and Condoleezza Rice, you'd think you were listening to old Herman Talmedge laying into some poor Black sharecropper. No matter how distinguished a member of a minority group may be, if he or she doesn't toe the party line, the hounds of the left can be counted on to start barking, "Oreo," "Uncle Tom" and "Sell Out." The irony, of course, is that they are all 50% blacker than President Obama.

For me, there was nothing like hearing a political hack like Ted Kennedy insisting that some honorable American wasn't "Black enough" or "Hispanic enough" to pass muster. Isn't it the least bit odd that Kennedy was allowed to hold down a job in the federal government for all those years even though one could have said with some justification that the Chappaquiddick Kid was never "smart enough" or "decent enough" or even "sober enough" to serve in the United States Senate?

Liberals speak out against special interest groups every chance they get, except of course their own. Exorbitant medical insurance fees, caused by outrageous jury awards, is driving doctors and surgeons out of business, and leaving the state of health care a shambles. However, trial lawyers are making billions, and funneling off a sizable amount to the Democrats. So, not a peep do we hear from the left side of the aisle.

Every objective study confirms that bi-lingual education is a rotten way to teach Spanish-speaking kids. At an age when mastering a new language is a snap, these children are weaned so slowly off their native tongue that many of them never catch up. But, in California, the teachers union, more concerned with its coffers than with the kids, pushed for a bi-lingual curriculum because they successfully lobbied for a contract that pays bi-lingual teachers a 10% bonus. They, too, in turn, tithe the Democrats.

Unlike trial lawyers, whom we all know to be immoral parasites, abettors to rapists and pedophiles, one would hope that teachers would be ashamed to sacrifice their charges for a handful of silver. But, liberals prove over and over again that they are shameless.

Just how hypocritical are those on the left? Well, Sen. Dianne Feinstein, who's made a career out of fighting against a private, law-abiding citizen owning a gun, was once discovered to be a pistol-packing mama. The Hollywood crowd made a big deal out of turning in some of their own artillery, but you may have noticed that their bodyguards never disarmed.

Actor Alan Alda used to give rousing speeches at NOW conventions and receive standing ovations for telling the ladies how he and his wife were equal partners. But for the first eight or nine seasons of "MASH," no woman wrote or directed an episode unless it was one featuring "Hot Lips," in which case Loretta Swit would insist on it. Yet nobody at NOW ever asked Alda, who pretty much ran the show after the first few years, why women weren't given a fair shake. But, then, liberals never put other liberals on the hot seat. Otherwise, they might have asked 75 Democratic congressmen, including Brad Sherman and Henry Waxman, why they voted to continue funding ACORN even after everyone, thanks to Glenn Beck, knew how absolutely vile the organization was.

Years ago, Norman Lear got a standing ovation as loud as Alda's at a NOW convention when he announced that he was donating $250,000 to the organization in the name of Edith Bunker. At the time, he had two vice-presidents in his company, two people who allegedly had equal power and authority. What wasn't equal was their salary. The man was paid $125,000-a-year; the woman, $75,000. So we have Lear, a wealthy contributor to liberal causes and election campaigns, giving away a quarter of a million dollars in the name of a fictional female character, while underpaying a female executive to the tune of fifty grand a year. For what it's worth, he was also widely known to under-pay the women who worked in his office.

Speaking of fictional characters, compare the way that liberals ridiculed Dan Quayle when he suggested it was a shame that Murphy Brown was sending young girls the message that having babies out of wedlock was no big deal, whereas the women in NOW blew kisses to Norman Lear when he donated a small fortune in the name of a fictional sit com character.

But the list goes on and on. Liberals complain that the rich get more money back than the poor when there's a tax cut, ignoring the obvious fact that if you pay more in, it makes sense that you would get more back. I have even heard some of them bemoaning the fact that the very poor wouldn't get any money back, even while acknowledging that low income earners don't even pay federal income tax! One can't help wondering in what bizarre universe these people dwell.

It's the same folks who saw no reason for Clinton to deal with Congress or the U.N. when he invaded Somalia, bombed Sudan and sent troops to Kosovo, who saw no inconsistency in demanding that Bush had to get approval from everyone, including the baseball commissioner and his third grade teacher, before blowing his nose.

Their juvenile placards and slogans insisted that Bush was rushing to war. We all know that he was doing anything but rush, but once liberals glom onto a line they like, they will repeat it, parrot-like, parading with their "No Blood for Oil" and "Bush = Hitler" placards until the cows come home.

Liberals, under the banner of the ACLU, will lead the charge for religious freedom. But when you check the record, you find that the religious practices they defend tend to be those that involve the smoking of marijuana, the ingesting of peyote buttons and the ritualistic slaughter of small animals. Where they draw the line is when it comes to the barbaric practices of hanging Christmas wreaths and lighting menorahs.

Liberals insist they love the Constitution, but they hate the Second Amendment like poison. They insist they love America, but they abhor patriotism. They point to Europe as the role model to which we should aspire, but they never move there. And invariably they fail to acknowledge that, for some crazy reason, people seeking freedom and liberty always seem to be headed our way and never in the opposite direction.

They tell us, when Clinton gets in hot water because of his sexual peccadilloes and his proclivity for perjury, that we should be as sophisticated as the French, and be above such things. They seem to forget that when the man they loved to hate, Richard Nixon, was driven out of office,

151

it was the very same French who couldn't understand what we were getting so excited about. Ah, the French, so continental, so sophisticated, so full of shit. It is my suggestion that the next time Germany or Switzerland or Luxembourg or even little, tiny Monaco decides to invade France, we let them.

I once observed that if liberals didn't have double standards, they'd have no standards whatsoever. Compare the media's approach to Obama with the way they dealt with G.W. Bush. From the very moment that Bush invaded Iraq, he was under constant attack. But now that Obama has his very own war in Afghanistan, I don't hear the same people referring to it as a quagmire, pointing out that the Taliban didn't attack us on 9/11 or demanding that President Obama announce a date for withdrawl.

While mulling over the man who sits in the Oval Office, I was reminded of a riddle from my childhood. You'd be asked what was black and white and read all over, and the answer was a newspaper. These days, I'm afraid the correct answer to what is black and white and red all over is Barack Obama.

A while ago, I saw Obamacare summed up rather succinctly by a picture of an elderly American set adrift on an ice floe. Of course, knowing David Axelrod, Rahm and Ezekiel Emanuel, John Holdren, Cass Sunstein and the AARP, as I have come to know them, I'm sure they'll find a swell way to sell it to us. My guess is that they'll simply call their final solution to the problem of all those pesky old folks wanting medical attention "Obama's Magical Ocean Cruises."

While it goes without saying that it's always open season on Republican politicians, nobody on the Left has ever voiced an honest word about Al Franken. If a Republican even half as dimwitted and obnoxious as Franken were ever elected, don't you think that Bill Maher or David Letterman would have observed how appropriate it is that he represents Minnesota, whose state bird happens to be the loon?

A while back, a blacklisted writer, John Sanford, died at the age of ninety. To his dying day, he remained a dedicated member of the Communist Party. One of his friends, quoted in a fulsome tribute printed in the L.A. Times, said that Sanford's political convictions were set in the 1930s and never wavered. That was intended as a compliment. Imagine a man whose politics were set so deeply in concrete that through seven decades of Stalin, the Hitler pact, the atomic spy trials, the massacres in Cambodia and Hungary, the enslavement of Eastern Europe, Khrushchev's speech to the Soviet Congress, etc., etc., etc., the man never entertained a single doubt that what he believed in his 20s wasn't necessarily so.

Priests have doubts. Nuns have doubts. Nuclear physicists have doubts. I suspect that even God has doubts. Only liberals are immune.

It was once observed, and with some justification, that a man who isn't a liberal at 20 has no heart, and that a man who isn't a conservative at 40 has no brain. And as I see it, if, at 50, he has neither heart nor brain, he'll very likely vote for Ralph Nader or Dennis Kucinich.

Most of the conservatives I know, including myself, started out somewhere else on the political spectrum, and evolved through time and knowledge and experience. I personally do not know of a single case of an individual evolving in the other direction.

I will leave it to the Darwinists to make of that what they will.

Years ago, when I was working in advertising, I was a copywriter on the Mattel account. It should have been fun because they made toys. But it wasn't, mainly because of all the restrictions the FCC placed on commercials aimed at children. In one of the spots I wrote, a little boy, playing with his Mattel racing car on the floor, imagined himself leading the pack at the Indy 500. It never got produced. Even though it would have been shot as an obvious daydream, and even though every little squirt playing with the car would imagine himself winning at the Brickyard, we weren't permitted to show the toys doing anything they couldn't actually do in real life.

So how is it that nobody else ever seems to get called on the carpet for their lies and exaggerations? How is it, for instance, that every liberal from John Kerry to Jesse Jackson can get away with pretending that American Blacks are still living like slaves, and that four decades after the Civil Rights Act, the only thing keeping Blacks out of the cotton fields are Democrats in Washington?

How is it that every rotten movie can get away with lying about how terrific it is? And, unlike other products, they never come with money-back guarantees.

And, finally, how is it that Jimmy Carter, that sanctimonious phony who was a disaster during his four years in the White House and a disgrace in the 30 years since, can pass himself off as equal parts statesman and saint? While most of us wished that he had simply slunk back to his peanut farm after Ronald Reagan whupped his butt in '80, we hadn't realized how starved he was for the spotlight.

A few years ago, you may recall, he was barnstorming all over the country, peddling his book, "Palestine: Peace Not Apartheid." Carter contended that his purpose in writing the book - in the unlikely event it was he and not some anonymous ghost who actually put Carter's vile thoughts on paper - was to open a dialogue about the Middle East. He called upon

America to take what he called a balanced approach to the Israeli-Palestinian problem. He claimed that America unfairly favors Israel because of the Jewish lobby. He also compared Israel to South Africa in the bad old days, equating the fence they've built as protection against suicide bombers with apartheid. What is most telling about all this is that Carter announced that he wrote the book in order to start a dialogue on the issue, but then consistently refused all offers to debate its contents.

One thing you have to say for Carter is that he's never been one to rest on his laurels. Perhaps it helps that he has no laurels upon which to rest.

Not too long ago, he announced, "The male religious leaders have had - and still have - an option to interpret holy teachings either to exalt or subjugate women. They have, for their own selfish ends, overwhelmingly chosen the latter. Their continuing choice provides the foundation or justification for much of the pervasive persecution and abuse of women throughout the world."

He went on to say: "It also costs many millions of girls and women control over their own bodies and lives, and continues to deny them fair access to education, health, employment and influence within their own communities."

Rolling up his rhetorical sleeves, he concluded: "At its most repugnant, the belief that women must be subjugated to the wishes of men excuses slavery, violence, forced prostitution, genital mutilation and national laws that omit rape as a crime."

If you're curious as to what ultimately opened Carter's eyes to the atrocities committed in the name of Allah by his erstwhile friends in the Islamic world, wondering whether it was the slavery, the denial of education and basic human rights or that old Muslim standby, genital mutilation, wonder no more. You see Carter wasn't condemning the barbaric way that Islamics treat their women, he was merely explaining why, at the age of 84, he was leaving the Southern Baptist Church!

Well, I, for one, am heartened that someone finally blew the whistle on the way those doggone Baptists are always forcing their womenfolk to stay in their kitchens for hours on end cooking up Thanksgiving dinners and 4th of July potlucks. It's simply intolerable that such things are still taking place in this day and age in what is allegedly a civilized nation. Even the Muslims can't imagine why Baptist women continue to put up with it.

I anticipate that the next news flash will be the announcement that the 39th president, aka Mr. Peanut, has converted and that, henceforth, he will be known as Kareem bin Carter.

Where does one begin to deal with all the lies foisted off by Mr. Peanut? Would he have called for a balanced approach to Germany and Czechoslovakia or Germany and Poland in the 1930s? Would he have carried Chamberlain's umbrella back from Munich?

Forgetting Jews in Congress and the Senate, why would any American, aside from Steven ("Munich") Spielberg, find a moral equivalency between Palestinians and Israelis? Israel keeps trying to trade land for peace, and they keep getting their school buses and pizza parlors blown up in exchange. For people who are traditionally known to be pretty sharp when it comes to horse-trading, this doesn't seem like a very smart way to conduct business. But, God knows, they keep trying.

Something that Carter, who has often boasted of his close friendship with Yasser Arafat, insists on overlooking is that prior to 1948, the "Palestinians" were in fact the Jews living on the land that was the basis for the modern state of Israel. It was land, mainly sand, they had bought at inflated prices from Arabs for over 50 years. The fact that it is now the Arabs who are known as Palestinians is the result of a clever P.R. firm that suggested if they wanted to picture themselves as underdogs in order to garner sympathy, they should stop calling themselves Arabs. After all, they were only about five million Jews in Israel and about 125 million Arabs surrounding them, and calling for their extinction.

Now, why on earth would Carter call for a balanced approach? After all, Israel, in spite of occasional differences with the U.S., is a staunch ally, one of the few nations that sides with us at the U.N., and is the only western democracy in a part of the world where Islamic Nazis run wild.

Whenever I hear an American claim that he favors Arabs in this ongoing conflict, a conflict perpetuated by a people who think Hitler left the job half-done, I wonder why. Whenever I hear an American claim that people who treat their women like garbage; who elect members of Hamas to leadership positions; who oppose freedom of speech and certainly religion; who cheered and danced on 9/11; and then, for good measure, insisted that Israel was behind the attack; and who pay homage to suicide bombers; are preferable to Israelis, a people who share our values and who are exactly like us, except that they're Jewish, I know that I'm in the presence of an anti-Semite.

Even if he happens to be a former president of the United States.

Somebody recently observed that it is a waste of time to argue with idiots because they drag you down to their level, and then beat you with experience. It's a good line, but not exactly true. What it fails to take into account is that there are so many idiots out there - liberals, Socialists, Obama groupies - that we sane ones get plenty of experience ourselves having to deal with the cuckoos each and every day.

For several decades we have heard that the Republican party is home to the fat cats so that even people who should know better accept the lie as gospel. It's a given that certain groups (the unions, ACORN, criminal attorneys, the oil industry, the environmental industry) will favor one party over the other, but when it comes to those really obese felines, I immediately think of such deep-pocketed lefties as George Soros, Norman Lear, Ben & Jerry's Ben and Jerry, Ted Turner, Bruce Springstein, David Geffen, Barbara Streisand, Oprah Winfrey, Steven Spielberg, Teresa Kerry and 95% of Hollywood's elite. Who are the comparable right-wingers who spring to mind?

The thing I dislike the most about defenders of illegal aliens is that they lie so much. They will say, for instance - with a straight face, mind you - that these people put far more into the economy than they take out in terms of social and health services, education and crime. That's true only if we're talking about the Mexican economy.

Compounding the problem, we see one hypocrite after another moving into Mexico's presidential palace. Calderon is shorter than Fox, but they are otherwise interchangeable. In one of his first statements after assuming the presidency, Calderon claimed that any fence we erect is comparable to the Berlin wall. Do you really think el presidente doesn't know the difference between a wall built to keep people in and one built to keep people out?

I'm not of the opinion that a person has to be perfect in order to point out the failings of others, but liberals take it to such an extreme that you have to wonder if they have any self-awareness at all.

I mean, when someone like George Soros, who collaborated with the Nazis, compared George W. Bush to Adolph Hitler, am I the only one who wondered if he meant it as a compliment?

Or take Janeane Garofalo, who says stupid things with such regularity you might take her for a sulky teenager even though she's in her mid-40s. Because she is an ignoramus and has the self-righteous attitude of an adolescent brat, she was a perfect fit for Air America, where she and Al Franken competed to see which of them could attract fewer listeners.

For those of you who have managed to go through life without ever having heard the nasty sound bites for which she's best known, your good luck is about to run out.

On one occasion, she said, "Our country is founded on a sham. Our forefathers were slave-owning rich white guys who wanted it their way. So when I see the American flag, I go, 'Oh, my god, you're insulting me.' That you can have a gay pride parade on Christopher Street in New York, with naked men and women on a float, cheering, 'We're here and we're queer!' - that's what makes my heart swell. Not the flag, but a gay naked man or woman burning the flag. I get choked up with pride."

Another time she announced, "The world would be better off with multiple superpowers. When the Soviet Union was a superpower, the world was better off."

I'm sure when she shared that thought with her fellow pinheads on New York's upper Westside, there was a lot of solemn head nodding and people turning to one another, martini in hand, and saying, "That little girl has a damn good head on her shoulders."

On the other hand, if she'd make such a moronic statement in Poland, Latvia, the Czech Republic, East Germany or Hungary, I'd like to think she'd have gotten her block knocked off.

It's usually difficult to figure out why anyone who grows up with all the advantages that go with being born in America and enjoying a moderately successful career, would hate the country as much as she does. But, at the risk of being tossed out of the layman's psychiatric association, it's hard not to view her as someone who has devoted her life to rebelling against mommy and daddy. After all, her mother worked as a secretary in the petrochemical industry and her father was an executive with Exxon!

Not too surprisingly, Ms. Garofalo is a confirmed atheist, toured on behalf of Code Pink and campaigned for Howard Dean. Take that, Mom and Dad! For good measure, in the early 90s, she got married in a Vegas chapel. Whether she and the groom, a fellow named Robert Cohen, were or weren't drunk at the time, they soon separated, although, for reasons of their own, never bothered getting divorced.

Although she came to be fairly well known because of her role in "The Truth About Cats and Dogs," she claims she despised the movie because she regards it as anti-feminist. One wonders why, that being the case, she didn't turn down the role after reading the script. But, for someone who is so vehement in her opinion about those she regards as hypocrites, the lady manages to cut herself a great deal of slack.

Ms. Garofalo is barely five feet tall, which meant that in "Cats and Dogs," because the star was Uma Thurman, she often had to stand on a soap box in scenes with the six-foot tall actress. She must have enjoyed the experience because in the 13 years since, she has rarely climbed back down.

Besides having had parents who worked in industries that Ms. Garofalo loathes, she isn't too happy about the hand or, rather, the size and shape God dealt her. As she says about prepping to be a stand-up comedienne, "I was a 36 C or D and at 5'1", I knew that being a small person with big boobs standing in front of an audience was not going to be easy. It would be really hard to get people to pay attention to me without mocking me. Getting a breast reduction to prepare for my career was no different from people who work to get good grades to get into a good graduate school to get a good job. I went down to a B-cup, and it was the best thing in the world."

Now, why would she assume people would mock her just because she was busty? Obviously, it's because if she were the one sitting in the audience, she'd be the one snickering and heckling. On the other hand, it's next to impossible not to mock someone who compares studying hard in college and graduate school to going to a plastic surgeon one afternoon for a breast reduction procedure. Funny, but when I think of something to compare it to, the first thing that comes to mind is a nose job.

She has directed much of her anger over the years at society for putting pressure on women to conform to body image ideals. However, in addition to the breast reduction, in pursuit of a feature role in "Jerry Maguire," she went on a diet and lost a good deal of weight, only to discover that Renee Zellweger had snagged the part.

One could almost feel sorry for her if she wasn't such a nasty piece of work. When speaking about Sarah Palin, Garofalo said, "There is definitely something wrong about her."

I assumed she had something in mind aside from the governor's being smart, attractive and happily married. But when she got down to specifics, the best she could come up with was that Gov. Palin was small-minded and mean-spirited, whereas she, herself, is obviously open-minded and a real sweetie pie.

She has also insisted that anyone who objects to Obama's policies is a racist, although I'm sure she wouldn't make the same claim about people such as herself who take exception to Justice Clarence Thomas's legal opinions.

When it comes to right-wingers in general, she brayed, "The reason a person is a conservative Republican is because something is wrong with them. That's science - that's neuroscience. You cannot be well-adjusted, open minded, pluralistic, enlightened and be a Republican. It's counter-intuitive." That's sure a lot of big words wasted only to prove what a small and petty mind she possesses.

About the tea parties, the all-seeing, all-knowing gnome, who naturally didn't attend one, said, "Let's be very honest about what this is about. This is not about bashing Democrats. It's not about taxes. They have no idea what the Boston Tea Party was about. They don't know their history at all. It's about having a Black man in the White House. This is racism straight up and is nothing but a bunch of tea-bagging rednecks. There is no way around that."

I can't help thinking when the surgeon reduced her breasts, he got carried away and also removed most of her brain.

As if it's not bad enough that she is such an arrogant, ignorant, self-satisfied little twit who, if she'd only grow a big red mustache, would look and sound a lot like Yosemite Sam, but she is also a major sell-out. How else to explain why she'd accept a role on "24," portraying FBI Special Agent Janis Gold, whose mission is investigating terrorists?

But just maybe Janeane Garofalo isn't quite as unaware of the sad truth about herself as she would have us believe. After all, it isn't as if her production company woke up one day and decided to name itself I Hate Myself Productions.

The only real difference between liberals and teenagers is that the people the teens idolize can sometimes sing, dance and/or play a musical instrument. Lefties would say the very same thing about conservatives, but, as usual, they'd be wrong.

Consider our icons for a moment. They tend to be people like Washington, Jefferson and Adams. In modern times, we have Ronald Reagan. When he was president, liberals called him an idiot and called for his impeachment. They claimed he was just another dumb actor, whereas Jimmy Carter, they insisted, had the IQ of a genius. Somehow, they managed to overlook the fact that the genius had allowed the Islamic terrorists to take control of Iran and hold American hostages for years. On the home front, he gave us near-record rates of inflation and unemployment. On the misery index, which is how economists measure such things, he had us at 20.5% when he left office. In human terms, that would be the equivalent of losing your spouse, your dog and your left arm. Not only did Reagan get the economy off life-support, but he managed to hammer the final nail into the Soviet Union's coffin.

Liberals, on the other hand, will put people such as Bill Clinton, Al Gore, Charles Schumer, Barney Frank and Patrick Leahy, on pedestals. Compared to them, teen idols Britney Spears, Miley Cyrus and Lindsay Lohan, don't look half bad.

But if grown-ups think its absurd and unseemly for the MSM to pant over Barack Obama, whose major achievement consists of having won a popularity contest against unpopular John McCain, that's nothing compared to their longstanding love affair with left-wing despots and traitors. Back in the 30s and 40s, the American left went gaga over Joseph Stalin. In the 50s, they demonstrated on behalf of the Rosenbergs and Alger Hiss. In the 60s, they wore little hats adorned with a red star and carried around the Little Red Book in homage to mass murderer Mao Tse-Tung, and, for good measure, sang the praises of the Black Panthers, Abbie Hoffman and the Weather Underground.

And let us not forget Fidel Castro and Ernesto Guevara, better known to his adoring fans as Che. By the way, people began calling him "Che" because it's the Spanish equivalent of "Hey," something he apparently said with even greater and more annoying frequency than John McCain says "My friends" or Caroline Kennedy says "You know."

Castro, lest it be glossed over by Sean ("Milk") Penn's infatuation with the bearded one, dealt with Cuba's homosexual population by either killing them or sticking them in concentration camps. Odd, isn't it, how much more noise the gay community makes about Reverend Rick Warren's giving an invocation than they ever have about the bloody tyrant who's spent the past half century presiding over a reign of terror a scant 90 miles from Florida?

In an article he wrote for the American Thinker, Humberto Fontava reminded us what some of the leading lights on the left have said about Castro, the man on whose behalf Che Guevara happily executed hundreds, perhaps thousands, of Cubans for no bigger sin than their not wishing to replace a dictator named Batista with one named Castro.

It was extortionist Jesse Jackson who said, "Viva Fidel! Viva Che! Long live our cry of freedom!"

Historical revisionist and sometime movie director Oliver Stone claimed, "Castro is very selfless and moral. One of the world's wisest men." Right - as if druggie Stone, good friend of Hugo Chavez, would know the first thing about morality or wisdom.

Ted Turner, who drinks a lot, informed us that Castro is "One helluva guy!"

Harry Belafonte, Hugo Chavez's favorite calypso singer, sounding like Howard Dean at his gooniest, proclaimed, "If you believe in justice, if you believe in democracy, you have no choice but to support Fidel Castro." Well, inasmuch as Castro has ruled over Cuba for 50 years without holding an election, you'd hardly regard him as the poster boy for democracy, but facts rarely get in the way once a pom-pom waving leftist goes into his cheerleading routine.

Jack Nicholson informs us that "Castro is a genius," but that's understandable because in Hollywood, any jackass who directs a movie or even delivers cocaine to a movie set is hailed as a genius.

Speaking of jackasses, another Hollywood ninny who doesn't worry about embarrassing his family and friends by opening his yap, proclaimed, "Fidel, I love you. We both have beards. We both have power and want to use it for good purposes." The speaker was not, as you might have guessed, Barbara Streisand or Arianna Huffington, but Francis Ford Coppola.

Never one to leave his stupidity in doubt, Chevy Chase claimed, "Socialism works. I think Cuba might prove it."

But it's not just those on the left coast who have made goo-goo eyes at Castro. Colin Powell, who should have faded away, as was the lot of old soldiers, according to a British war ballad, instead took the time to tell us, "Castro has done some good things for Cuba." Powell never quite got around to telling us what those things were. Instead, he wound up sounding like the apologists for fascism during the 1930's who never got tired of reminding the world that, thanks to Mussolini, the Italian trains ran on time.

The late Norman Mailer, the moral conscience of New York's upper Westside, who stabbed his wife and also led the campaign to get killer Jack Abbott out of jail, so that, quite predictably, he could murder again, unequivocally stated: "Fidel Castro is the greatest hero to appear in the Americas."

Not one to be left out of any major gathering of morons, George McGovern proclaimed, "Castro is shy and sensitive, a man I regard as a friend."

The fact that Castro has probably defiled more women than Saddam Hussein and his sons, Qusay and Uday, put together doesn't mean a thing to his legion of fans, male and female alike, any more than the fact that Stalin and Mao had more blood on their hands than Hitler. For that matter, I'm sure that the millions of innocent South Vietnamese and Cambodians who died at the hands of the North Vietnamese and Pol Pot's Khmer Rouge never caused Jane Fonda to lose a single night's sleep.

The final irony is that a great many of the same fools who spent eight years carrying signs in the streets condemning George Bush as a warmonger, a man who trashed the Constitution, traded American blood for Arab oil and who, worst of all, mispronounced "nuclear," go home to walls that are covered with pin-up pictures of Castro and Guevara.

For that matter, would any of us be terribly surprised to learn that just looking at his Che poster sends a shiver up Chris Matthew's leg?

Speaking of Chris Matthews reminds me there are two kinds of awards in this world - good ones and bad ones. It is simple enough to distinguish between them. I am the recipient of the former and other people are recipients of the latter. But if it were up to me, there would be a moratorium on all of them. They just keep getting dumber and dumber. I mean, I refuse to believe that I'm the only person who is sick and tired of seeing the likes of Michael Moore, Al Gore and "It's Hard Out Here for a Pimp" win Oscars and people like Yasser Arafat, Jimmy Carter and Al Gore, taking home Nobel Peace Prizes.

Let's face it, if they simply drew names out of a hat, the folks who hand out these things could hardly do worse. At least on "Dancing With the Stars," the winners have to know how to do a mean tango.

Out here in Los Angeles, the sidewalks of Hollywood Blvd. are not only lined with bums and pimps, but with bronze stars commemorating celebrities, past and present. What they don't tell the tourists who stand gawking at names of people they've never heard of is that the honorees have to fork over thousands of dollars to defray the cost of installing the star and the ceremony that goes with it.

But of all the silly awards, the most mind-boggling that I've come across recently is the Emery Reves Award for Lifetime Achievement in Journalism that was bestowed to - hold on to your hats, ladies and gentlemen - Chris Matthews!

Because the late Mr. Reves, born Revesz Imre in Hungary, was Winston Churchill's friend and literary agent, the award allegedly honors "excellence in writing or speaking about Churchill's life and times, or by applying his precepts and values to contemporary issues among the English-speaking peoples." It reminds me of a line from "The Maltese Falcon": "The cheaper the crook, the gaudier the patter."

In any case, Mr. Reves has been dead since 1981 and, so, he's in no position to point out that Churchill would be spinning in his grave if he thought that anyone in his right mind would confuse his precepts and values with those of a jackass like Matthews. One can almost hear the old man thundering: "They must have me confused with that umbrella-toting ninny, Neville Chamberlain!"

At the awards dinner, someone actually stepped up to the microphone and, with a straight face, said: "Mr. Matthews' passion for a free and open press and the public debate that it sparks is legendary. He is an enthusiastic supporter of democracy and has been a learned member of the news reporting fraternity throughout his distinguished and prolific career."

But, nary a word about the fact that he is a knee-jerk mouthpiece for the Left and should, by all rights, be drawing a weekly paycheck from the DNC, or that he can't manage to get through a single sentence without spitting.

Next year, rumor has it, Matthews is on the short list for the Nobel Peace Prize. Now that Barack Obama has his, so far as I can see, his only real competition is Mahmud Ahmadinejad.

One of the obvious differences between liberals and conservatives

162

is how they regard the United Nations.

My wife would like to see us kick the United Nations out of the United States. I, for one, think it's a swell idea. What's more, I'm certain that most New Yorkers feel the same. After all, for the past six decades this gang of scofflaws have taken advantage of their diplomatic immunity to be the worst kind of guests. Double-parking is the least of it.

My own reason for wanting the U.N. padlocked is because I object to corruption and hypocrisy being passed off as high mindedness. I heard rumors that Kofi Annan, which sounds like a 12-step program for caffeine addicts, collected a nice piece of change out of Iraq's phony oil-for-food program. But my problem with the organization is more basic than that, although it does explain how it is that Mr. Annan seemed to have a more expensive wardrobe than George Clooney.

People such as John Kerry are always eager to get the U.N.'s good housekeeping seal of approval before America makes a foreign policy decision. Or at least Kerry and company do when there's a Republican in the White House. I don't seem to recall its having been quite so imperative when Clinton and Lewinsky were holding down the Oval Office.

Be that as it may, what nation in its right mind would surrender even a scintilla of its sovereignty to a group as loathsome as the member states of the U.N.? I would sooner trust the Mafia to call the shots. You think I'm indulging in hyperbole? At least I have no reason to think that, for all its faults, the Costa Nostra hates America. I mean, consider that among the regimes having votes are the likes of Cuba, China, the Democratic People's Republic of Korea (North Korea to you), Laos, Cambodia, Rwanda, Myanmar, Sudan, Uganda, and several dozen Muslim-dominated dictatorships running the gamut from Bahrain to Yemen. And that's not even counting France.

Understand, the U.N., while going ballistic over America's rescuing Iraq from Saddam Hussein's iron grip, did nothing about genocide in Rwanda and the Sudan. The U.N., while taking every opportunity to chastise Israel, treated Yasser Arafat as if he were another Mother Teresa and his gang of suicide bombers were just so many good Samaritans going about their business.

But even aside from all that, I counted 33 member nations with populations under 1,000,000. In fact, there are a baker's dozen with populations under 100,000! We don't call places that size countries, we call them counties or neighborhoods. The total population of those 33 countries, ranging alphabetically from Andorra (67,509) to San Marino (24,521), is slightly in excess of 10 million, the same as Seoul, Korea, for crying-out-loud! If you can believe it, there are only 16,952 people in Palau. Palau has a seat in the United Nations, and, what's more, their ambassador can park anywhere he damn well pleases!

It so happens Palau is an ally of America's, but do you really want, say, San Marino having a say in matters of America's foreign policy? On top of all that, the U.S. not only pays most of the freight for the U.N., but we don't even charge them rent. Can you imagine what someone like Donald Trump would pay for that piece of real estate?

So, give me one good reason why these good-for-nothing freeloaders shouldn't be sent packing. Let them set up camp in the Hague or Geneva or Fallujah, for that matter.

If someone feels the absolute need for America to belong to a fraternal organization, I would suggest something a tad more selective, something like the Elks or a summer bowling league.

At this time, probably the most controversial part of our Constitution is the Second Amendment, and, frankly, I can't understand why liberals are so opposed to Americans owning guns.

First, though, I have a terrible confession to make. You see, even though I am not a hunter, never really considered Charlton Heston a very good actor, and only recently joined the NRA - mainly so I could wear their cap and annoy my liberal acquaintances - I have no objection to my fellow citizens owning guns.

Besides, with a kazillion guns already in circulation, Brady Bill or no Brady Bill, I'm afraid we'll never again see the day that criminals have to make do with rocks and sharp sticks.

Oddly enough, it's often the very same people who get irate about their neighbors having the means to defend themselves who are the folks most opposed to mandatory sentences for gun-toting felons. It's as if they're against the possession of guns by amateurs, but hate the idea of denying professionals the necessary tools of their trade.

Where guns are concerned, statistics and common sense rarely have the power to sway a liberal's opinions. They simply won't accept the idea that guns are ever used defensively to safeguard the innocent. So far as they're concerned, the Founding Fathers were all drunk the day the drafted that part of the Bill of Rights having to do with bearing arms.

In terms of public relations, I think it would be wise if just once, when some kid blasts a schoolmate, Michael Moore and the rest of the anti-gun crowd didn't take such obvious delight in using the incident to beat the opposition over the head. In a nation of 300 million people, probably close to 7 or 8% of whom are here illegally, bad stuff is going to happen.

It's a rotten shame, but it's unavoidable. Believe me, schoolyard bullies and math exams are a far bigger source of terror to most of our kids.

There is conclusive proof that the anti-gun zealots are less concerned with the safety of young people than they are with their own holy mission; otherwise, they would put guns on the back burner and concentrate, instead, on getting teenagers off the road. In a country where millions of adolescents are encouraged to start driving cars - cars fueled by a deadly mixture of gasoline and high-octane hormones - one can only laugh at the anti-gun crowd's pretense that public safety is their number one priority.

The battle, for the most part, comes down to liberals vs. conservatives. As usual, liberals turn their backs on common sense, preferring to appear compassionate.

Because they are stuck with an agenda, liberals are forced to parrot anti-gun propaganda even when, like the late columnist Carl Rowan and Sen. Dianne Feinstein, they, themselves, are discovered to be packing heaters. And surely I wasn't the only person who yawned when Sharon Stone made such a big deal of turning in her roscoes. The point might have been made more forcefully if her bodyguards had turned in theirs.

Do I think everyone should have a gun? Of course not. But is that something that keeps me up at nights? Hardly.

Of far greater concern to me are the yahoos driving around in those lethal, over-sized, gas-guzzling, lane-straddling, sport-utility vehicles. Armed with a feisty attitude and a few tons of steel, every soccer mom has become a full-fledged menace to society. I swear, there are more tanks to be found in the parking lot at the local supermarket than Gen. George Patton had to face during the entire North African campaign.

I don't know how long urban legends have been with us, or why it is we never hear about rural or even suburban legends, but it seems to me there's been a major change in these silly things over the past few years.

It used to be that one would hear about little carnival lizards being flushed down toilets and morphing into huge man-eating alligators in the city's sewer systems. Or occasionally one would hear tell of a boa constrictor mysteriously showing up in some city dweller's apartment. Another popular urban myth concerned a cuckold filling up his rival's car, typically a convertible, with cement.

But these days, the most common folk tale is that every kid who is killed by a cop or a gang member is an honor student, sort of the way that tabloids used to identify every hooker who was ever arrested or murdered as a Hollywood starlet.

I first became aware of this phenomenon when my son was in high school. At least every other month, or so it seemed, I would read about some poor innocent teenager, invariably an honor student, being shot down in the street. Nearly without fail, when I'd ask my son if he knew the victim, he'd inform me that the 10th or 11th grader was a known drug dealer.

In the area of youthful criminality, things have become so absurd that whenever a Black or Hispanic teenager is arrested, we are assured by his mother, his attorney and a complicit media, that he's the one who is the victim - a victim of a bigoted white society and a racist police force. Not too long ago, a 13-year-old punk here in L.A. swiped a car, went joy-riding, and when he was finally cornered, tried to drive over the cops . When an officer shot him in self-defense, his mother was treated like the parent of a martyr. Nobody dared ask her where she was and what she was doing when the adolescent was out on the streets committing mayhem at 4 a.m.

Funny, for years whites were told we were never to refer to Blacks, no matter their age, as boys. But let one of these teenage gang-bangers get collared for anything from rioting to rape and, suddenly, everyone from their lawyers to the editorial staff at the L.A. Times is insisting they're only boys, just tots, mere toddlers.

The other big lie that's caught on in a big way is global warming. I suspect this is strictly an urban legend because in rural America, farmers have the experience and the common sense to recognize the cyclical nature of climate.

Because of the unusually cold winter we've been having here in Southern California, I've given a good deal of thought to the subject. What I find so fascinating about it is that Al Gore's disciples are able to explain all types of weather as a result of it. If it's unreasonably warm, we not only know why, but we know we can lay the blame on those good-for-nothings driving their gas-guzzlers to the supermarket. It might even sound reasonable if you were unaware that changes in the earth's weather occur on an irregularly regular basis, and that just a short time ago these same junk scientists were warning us about global cooling and an impending modern Ice Age.

As I'm sure you've noticed, freezing cold weather is also blamed on global warming! In other words, no matter what the result is, the cause remains the same.

In a way, it reminds me a lot of religion. The true believer gives God credit for everything. If something wonderful occurs, it's because of God's innate goodness. But when it's something awful - something like an earthquake, childhood leukemia or a holocaust - the faithful will insist, "God moves in mysterious ways. We can't hope to read His mind, but we know He had His reasons."

166

I am not a religious person, but if I'm going to accept anything on faith, I would prefer to lay my money on an invisible force than on Al Gore. God, we're told, somehow managed to create the seas and the stars, dogs, deer, peaches, sunsets, and man, himself, and also found the time to act as a muse for Johann Sebastian Bach, Thomas Jefferson and, I suspect, the fellow who invented baseball. On the other hand, we have Al Gore, the pumpkin-headed schnook who couldn't even carry his home state in a presidential election and claims to have created the Internet, but never quite got around to getting a patent.

On top of all that, God doesn't live in a mansion with just Tipper for company, doesn't fly all over the world in fuel-guzzling private jets and hasn't become a multi-millionaire by scaring children and gullible adults with tales of rising oceans and vanishing species.

Before the last presidential election, I heard a great many people say that, thanks to the media running interference for Barack Obama, they didn't feel they knew very much about the man. I, on the other hand, felt I knew more about him than any candidate who had run in my lifetime!

I knew that he believed in the Marxist principle of sharing the wealth through coercion, and I knew that didn't refer to his own wealth, but to everybody else's. I knew that he shared Mrs. Obama's lack of pride in America, and that, in his gut, he believed America is a racist nation.

I knew he shared Rev. Wright's hatred of white people. Because he depended on their votes, he kept that belief under wraps, but it certainly came through loud and clear in his books.

I knew that the people he surrounded himself with, people like Wright, Father Pfleger, Louis Farakhan, Tony Rezko and Bill Ayers, were vile. And the ones whom he was forced by circumstance to be allied with, people like Ted Kennedy, Nancy Pelosi, Harry Reid, Henry Waxman, Maxine Waters and John Murtha, weren't much better.

Because even his disciples realized that Sen. Obama could barely identify such places as Iraq, Syria, Israel and Afghanistan, on the map, he selected an old political hack like Joe Biden as his running mate. Joe Biden was supposed to supply the foreign affairs expertise Obama lacked. It reminded me of the days when I was working in TV and was trying to get comedies on the air. The problem was that the networks only wanted to produce pilots written by people who had experience producing sit coms. So, even though I had written for the likes of MASH, Bob Newhart, Family Ties, Mary Tyler Moore and Rhoda, they preferred being in business with people who had written and produced lousy sit coms. So it is with Joe Biden. The man has plenty of experience, but the problem is that he has always been wrong. Just one major example was his vote against Desert

Storm. He would have gladly stood by while Saddam Hussein took over the oil fields of Kuwait. He never has bothered to explain his reasoning, but when it only takes about 200,000 votes to win a senatorial election in Delaware, I guess all it takes to be elected are hair plugs and painted teeth.

It occurs to me that politicians continue, as a matter of P.R., to refer to themselves as public servants. If so, they are the only servants in the history of mankind to not only make more money than their masters, but are the ones who insist on giving all the orders.

Because we saw this election as the most important in our lifetime, my wife and I cast our absentee ballots several weeks early. We wanted to be certain that our votes would count even if we died in the meantime. It's nothing new. Heck, dead Democrats have been casting votes for years and, thanks to ACORN and complicit state governments, they still are. ACORN even registered cartoon characters. In at least one case, Barney Frank, we even have an example of a cartoon character who managed to get elected to Congress.

It astounds me that Democrats continue to paint Republicans as plutocrats when actual plutocrats like Boxer, Feinstein, Schumer, Kerry, Clinton and even a guy named Rockefeller, sit in the Senate, and people like George Soros, Barbara Streisand, George Clooney, Warren Buffet, Bill Gates and Oprah Winfrey, fill their coffers. I used to wonder why Soros, a bottom-feeder who made his fortune in the questionable business of currency trading, would align himself with the far left wing of the Democratic party. Then, one day, it occurred to me that I used to describe John Howard Lawson, a hack screenwriter who once ran the Communist party in Hollywood, as a man who was born to run a gulag. I now believe that Soros sees himself as a major honcho in a new Soviet United States, a man in charge of the brutes who would run the gulags.

During the presidential campaign, we were told that Barack Obama was another Lincoln. At the time, I recall thinking that he might very well be another Lincoln, but certainly not Abe. Then we were told he was another FDR, which was certainly closer to the truth, and not just because they both smoked cigarettes and made Narcissus look like a shrinking violet. But, now that he's been in office for a while, he mostly reminds me of Wile E. Coyote. He thinks he's very clever, but he keeps falling off the cliff while holding the anvil he intended to drop on the Roadrunner.

I felt that those people who insisted in 2008 that, down deep, Obama was a Muslim were being unfair. While I had to question what sort of Christian would have sat in Jeremiah Wright's church, soaking up all the racist swill for 20 years, at least the Trinity United Church of Christ wasn't a mosque. But I have to confess Obama seems to be doing everything he can to make me question my earlier judgment.

At a time when Iran, not to mention North Korea, is shaking a nuclear-armed fist at the world, Obama is telling Russia he'd like to dismantle our nuclear weapons. I'm afraid that, as a means of providing America with a viable national defense, his approach verges on the suicidal. On the other hand, if it was his intention to join the likes of Kofi Annan, Yasser Arafat, Al Gore, Le Duc Tho and Jimmy Carter, as Nobel Peace Prize winners, it proved to be an absolutely brilliant strategy.

As if his kowtowing to Saudi Arabia's King Abdullah wasn't contemptible enough, Obama then flew to Turkey, where he announced: "We convey our deep appreciation for the Islamic faith, which has done so much over so many centuries to shape the world for the better, including my own country."

Even those of us who never entirely bought the notion that Obama had been born in Kenya began giving it careful consideration after that asinine remark. For years now, atheists have balked at the idea that the United States was created by a group of extraordinary Christians who shared Judeo-Christian values. But even they only went so far as to insist that some of our forefathers weren't Christians, but were merely deists. But until now, nobody had ever seriously suggested that Washington, Jefferson, Adams, Madison and Monroe, drew their inspiration from the Koran.

It is at such times that one can easily understand why the question about Obama's citizenship continues to plague so many people. Which leads me to admit that I have always been befuddled by the notion of dual-citizenship. As a concept, it's illogical. As a matter of national policy, it's insane. What truly confounds me is how it's possible that dual citizenship is legal, but bigamy isn't.

As if all these gaffes weren't bad enough, we have the current administration bowdlerizing the language. There are thousands of American G.I.s being deployed to Afghanistan, but nobody is permitted to call it a "surge" because it might remind people that Sen. Obama voted against the surge in Iraq.

God forbid we mention "Islamic fascism," lest King Abdullah forget how cute our president looked bowing and scraping to him. Furthermore, we are no longer supposed to call "the war on terrorism" the war on terrorism because, I suppose, it might give certain people the idea that we actually hold a grudge against the barbarians responsible for 9/11.

So far as I'm concerned, the only term they've come up with that I approve of is "man-caused disaster," which was invented by Janet Napolitano. Understand, I don't sanction her using it as a euphemism for 9/11.

The only reason I like it is because I think it so perfectly defines the Obama presidency.

Along similar lines, I have long wondered how it is that something as asinine and clearly un-American as the Congressional Black Caucus can exist. I mean, as embarrassing as the rest of Congress is, these jackasses take the prize. The idea that members of the House should be separated on the basis of color, even on a voluntary basis, is undeniably racist. Still, I can see where if I were a congressman, I would welcome any excuse to be as far away as possible from the left-wing lunkheads who make up the Caucus.

Six of its members, Barbara Lee, Bobby Rush, Melvin Watt, Laura Richardson, Marcia Fudge and Emanuel Cleaver II, flew down to Cuba on a junket and came home raving about their visit to Castroland.

In their collective ability to turn a blind eye to the victims of this 50 year old Communist tyranny, the dirty half dozen remind me of the dupes who came back from the Soviet Union in the 1930s, rhapsodizing about the glories of the workers' paradise, while managing to overlook the intentional starvation of millions of peasants, the torture and executions of anti-Communist intellectuals, the Siberian gulags, rampant anti-Semitism and political assassinations.

Behind their backs, Stalin parroted Lenin, referring to them as useful idiots. However, I think when it comes to Barbara Lee and her fellow loonies, even Stalin would have been hard-pressed to call them anything but useless.

Judging by my email, a great many conservatives are counting down the days until they next get to vote in 2010. They hope and pray that Americans will come to their collective senses and undo some of the horrors unleashed by the last presidential election.

Naturally, I hope they're right. But I'm not sure that it will be enough to sound the alarm that the sky is falling because, by then, I suspect it may have already fallen. Besides, I'm not convinced that most of my fellow citizens have a problem with the direction that Obama, Pelosi and Reid, have taken us during this past year. At the rate that Obama and the liberals are going, when it comes to piling up the national debt; nationalizing banks and major companies; scuttling our missile defense system; reaching out to Islamic and Communists tyrants; breaking our promise to defend Poland and the Czech Republic; funding the SEIU, ACORN, AmeriCorps and Hamas; discussing nuclear disarmament with Russia at the same time that Iran, Pakistan and North Korea are gearing up; talking tough to Israel while currying favor with the Arabs and the Islamics; I have no idea what will be left to salvage by November, 2010.

Still, if you know where to look, there are certain ironies one might find amusing. For instance, ever since Obama came on the scene, his supporters have insisted that, unlike George W. Bush, Obama would have influence with the other world leaders, particularly with those who speak German, French, Spanish and Italian. How surprised his disciples must have been when Obama begged for European cooperation in fighting the Taliban in Afghanistan and all he heard was a chorus of nein, non, nunca and nospeaka the English.

But, then, anyone who seriously expects the Europeans to take up arms is the same person who believes that rabbits lay Easter eggs. No western European nation would want to risk its well-deserved reputation for unenlightened self-interest by ever doing the decent thing.

You might think there would be some small feeling of obligation to the country that saved Europe from the Nazis in the 1940s and from Soviet domination over the following four decades, but that would be asking the impossible of governments that regard gratitude as an unseemly emotion and confuse arrogance with sophistication.

Frankly, if it didn't constitute such a direct threat to the United States, I would rather enjoy the ongoing spectacle of the Muslims finally, after a thousand years, conquering Europe.

Speaking of Muslims, about whom Obama, as was the case with Bush, can never say enough nice things, I'd like to know why America has decided to sign on as defenders of the faith. We went into Kosovo, Kuwait, Iraq, Somalia and Afghanistan, to protect people who despise us and want us dead. For good measure, when a tidal wave hit Indonesia, we sent over a billion dollars in aid. That was back before Obama, when a billion dollars was still a lot of money, and was far more than any of the oil-rich nations sent to bail out their fellow Muslims.

To top things off, we elected a fellow named Barack Hussein Obama, who rushed off to Turkey on the taxpayers' dime to tell them how large a role Islamics have played in American history.

One thing I must say for Obama is that he has become very adept at bowing. First there was that memorable kowtow to King Abdullah, and he quickly followed that up by taking numerous bows for the rescue of Capt. Richard Phillips. We were all delighted that, thanks to the U.S. military, the captain was saved from Somali pirates, but the only people who deserved congratulations were Commander Frank Castellano, the Navy SEALs and the fantastic marksmen who hit their three targets. The only thing the Commander in Chief did was to prolong the nightmare for Capt. Phillips and his family by saying that no action should be taken unless the hostage's life appeared to be in imminent danger.

If this is the administration's approach to hostage negotiations, we can better understand why Obama and Biden are insisting that Israel take no preemptive action against Iran. Apparently, no imminent danger can be assumed until Tel Aviv is nuked off the face of the earth.

It pains me to admit it, but there are certain times when I find I am ashamed of my beloved country. One of my saddest moments was watching the last helicopter lifting off from the roof of that CIA safe house in Saigon, leaving behind our South Vietnamese and Cambodian allies to the tender mercies of Pol Pot and Jane Fonda's other murderous chums.

Another occasion was when our president went to Europe and, doing his rather uncanny impression of Michael Moore, apologized for American arrogance. Naturally, his own arrogant words were greeted with great applause from a pack of jackals who would have been under the boot of Hitler or Stalin, except for America's hatred of tyranny, its unrivaled display of courage and fortitude, and its sacrifice of treasure and blood.

The way that liberal politicians and Hollywood celebrities carry on over the plight of poor people, you might easily get the idea that they actually know some. They don't. Why would they when they only hang around with each other?

Those two groups are made up entirely of narcissists. Who else would want or need to exist entirely in the spotlight? They're like moths. The irony is that, physically, the two groups couldn't be more different and, yet, on a per capita basis, they probably spend the same amount on Botox, collagen and plastic surgery. When it comes to nips, tucks and hair transplants, alone, Hillary Clinton, Nancy Pelosi and Joe Biden, have spent enough money to keep several poor families in vittles for years to come.

Speaking of appearances, I can see the attraction of politics. In no other field, except perhaps for rock and roll, are so many homely people described as highly photogenic sex symbols. I first became aware of this phenomenon when John Kennedy, a man who in his early 40s already had an impressive set of jowls, was sold to us as a combination of Tyrone Power and Cary Grant. Then along came Bill Clinton, a pudgy fellow with a big red nose and little piggy eyes, who most closely resembled W.C. Fields, and yet even he apparently made liberal women swoon. Now we have Barack Obama, a man boasting ears that would put Dumbo to shame, a man who looks like he could leave Air Force One in the hanger and just let a strong breeze carry him wherever he wants to go.

It's not just the politicians, but also their mates, so long as they're Democrats, who get the star treatment. Take Michelle Obama ... if you would be so kind. Every time I turn around, there she is on a magazine cover. Now, normally, like the Mafia, I lay off the spouses, but inasmuch as this particular spouse attended the same racist church as her hubby for 20 years, I'll make an exception in her case. After all, in spite of the fact that affirmative action got her an Ivy League degree and her hubby's crooked Chicago cronies got her a $7,000-a-week salary and that, moreover, America has sent billions of dollars for no particularly good reason to Africa, she insisted this is a mean country and that, until Barack ran for president, she had never been proud of America.

Naturally, the liberal media is now trying to convince us that she has all the allure, glamour and fashion sense of Jackie Kennedy. I have even heard her upper arms described in the sort of language Wordsworth devoted to flowers in the morning dew and that Keats lavished on nightingales. Frankly, if I were Mrs. Obama and the geeks started rhapsodizing about my triceps, I might consider wearing sleeves.

But there's no getting around the fact that Barack is the bigger menace. His latest money-burning crusade is universal health care. It was bad enough when the Clintons pushed for it 15 years ago. It hasn't improved with age.

If it were up to me, basic health insurance would only cover catastrophic injuries and diseases. If hypochondriacs feel they have to see a doctor every time they sneeze, that kind of coverage can be handled the same way as car, life and fire insurance. People could write a check and pay for it themselves. As P.J. O'Rourke observed: "If you think health care is expensive now, just wait until it's free."

A friend of mine thinks that one way to lower the price of medical care is through tort reform. He thinks that so long as lawyers can put physicians through the meat grinder, doctors will be forced to keep raising their fees in order to cover their insurance bills. It was my friend's suggestion that if somebody sues a doctor for malpractice and loses the case, he should be liable for all the court costs. I pointed out that no poor person, no matter how badly maimed, could then afford to sue and run the risk of losing, and that no lawyer could afford to take the case on a contingency basis.

My solution was that no lawyer would be allowed to sue a doctor if he had sued a medical practitioner, say, twice before and lost. That would at least prevent the worst sort of shyster from making a career out of chasing ambulances.

One of the things that concerns me about Obama's presidency is that every time he opens his yap, he sounds so darn naive. A while ago, he spoke about reaching out to moderates in the ranks of the Taliban. A moderate in that society is a cretin who wants to murder Christians, Jews and any woman who refuses to wrap herself in a bed sheet before leaving the house, but who draws the line at beheading his victims for Al-Jazeera's TV cameras.

I find it hard to believe that the majority of saps who voted for Obama would do it all over again even though he has been spending money in a way that would give drunken sailors a bad name, while Wall Street and Main Street both begin to resemble Tobacco Road. It seems that when people described Obama as charismatic, they didn't mean he was particularly bright, only that he was able to convince a lot of dummies that liver-and-onion flavored ice cream tastes better than chocolate or vanilla.

The way things are headed, it seems that Khrushchev almost got it right. The Soviet Union didn't bury us, as he predicted, we simply dug our own grave. We went Socialist without a bomb being dropped or a shot being fired. The coup took place in election booths all over America, and anyone who doesn't regard it as a tragic event didn't deserve being born here.

Recently, the following message has been all over the Internet: It's a Recession when your neighbor loses his job. It's a Depression when you lose your job. It's a Recovery when Obama loses his.

Amen.

CHAPTER ELEVEN

A Few Concluding Remarks

Liberals have become so accustomed to having only their own points of view disseminated by the mass media that they now believe that any opinions in conflict with their own is an infringement on their right to free speech. So not only do they feel entitled to spout off ad nauseam, but honest disagreement is regarded as censorship!

What they enjoyed before talk radio and the Internet bloggers came along was a virtual news monopoly, consisting of the New York Times, the Washington Post, and the three major networks. All of which could be counted on to parrot the liberal line. Now, like spoiled two-year-olds being forced to share their toys, they can't stop whining.

Frankly, I'm amazed that liberals can be wrong so often about so many things. One of the few issues they are occasionally right about is protecting the environment. But even in that area, they manage to botch it. The radical element that infests their ranks are always trying to stop any and all forms of development, the source of homes and jobs for those of us who don't want to live in caves. Their love for Mother Earth leads them to blow up buildings, bomb car dealerships, and sabotage logging sites, all with an air of moral superiority. They don't, in fact, love snail darters, spotted owls or Alaska's caribou, anymore than the rest of us; they merely hate western civilization in much the same way that Islamic fundamentalists do.

A fact worth noting is that during LBJ's administration, a group of tree huggers got an injunction to prevent the feds from working on a certain project down South, for fear it would harm the environment. The project involved shoring up the levees of...New Orleans.

I would think the hardest part of being a liberal is always having to remember to spout the party line, just like old-time Stalinists. For instance, they must always remember to parrot the propaganda that they, every bit as much as conservatives, support a strong military.

The basic difference, of course, is that they don't want it to do anything.

Sometimes, people ask me why I invariably identify myself as a conservative, and not a Republican. The first, I point out, is a philosophy, while the latter is a political party. A philosophy can afford to be pure as the driven snow. A party, on the other hand, has to deal with the nitty-gritty of fund-raising and electing candidates. I accept the realities of politics. Furthermore, I know too much about human nature to ever have my illusions shattered. Unlike my fellow conservatives, I don't believe it when an office seeker of any political persuasion vows he'll cut spending and clear out all the bloated bureaucracies once he or she is elected and goes off to Sacramento, Springfield, Albany, Montgomery, Austin, or especially, Washington, D.C. It simply goes against every instinct known to man to seek office with the intention of having less money, power and influence, than one's predecessor.

I have no way of knowing whether the Republican party will go the way of the Whigs, the Bull Moose and the dodo bird. But perhaps it should. After all, when they held control of the House, the Senate and the Oval Office, for the first six years of President George W. Bush's administration, they were lazy, inept, corrupt and dedicated to expanding the federal government and spending every last tax dollar they could lay their hands on. In other words, they behaved just like Democrats.

To give Bush his due, he prevented a recurrence of 9/11, a notable feat when you realize how desperately the Islamics wanted it to happen again and again. However, he did nothing to prevent the financial crisis from taking place. What's more, when it did occur, he, like McCain, never laid the blame for it at the feet of people like Obama, Chris Dodd and Barney Frank. I never could figure that out. Just as I could never figure out why Bush kept paying lip service to Muslims. Was he afraid he and Laura wouldn't be invited to the really cool Ramadan parties?

God knows I kept trying to give sound advice to McCain once he got the nomination, but I guess he was too busy studying the campaign strategies of George McGovern, Michael Dukakis and Bob Dole, to notice.

If there is one thing that the next Republican presidential candidate should take away from this latest debacle it's that, for all the pandering that Bush and McCain did with their open border policies, McCain, aka Mr. Amnesty, only received a smidgen of the Latino vote. So, while in some parallel universe, a Republican might be cutting into the Jewish, Black and Hispanic blocs, here in America, for all the feel-good chatter about the big Republican tent, going after those votes is time and money misspent. Frankly, when you look at the demographics, the forecast for conservatives in America is none too bright. Democrats, after all, breed at a far faster rate and young people just keep getting dumber.

I hate to be a gloomy Gus, but Obama's victory really got me down. The inspiration for other presidents was often supplied by the likes of

Washington, Adams, Jefferson, Franklin and Lincoln; we now have a guy who draws his moral and intellectual concepts from the likes of Wright, Ayers, Rezko, Pfleger, Alinsky and Khalidi.

Liberal minorities in Congress were bad enough, but with a radical leftist in the White House, one can imagine the judges who will be appointed to lifetime sinecures on the Supreme Court and the various courts of appeal. You think Stevens, Ginsburg and Kennedy are bad? You ain't seen nothing yet.

This brings us to Sonia Sotomayor. The truth is I would have been opposed to any judge appointed by President Obama. That's not to say I was sad to see Justice Souter leave. In fact, I thought his decision to retire was the first good decision he'd made in 19 years. But how could any member of Congress vote to seat Ms. Sotomayor on the Supreme Court after hearing her say that the courts are where policy is made? What did she think those various senators and congressmen were paid to do? Okay, bad question; I admit I don't know, either. But I do know that judges aren't supposed to make policy decisions.

Furthermore, the fact that she also believed that her experience as a Latina would not only cause her to rule differently from other jurists, but that, being a Puerto Rican woman would make her a better judge than a white male not only argues against her superiority, but defines her as a sexist and a racist. I was curious which particular white males she had in mind, and found myself wondering if her new colleagues on the Court were asking themselves the same question.

I have liberal friends - mea culpa! - who are euphoric because they're convinced that, thanks to Obama, the world will now love America. For all my bantering, they refuse to cough up the names of those countries that were ready to divorce us, but are now eager to rush off on a second honeymoon. I do find it fascinating, though, that while we've now elected a Socialist, many of the European nations, having learned their lessons the hard way, have begun electing conservative leaders.

How long, I wonder, will it be before the Democrats turn Charles Schumer's wet dream, otherwise known as the Fairness Doctrine, into a 1st amendment-shredding reality? And how long until Obama carries through on his campaign promise to fund the U.N.'s crusade to end global poverty to the tune of a trillion dollars?

For the longest time, I had heard that in America anyone could grow up to be president. Now, when I consider Obama's background, his friends and associates, and his views regarding wealth distribution, I can see they weren't kidding. They meant absolutely anyone.

Years ago, I suggested that any man or woman who was convinced he or she should be president was clearly insane. For that reason, and because I was already fed up with all the lawyers being elected, my solution was to draw a name out of a hat. I was convinced there was a better chance of winding up with a sane, decent, honest man or woman in office if it turned out to be my next door neighbor or the nice lady who lives around the corner. Clearly, voting is one area where practice doesn't make perfect. Holding elective office is another.

At this point, if I can't have my lottery, I'd settle for two things. One, I'd limit voting to those people who pay income or property taxes. It's just absurd that millions of Americans who have never held down a job or served in the military and are still receiving an allowance from their folks can cancel out the votes of their parents. Two, I'd make term limits mandatory for every elected office in America, and I'm talking about single terms. No more lifetime careers in politics. If you want to get rich, back off from the public trough and get an honest job.

Frankly, I don't know if we could actually get by without politicians, but wouldn't it be fun to try?

While it's true that I invariably vote for Republicans, I never fool myself into thinking they'll be wonderful, but merely better than their Democratic opponents. Those people who are hurt by such political facts of life are to be pitied. It's like a child's discovery that Santa Claus and the Easter Bunny aren't who they've been cracked up to be. To such conservatives, all I can say is: Grow up.

Looking back on my own political metamorphosis, I realize how typical it is that, as one matures, takes on responsibilities, deals with tragedy and loss, one tends to drift from left to right, and how rarely the reverse occurs.

In all of history, so far as I'm aware, there had only been two famous tea parties. At the first one, Samuel Adams and a few of his freedom-loving friends pitched several crates of tea into Boston Harbor. The second was the one Lewis Carroll wrote about, a madcap affair with the March Hare, the mad Hatter and the narcoleptic Dormouse, ganging up to give Alice a hard time.

All of that changed on the 15th of April, 2009, when a series of tea parties took place all across America. Even I, who try to avoid crowds, attended a gathering here in the San Fernando Valley.

If you believe the creeps in the MSM - and why would you? - we were all dues-paying members of political fringe groups, and none of us would think about leaving the house without first donning our little aluminum hats. If you believe Janet Napolitano - and how could you? - we were not merely man-created disasters like Somali pirates and Islamic butchers, but full-fledged terrorists. Some among us even confessed to being - yikes! - military veterans.

Well, either she is very wrong or I am. To me, the 3,000 people who showed up at the Van Nuys Civic Center looked like pretty decent, average Americans. But, not being the head of Homeland Security, I can't claim to be an expert when it comes to spotting terrorists. Heck, all I know is what when I look at the likes of Charles Schumer, Barney Frank, Chris Dodd, Barbara Boxer, Harry Reid, Patrick Leahy, Henry Waxman, Nancy Pelosi and Barbara Lee, my blood runs cold, and when I hear Barack Obama pushing his socialist agenda and reaching out to the likes of Castro, Chavez and Ahmadinejad, the little hairs stand up on the back of my neck. It's like watching one of those really creepy movies, but instead of all the scary stuff taking place on Elm Street, it occurs on Pennsylvania Avenue.

At the get-together I attended, we were rallied, aroused and amused, by such speakers as comedian Evan Sayet, actress Morgan Brittany and L.A. talk show host Kevin James. In fact, my only problem with the event, aside from my decision to wear tennis shorts on a night the temperature dipped into the low 50s, was that the entire focus was on Obama's insane fiscal policy. I in no way wish to suggest that the bail-outs, the budget and the so-called stimulus package, don't remind me of something Dr. Frankenstein would have cobbled together in the castle's basement if his master plan, like Obama's, had been to destroy capitalism.

However, there are so many other things about the man and his mission that I find terrifying. I hate to have us so busy concentrating on his left hand while, with his right, he muzzles the conservative media; destroys our missile defense capability; funnels funds to ACORN, AmeriCorps and Hamas; nationalizes the banks and takes control of the automotive industry; and, for good measure, discusses nuclear disarmament with Russia while trusting the U.N. to deal with Iran and North Korea.

So, while I regard Obama's plan to use the tax code to impoverish productive Americans while using tax rebates to bribe those who don't even pay income taxes as a vile left-wing plot, I'd hate to have my fellow conservatives so completely focused on this one area that they fail to see all the other tricks this con artist and his left-wing cronies have up their sleeves.

Something that has bothered me over the years is the way the lame-brains in the left-stream media invariably turn into unlicensed shrinks whenever a Republican is in the White House, but toss a dust cover over the couch as soon as he's replaced by a Democrat.

For instance, how many times did we hear liberals babbling about the psychological demons George W. Bush had to contend with because of his allegedly troubled relationship with Dad? But the fact that Bill Clinton's father was a drunken bully apparently left no emotional scars on Bill's impenetrable psyche. Furthermore, I have yet to hear such eminent Freudians as Bill Maher, Chris Matthews, Rachel Maddow, Frank Rich, Maureen Dowd or Keith Olbermann, even suggest that being deserted by both his father and his step-father, spending his formative years in the alien culture of Indonesia, only to be dumped, at the age of 10, on his white relatives in Hawaii, may have turned Obama into a smooth-talking, narcissistic psychopath incapable of telling the truth even if it's about something as relatively inconsequential as sending his kids to a public school and getting them a mutt from a shelter.

Now, of course, I'm not saying he is any of those things. But don't you think if he had wound up after experiencing all that early trauma as somebody who believed in a free market economy; in supporting Israel against the barbarians; in opposing late-term abortions; in calling terrorism by its rightful name; in attending a church that had more in common with Rick Warren's than with Jeremiah Wright's; and in sharing the Constitutional interpretations of Justice Roberts, Alito, Thomas and Scalia, the media would have long ago concluded that even if he wasn't exactly the Manchurian Candidate, he was definitely a booby who needed to be hatched?

CHAPTER TWELVE

A 12-Step Program for Recovering Liberals

When a person quits smoking, it's said that food tastes better and the air smells sweeter. In similar fashion, when a person stops being a liberal, facts take on greater importance and logic finally trumps emotion.

Most 12-step programs start out by requiring people to understand that they're powerless over their addiction and that only by turning their lives over to a Power greater than themselves can they be restored to sanity. Far be it from me to suggest that I am that Power, but clearly someone has to step up and try to rescue these poor liberal saps. Even the most hare-brained among them deserves that much.

First, though, they have to acknowledge that John Kerry, Nancy Pelosi, John Murtha, Dick Durbin, Charles Rangel, Harry Reid, Henry Waxman and Charles Schumer, are not moderates, but rather, leftists with a Marxist agenda. Furthermore, they must recognize that the New York Times, the Washington Post, the L.A. Times, CNN, the three major networks, the news magazines and the New Yorker, are not objective in their reporting of political events, and neither are Chris Matthews, Keith Olbermann, Rachel Maddow and Bill Maher, in their commentary.

Step #1: It is high time that every American be guaranteed the right to speak freely. It is not meant solely for left-wing college students who wish to take advantage of the First Amendment to shout down conservatives. At the same time, they must not construe the conservative's right to dismiss them as arrogant airheads as constituting censorship.

Step #2: Affirmative Action argues that African Americans and Latinos are intellectually inferior and are unable to compete academically unless other students are handicapped because of their race. Interestingly enough, when Black and Hispanic students are given their unfair advantages, it's rarely at any cost to white students, whose rate of college admissions remains constant; instead, it's nearly always another minority group, Asians, who pay the price. This is what left-wingers refer to as leveling the playing field.

Step #3: Liberals always claim to be in favor of higher taxes, agreeing with Bill Clinton that the government invariably spends money more wisely than those people who actually earn it. However, such prominent proponents of higher taxes as George Soros, Dianne Feinstein, members of the Kennedy clan and Mr. and Mrs. John Kerry, protect their own otherwise taxable income through trusts and offshore accounts. Obviously, any American who believes higher taxes are a good thing can do the honorable thing by spurning all deductions and paying Uncle Sam everything up to 100% of his or her income.

Step #4: Even the most secular of liberals seems to believe that Jimmy Carter is a saint. The evidence for this seems to be that he has on occasion posed with a hammer in his hand at Habitant for Humanity building sites and is constantly walking around with an expression on his face that suggests he has just forgiven Pontius Pilate for betraying him. This is the same fellow, let us never forget, who called Yasser Arafat his good friend and who has accepted untold millions of dollars from Arab cut-throats, who ask nothing in return except that he go on insisting that there would be peace in the Middle East if only those darn Israelis would just disappear from the face of the earth.

Step #5: Stop insisting that all wars are bad. It only makes you sound daft. Carrying signs that equate a U.S. president, any U.S. president, with Adolph Hitler is not only rude, but suggests you're certifiably nuts. So far at least, every president has left office right on schedule. Aside from FDR, who just happened to get elected four times, not one of them has remained in office beyond eight years. On the other hand, Hitler ran Germany for 12 years and only death and the allied forces brought that to an end; Stalin ran the Soviet show for 31 years; while that hero of the left, Fidel Castro, has held the reins, not to mention the whip, for about 50 years.

Step #6: Repeat after me, "Separation of church and state" exists nowhere in the Constitution. The first amendment does not require the removal of Christmas trees from the village green, the 10 Commandments from courthouse walls or "under God" from the Pledge of Allegiance. All it does is forbid Congress from establishing a state religion such as the Church of England, and anybody who tells you otherwise is a liar and, most likely, a card-carrying member of the ACLU.

Step #7: Stop using the word "big" as a pejorative. There is nothing intrinsically bad about big oil, big agriculture or big pharmaceuticals. Overall, they do a very good job of keeping our cars on the road, food on our table and most of us over 65 alive and functioning. On the other hand, big government, which so many liberals simply adore, represents a usurpation of the allegedly inalienable rights of individuals. A quick perusal of the Constitution should convince you that beyond declaring war, forging treaties, overseeing patents, printing money, running the post office, collecting taxes and protecting our borders - and a few other things that

Washington doesn't do at all well these days - the federal government has very limited responsibilities.

Step #8: Acknowledge that the United Nations is, in the main, an aggregation of venal diplomats who live high off the hog in New York City while representing the most corrupt and vicious regimes in the history of the world. Only a fool or a diplomat would continue to suggest that this gang of well-dressed thugs possesses anything resembling moral authority.

Step #9: Do not keep insisting that at a time when nearly all the large scale evil in the world is being perpetrated by Muslims that racial profiling is anything but a sensible approach to airport security. During WWII, Swedish Americans were not suspected of performing espionage for the Axis powers and for a very good reason; namely, because they weren't performing espionage for the Axis powers. These days, their Swedish American children and grandchildren are not suspected of trying to blow up airlines, but the smarmy bureaucrats insist on pretending that they're every bit as likely to be up to mischief as a bunch of 25-year-old Osama bin Laden look-alikes from Yemen and Saudi Arabia.

Step #10: Stop trying to pretend that illegal aliens are the same as legal immigrants just so you can claim the moral high ground and accuse those of us who are opposed to open borders of being racists.

Step #11: Once and for all, stop forgiving murderers. Whether or not you're in favor of capital punishment, only the victim of a crime has the right to grant forgiveness. And inasmuch as the killer has deprived his victim of that ability, don't take it upon yourself. It doesn't prove how compassionate you are, only that you're as sanctimonious and as self-aggrandizing as, say, Jimmy Carter.

Step #12: Stop bashing the U.S. military and the Boy Scouts. The only reason you have the ability to shoot your mouth off is because men and women braver and better than you sacrificed life and limb for your right to do so. As for the Boy Scouts, they are absolutely right to keep homosexuals from taking youngsters on camping trips. While it's true that many gays are perfectly fine people and that very few homosexuals are pedophiles, there's no reason on earth to take unnecessary risks just so we can all prove how broadminded we are. For what it's worth, as decent as most Catholic priests are, I wouldn't let them take youngsters into the woods, either. It's fine to be compassionate and understanding, but let the gays among us be understanding for a change and acknowledge that, every so often, common sense should trump political correctness.

And, finally, making this a baker's dozen, Step #13: Let us all agree that while being a woman, a Black, a Jew, a Catholic, a Mormon or even a gay, for that matter, should in no way preclude anyone from being elected president of the United States, none of those things constitutes a very good reason to vote for someone.

CHAPTER THIRTEEN

In Appreciation

In the days and weeks following 9/11, friends and neighbors saw the American flag flying by my front door and assumed it was in remembrance of the people murdered by Islamic terrorists. I didn't bother correcting them because, by then, that was certainly part of my intention. The thing is, the flag had been out there for several months, but they just hadn't noticed. Or maybe they thought it was corny and didn't want to comment. But, now, I think, is a good time to set the record straight.

I went out and bought the flag because of my grandparents. I should explain I had never known my dad's parents, both of whom died before I was born. I knew my mother's parents, but could never speak to them. Although they had come to America in 1921, they had never mastered English. They could speak Russian and Hebrew, but they preferred Yiddish. I couldn't converse in any of those languages. And, so, to me, my grandmother was this little old woman who would give me a wet kiss on the cheek and slip a quarter into my hand. My grandfather was a very quiet, bearded man who always wore a black frock coat; he looked like a short Abe Lincoln. He went to shul twice a day. When he was home, he was either reading the Torah, shelling lima beans or sipping tea through a sugar cube held between his front teeth. In short, if my life were a movie, they'd have been dress extras.

So why did I buy a flag because of those four people - two of whom I had never met and two of whom I had never really spoken to? It's simple. Because of sheer, unadulterated gratitude.

You see, one day, on my way home, I began to think how lucky I was to have been born in this country. Through no effort of my own, having made no sacrifice, taken no risk, I was the beneficiary of freedom, liberty, education, comfort, security and, yes, even, to some extent, luxury. It was not the first time I had acknowledged this good fortune. The difference this time is that, for some reason, it suddenly occurred to me that my good luck hadn't just happened. It had been the direct result of these four people pulling up stakes and moving thousands of miles across an entire continent and the Atlantic Ocean, to a new country, pursuing a dream that their children and their children's children, of whom I am one, might, just might, have better lives.

There were no guarantees. That was my epiphany. They had been denied the assurances of hindsight. They had done all this on a roll of the dice, only knowing for certain that there would be no turning back.

My father's parents were illiterate peasants. My mother's parents not only never spoke a word of English, but her father - although he owned a small grocery store in Chicago - never, in 30 years, spoke on a telephone because he didn't want to embarrass himself. But their grandson, bless their hearts, has enjoyed a career as a successful writer. I doubt if any of them imagined anything so specific or anything quite that wonderful when they snuck across the Romanian border in the dead of night, but they had certainly heard a rumor that in America anything was possible.

The fact is, had those four people, all of whom were poor and barely, if at all, educated - their little children in tow - not somehow found the courage to make the journey, I would have been born a Jew in the Soviet Union. Between Stalin and Hitler, the odds are likely I would have wound up a slave in Siberia or a bar of German soap.

So it happened that day when I was out driving and thought about the enormous debt I owed those four immigrants, a debt I could never possibly re-pay, I decided to pull in at the local hardware store and buy a flag. I thought it was something they'd have wanted me to do on their behalf. It wasn't nearly enough, I know, but it was something.

The Author

Burt Prelutsky was born in Chicago and raised in Los Angeles. He was born a liberal, but managed to come to his senses along the way.

He has been a humor columnist for the L.A. Times and the movie critic for Los Angeles magazine. On a freelance basis, he has written for the NY Times, Modern Maturity, TV Guide, the Washington Times, the L.A. Daily News, Human Behavior, Esquire and Sports Illustrated.

For TV, in addition to several award-winning movies that starred the likes of Jean Stapleton, Keith Carradine, Martin Balsam, Jean Simmons, Ed Asner, Jack Warden, Sharon Gless, Lillian Gish, Barnard Hughes and Sylvia Sidney, he has written for Dragnet, McMillan & Wife, MASH, Mary Tyler Moore, Rhoda, Family Ties, Bob Newhart, Dr. Quinn and Diagnosis Murder.

He is the author of "Conservatives Are From Mars, Liberals Are From San Francisco," "The Secrets of Their Success" and the upcoming "If Life is a Test, These 60 People Aced It" (interviews with the likes of Charles Krauthammer, John Stossel, Newt Gingrich, Carl Reiner, Gov. Rick Perry, Gary Sinise, Pat Boone, Joseph Wambaugh, James Woods, Rep. Michele Bachmann, Ralph Peters, John Bolton, Walter Williams and the late Karl Malden.

He plays poker and tennis, and rarely cheats at either.

He resides in the San Fernando Valley with his wife Yvonne and his dog Duke.

Dear Reader

If you enjoyed this book, write to me at BurtPrelutsky@aol.com and let me know. Better yet, recommend it -- don't lend it! -- to your friends, neighbors and relatives.

If you wish to purchase autographed copies, please send a check or money order in the amount of $15, plus $5 shipping and handling, to Scorched Earth Press, 16604 Dearborn Street, North Hills, CA 91343-3604. California residents, add $1.50 sales tax.

(Hey, it's not my fault you live in California. It's only my fault that I live here.)

Best wishes,

Burt Prelutsky

Other Books by Burt Prelutsky

Conservatives Are From Mars, Liberals Are From San Francisco
(A Hollywood Right-Winger Comes Out of the Closet) Scorched Earth
Press

Conservatives Are From Mars, Liberals Are From San Francisco
(101 Reasons Why I'm Happy I Left the Left) WND Books

The Secret of Their Success
(Interviews With Legends and Luminaries) Expanding Books

If Life is a Test, These 60 People Aced It
(a collection of interviews due out in the Spring of 2010) WND Books